Bijan has truly shared a remarl
darkest places of the New Age
regime and mindset to a life or freedom in Christ Jesus. His use of
metaphorical language and parallels creates for the reader, an opportunity
to discover truth in an interesting way. I encourage you to join Bijan
on this amazing journey that will leave an indelible mark on your life,
confirming that in Christ, there are new beginnings!

Rev. Giulio Gabeli
National Director of Canada Celebrates
Israel Network, Apostle and Senior Pastor,
Westwood Community Church

"A remarkable account of a life! A completely intriguing and captivating
memoir of a soul searching for truth, and the ultimate testimony of the
saving grace of Christ in a culture that is still fairly unknown to a western
world. A great read!

Marika Siewert
Canadian Singer/Songwriter
President of Emerton Records

I clearly remember the day when you and I went to hear Paulo Coelho,
not in Rio de Janeiro, but in our own city, from the balcony of the famous
Hall of Solidarity in Tehran. It was as magical as the day, at the Book
Exhibition, when you brought the heaven to earth by offering me the
gift of Christ with a small Bible you gave me out of your backpack. And
I wondered what I could possibly offer you in return, except, perhaps to
become a force to push you toward reaching your dreams!

Tell me now, how can I look at you and the fulfillment of your dreams
today and would not say, "Another 'Alchemist' is on the way; another
pilgrim, but this time, with a true story to tell.

M. Ramez (a.k.a Brida)
Poet, Literature Editor, and a dreamer

Journey back from Ixtlan

A Non-Ordinary Transformation Account of a Persian Enchanted Soul

Bijan Ilyaie

WESTBOW
PRESS
A DIVISION OF THOMAS NELSON

WestBow Press books may be ordered through booksellers or by contacting:

WestBow Press
A Division of Thomas Nelson
1663 Liberty Drive
Bloomington, IN 47403
www.westbowpress.com
1-(866) 928-1240

Because of the dynamic nature of the Internet, any web addresses or links contained in this book may have changed since publication and may no longer be valid. The views expressed in this work are solely those of the author and do not necessarily reflect the views of the publisher, and the publisher hereby disclaims any responsibility for them.

Any people depicted in stock imagery provided by Thinkstock are models, and such images are being used for illustrative purposes only.

Certain stock imagery © Thinkstock.

ISBN: 978-1-4497-4961-3 (sc)
ISBN: 978-1-4497-4960-6 (hc)
ISBN: 978-1-4497-4962-0 (e)

Library of Congress Control Number: 2012908907

Printed in the United States of America

WestBow Press rev. date: 5/17/2012

To all who touched my life and soul during my journey,
to those who helped my dreams come true,
to you who read this book and will continue its legacy,
and to Brida.

"And no one puts new wine into old wineskin;
Or else the new wine will burst the wineskins and be spilled,
and the wineskin will be ruined.
"But new wine must be put into new wineskins,
and both are preserved.
And no one, having drunk old wine,
immediately desires new; for he says,
'The old is better.'

Gospel of Luke 5:37-39

Contents

Preface

MY DEAR FRIEND MARINA NEMAT, the Iranian-Canadian author of the bestselling book *Prisoner of Tehran* (Penguin Canada, 2008) says in her blog, "*Literature is not to serve a certain ideology, but to become the honest bearer of the human experience and condition.*" (www.marinanemat.com/ esseys Dissidence and Literature). That was what I believed before I started writing this memoir. But during the process, something changed in me. My intention, at the beginning, was (and still is) not to go into details regarding my belief system, but the writing process compelled me to be more specific on occasions for it was my faith that kept me alive when I walked through the valley of the shadow of death, even up to this very moment.

An experience can only be as valid as our belief system and can be defined within the context of our conviction. I'm still convinced that literature should be an honest bearer of the events that we face in life, but it cannot transfer the perception of an experience itself detached from who we are and what we already believe in. My comprehension of any new experience is based on analyzing its specific elements according to what I've already chosen as my belief system. Pain, sorrow, and happiness are defined according to our belief system, like in Buddhism. Meanwhile, in many cases, belief gives its place to a genuine and living faith—faith in people, faith in an ideology, faith in a better future for humankind, faith in our country, faith in freedom and democracy, and finally faith in a much higher, compassionate, and far greater force in the universe—God. We all represent an ideology, with or without an "ism," whether it's in the form of politics, religion, or philosophy. Faith makes life worth living, regardless of the hardships, sufferings, and rejection—and even the torture in a prison cell. Faith helps us endure the hardships of life. Only faith can give us a hopeful picture of a better world in the future, and it keeps us trying, testing, and moving forward until we reach what we hope for. There I said it—hope. We are here on earth in this moment, right where we are, in order to give hope to someone who desperately needs it. Yes, that is our reason to be. And it starts with having faith in the things that we personally hope for.

My deepest desire is to see this memoir serve as a means to communicate the truth that *no matter where we are born or grow up, similarities of human experiences can be the most essential and effective means of perceiving life and the behavior of people around us, as well as our own. By understanding life we can make it more understandable for others, especially for those we are destined to meet on our journey.* There is hope in this, a divine and unshakeable hope for those who feel they have to fight this battle all alone. We are connected to each other through the chains of common experiences. Knowing this truth helps me believe I'm not alone in my battles.

In 1972, Carlos Castaneda (an anthropologist who met with a Yaqui Shaman) published his third book called *Journey to Ixtlan*. He chose this title to refer to a non-ordinary state of mind (or reality, figuratively Ixtlan) into which he entered many times while being taught the secrets of Yaqui Shamanism by an old Indian sorcerer called Don Juan Matus. As a result of this magical experience, the foundation of the world we call reality became, for him, a mere phantom. I travelled to my own Ixtlan through practicing sorcery for years but, at the end, my experience convinced me otherwise.

Journey Back from Ixtlan is the account of a man, a hunter of knowledge, who lived in a realm of magic long enough to understand that his true battle awaits him in the real world. In this story, he comes to grasp the reality that what he used to call "ordinary" (and tried to surpass) is in fact the extraordinary destiny he has to face and fulfill as a warrior in search of the ultimate truth of life. And here is how he starts his *Journey Back From Ixtlan.*

Meeting the Warrior

I GUESS IT WAS A late spring night in 2000; his first trip to Iran. Mehrabad International Airport was filled with young people crowding here and there, talking about him on every corner. His books were on the top of the international bestseller lists. Presumably his Iranian Publisher had changed his flight date a few times to avoid any trouble possibly caused by his young fans, but still they had managed to figure out what day and what time he would arrive, just as I did. He was a phenomenon. In just a couple years, his fame as an author had reached the highest rating as a bestselling author in his country, in Iran, and around the world.

A huge crowd of young people had showed up in groups, hoping for a chance at an autograph or a moment with him on camera.

As I squeezed the letter tightly in my hand, I noticed how exited I was. I wasn't sure if I would be able to hand him the letter, but it was worth a shot.

For some reason, rather than the regular butterflies we all feel in our stomachs at such times, I had the thought that something was not right! I went out to have some fresh air and to rehearse my sentences—the things I wanted to tell him, like how I admired him and how his writings had inspired me in the toughest times of my last few years.

I was reviewing these thoughts when that butterfly feeling hit me again. This time it was very strong. All of a sudden I knew for sure he wasn't going to show up at the International Arrivals Terminal. Suddenly I found myself running toward the Domestic Arrivals, which was about a five minute walk from where I was. As soon as I got there, I knew I was at the right place. Apparently I wasn't the only one with that weird feeling.

About fifteen to twenty other young adults were also there waiting for him.

All of a sudden, we heard a whispering all around us; *is it him, is it him?* My heart beat accelerated. I saw him coming out, surrounded by some huge men, probably his bodyguards or the publisher's people. I recognized him. He had finally showed up; it was him—Paulo Coelho!

People from his Farsi publishing company quickly surrounded him with baskets of flowers and handshakes. Without a second of delay, they led him toward the exit door. One of the publisher's men told him, "Mr. Coelho, we had to change the terminal because there are hundreds of young people at the International Arrivals. It may get out of control. Please accept our apologies."

Paulo smiled and said, "I understand."

I thought, *Come on, guys. I'm sure he wanted to see that young, passionate crowd. You guys don't know him at all.*

It was one of the most anticipated moments of my life. As soon as they grabbed his luggage and moved toward the exit door, I made up my mind and ran to him with the letter in my sweaty hand. I greeted him passionately, welcoming him to Iran. I told him that he had no idea what his visit to Iran meant to our younger generation. He listened to me attentively. Then I asked him if I could give him a letter. He smiled, shook hands with me, and said, "A letter? For me? Wow, of course you can. I'm honored. No one has ever given me a letter in an airport before. I'll definitely read it. Can't wait to see what's in it!"

I wasn't sure if he was just trying to be nice or if he actually cared. But now, after almost 12 years, I think he really meant it. Everything happened so quickly. A man from the publishing company ran to us as soon as he saw us talking. (It was Arash Hejazi, Paulo's Iranian publisher. I met him later.) He appreciated my enthusiasm first and then turned to Paulo and said to him that they had to leave before others found out where he was. I told Paulo that inside the letter was my contact information, in case he wanted to contact me. He said he would read it gladly, and we shook hands again. Then they got in the car. Others were watching us, giving me their thumbs up as a sign of a good job. Maybe they thought I was very bold and courageous to approach him in that situation. Or perhaps they thought he was too famous or too unreachable to get close to. I think some of them really envied me.

Paulo never knew who he was for me. He and his real or fictional characters were among my few remaining intimate friends in the painful years leading up to that moment in the airport, and even until a little while later. Without them I wouldn't be able to go through some of the toughest things that had happened to me. No, he didn't know that. No one knew, except one person: Brida.

I left the building dancing and singing "Hallelujah." It was one of the most exciting nights of my life. There were, of course, better days, but this one was somehow different. Maybe it was because of the similarities I shared with Paulo—not only in thoughts, but also in the events that had led my life to that exact moment—things that affected my life forever.

Pursuing our personal legend, our journey of life, seeking and searching, keeping the dreams alive, and experiencing life with all of our heart and soul were the key themes in all his writings. And that's what I've been trying to do in my last 22 years. Of course, when I met with the warrior, I still had a long way ahead.

Once an old Buddhist guru predicted to me that I had two totally different destinies waiting for me, based on two options I faced at the moment. To give you a clear picture of those two choices, I am arranging the account of my life chronologically instead of through flash backs and flash forwards (except in two or three chapters where the story requires such a style). But I assure you that you will still be surprised at the true twists and turns in the story.

If you want to know what led to that wonderful night at the airport and what happened after that close encounter with the warrior, and if you want to know what two choices I faced, then take a deep breath. We are about to enter the rabbit hole!"

The Little Warrior's World

As far as I know, within the circle of those I've met so far, I was the only one who, at his twentieth birthday, was officially working for the Ministry of Defense, was a voodoo practitioner and medium, was a spiritual Guru with actual disciples, and was a heavy drug addict and dealer.

I was a shy boy. I rarely played football or any other tough sports or games. Since learning how to write and read, I always preferred being alone and reading books or articles about supernatural events, mysticism, magic, secret religions, and even UFOs and Eric Von Daniken's theories about aliens and their prehistoric presence on the earth.

I was known among my relatives and friends as a nice and kind boy. I guess that was why some kids didn't like me much and called me "mommy's boy." I always hated when they called me that. I was also what all parents always longed to see in their kids: a very good student. The first thing I did when I arrived home from school was my homework. Up to grade four, I was the best student in all my classes and always came first or second in exams.

My parents were the nicest in the family. They were well spoken of for their close relationship—you know, like lovebirds. I had two younger sisters, one eighteen months younger and the other one eight and half years younger. The older one was my polar opposite. She couldn't stay at home. She was always late to and from school and was a sort of rebel. She was outgoing and social, while I always liked my solitude. She had a heart as big as an ocean, and she was, and still is, a joy to the people around her. We call her Sherrie, which is a shortened version of Sharareh; it means "sparkling flames." Yes, that's what she is!

The youngest one, which I prefer not to mention her name because of safety reasons for she's still living in Iran, was something between me and Sherrie, more moderate, I may say. But as time passed, I began to see more similarities between her choices and mine, and that made me more proud of her. For instance, in music, her taste was much closer to mine; I was very proud of my musical choices. My relationships with both of my sisters were based on honesty, love, and respect. We were so close that I was almost the first to know if they were interested in any guys. I even remember giving them advice on how to solve their relationship problems in some cases. That was not good for my reputation as a guy or a brother, but I didn't care. I've always respected girls. I guess it is sometimes counted as a weakness, both in the eyes of guys and girls.

One of the reasons I wanted to be nice to everyone was because I didn't like conflict. In fact, conflict was the only thing I always ran away from. I always thought respecting others could diminish all the conflicts between people. But later, as I grew, I found out that life is not that simple. People are able to create conflicts out of nothing and then easily blame them on you.

My father was in the military. Even though he was not a very high-ranking officer, he was highly respected. He was even allowed to enter the four-star generals' offices without an appointment or any permission in advance. He had connections in all of the military bases around the country. He was known by everyone at the Ministry of Defense. Because of the nature of his work, almost all other military personnel under his authority, or even above him, respected him. In fact, most of the respect he received wasn't because of his position, but because of his character. He was loved for his kind and fair approach to everyone. I remember many times when his associates at work asked him to be the judge in their disputes, whether it was a family issue or a work problem. At the same time, he was also very authoritative. No one ever disobeyed him, as far as I knew. Every year during the summer, when the school was closed, he took me to his work place, and I personally witnessed how he treated others and how they respected him. He treated everyone with dignity and justice. I was a witness to that even as a young child.

I still clearly remember those days when I used to run in the long and empty labyrinths of the Ministry, playing hide-and-seek with the guards. Actually, they never played with me because they were like the guards at Buckingham Palace; they never moved from their stations. But still, it was fun to tease them. Sometimes they would scare me with a sudden move, and I would scream and run. There were times, when I was running in hallways or jumping up and down the stairs, when I would hear the sound of footsteps in the corridors. I had learned how to tell from the sound of the footsteps and the shouts of the guards how important the person was. Sometimes I had to quickly hide behind the huge velvet curtains until they were gone. I had probably seen two or three Ministers of Defense during my reign in the Ministry. As a child, I used to think I was the prince of that glorious palace—that my father was the most important person in the whole world, and I was second to him. I knew every corner and every hiding place in the Ministry.

On one occasion, I was seen by the Minister himself. I ran like I had seen a Jin. I was scared, for I'd always thought he and all other generals were bad people and that my father was the hero who was supposed to save others from their wicked hands. A couple minutes after I was seen by the Minister, everybody was talking about this little kid who was running around the Ministry. A search began, but as soon as my father heard about it, he called the Minister and told him that it was his son, who he had brought to the building for a tour. The Minister wanted to see me, so my dad took me to his office; I was scared to death. Sometimes I wondered why my father did not destroy them all in a wink of an eye! I was only six years old when that happened.

I was very popular among those who had been working under my father's supervision. Everybody was ready to help and rescue me in case I was in trouble, even though it was dangerous for them. That was how I knew who was a friend and who was with the enemy. There were times when they had to hide me under their desks when a general would unexpectedly decide to check the departments. It was frightening and exciting at the same time.

Every summer for at least six consecutive years, from the ages of five to eleven, I had the chance to be in this magical palace, living in my tales of wicked rulers who were mean to their people and the savior (my dad) who was always there to bravely save his people from the hands of these monsters. Of course, as I grew up, I found out that things were a little bit different. They were not as bad as I used to think. Reality is, we all have to leave childhood behind and come out of the bubbles we build around ourselves. But soon we figure out that we have to build and live in another bubble called adulthood, which comes with responsibilities. That's why most of us want to stay in the bubble of childhood; responsibility sucks!

My dad had a very gentle side, too. He played the santur, an original Persian musical instrument with seventy-two to one hundred strings that is played with two light, oval-shaped mallets. At most weekend parties with friends and family, he was asked to bring his santur and play while others sang old Persian songs. Every Iranian around the world has great memories of those days in the times of Shah, king of Iran. Those gatherings were like a tradition for all of us. Every Thursday night, which was like Saturday night in the West, all the uncles and aunts from both sides, along with the grandmas and grandpas and all cousins—young and adult—used to gather in one place, playing card games, dancing, singing, drinking (only the adults), and doing other fun stuff. At the end of night, when most of the adults were happily drunk, it was time for the santur and poems from Hafez and Rumi, or some current famous poets, to be sung in a traditional Persian atmosphere. I liked it very much, and I promised myself to learn to play the santur when I grew up. I even gave it a try for a while, but I guess I was made for something else, as you will read later. I personally do not know any Iranian who does not miss those fun, simple, and care-free nights in Iran in the times of Shah.

My mother was the sweetest of all and a very beautiful dancer. She, like most moms, was our secret keeper. She was another hero, but back at home. She was the one who always rescued us from the hands of bullies at the school, the one who protected us in the marketplace, and the one who found us if we were lost in the crowd. As we grew, we began to do the things we were not supposed to do, but she kept protecting us when our dad was angry at us because of all those so called "bad things" we used to do as kids.

Women are natural defenders. No matter the culture, the number of wives who have sacrificed their own dreams and desires to protect their families is much higher than the number of men who have done the same. We men tend to think we are the centre of the universe, and most of the time, we ignore and neglect our responsibility, not toward the family, but directly regarding our wives. But that wasn't the case for my parents.

In general, and in comparison to other parents I've met, my parents were the best. I will always be thankful for all they did and went through to raise us up to be who we should be. Of course our own personal choices, as free human beings, can always change the course of our lives and lead us to places no parents want for their children. As we grow up we begin to make wrong choices but at the time of facing the consequences we tend to put all the blame on our parents because, as human beings, we don't want to admit our mistakes or acknowledge our wrong choices. My parents really did their best for us and I personally do not blame them for the consequences of my own choices in life

When I finished grade four, at the age of nine, my parents enrolled me in an extra summer school for the talented. They wanted me to pass grades five and six in one tough exam and then go to junior high. I wasn't sure if I was fully ready for such a great step, but I was only nine at the time. What could I possibly do? They just wanted to boast about me before the family. I couldn't let them down. So during that long summer, I did my best, and I passed the big exam. Then, without having an exciting summer vacation, I entered junior high the same year.

I felt such pride walking among kids much older than me, but at the same time, the sudden immersion in junior high had its damages on me too. Because of my interest in history, geography, physics, English language, and literature, I was the best in my class, but not everybody likes geeks!

I was the youngest and smallest in my school. All other students looked at me as a geek, but I wasn't one. That's when some of them began to bully me and few others tried to protect me. Being someone who knew all the answers to the teachers' questions caused many students to start close friendships with me. But as we all learn through life, popularity will also make enemies; some guys began to develop a jealousy of and hatred toward me, about which I could do nothing.

Back in those years, in the old educational system in Iran, almost all junior (middle) and high schools were one and were called high school. As a result, many of the students in my school were eighteen years old, and I had friends ranging in age from twelve to eighteen and, in some cases, even older!

I could tell you many stories of different occasions when I was picked by various groups and gangs in our school for different reasons— maybe because I was too small and fit for a game, or because my grades were great, or simply because they wanted to laugh at me. For whatever reason, everybody liked to have me in their gangs, and that was enough to make me feel important. I really liked it very much when older boys in our school approached me and asked me to help them with their grades. I was so naive that I always thought I was the greatest in our school, and because of my age, it never even occurred to me that they could have had other intentions!

As I mentioned, my desire to help others and my boastful feelings of being the best in school became my weakness and left me almost defenseless on countless occasions. When older guys began to approach me and ask me to help them in their studies, in private or at their place, most of the time I was happy to do it. But after a while, I began to understand that what they wanted was not my knowledge, but in fact, my body!

In several occasions, these guys tried to make me show my private areas to them. Some of them even used force. I was always quick to react and was able to escape. But on a few rare occasions, they succeeded in partially abusing me for their own pleasure. I didn't like what they were doing, but I decided not to tell anyone about it. I sincerely believed that all they wanted was me helping them in their homework! One day I finally realized that I didn't like what was going on, and I told myself, "I won't help anyone with their grades anymore!" Of course, girls were an exception, as you may know.

By the time I reached the age of twelve, I began to notice new stuff about my own body and saw myself changing, not only physically, but also emotionally. The most important thing was that I wanted to be with girls more than I wanted to get better grades! I just longed to be with them every second of my life. I didn't know what was happening to me, but it was so pleasant that nothing else could be compared to it. So I began to shift my focus from reading weird books on the supernatural to something even more exciting, breathtaking, adventurous, mysterious, and unpredictable—girls.

I learned that I could use my talents and charms to attract some of the most popular girls in our big family circle, as well as in neighborhood schools (even in the times of Shah, boys and girls were mostly in separate schools). It was a great discovery, much better than being picked up by any school gang or group. I felt there was something very special about girls, something as special and mysterious as reading mystical books. I was only twelve, but I knew many things about ancient civilization and the mysteries of the world, like the Mayas, ancient Egypt, Indian cults, Sufism, and UFOs! Girls produced the same chemical activities and excitement within me as studying these fascinating mystical subjects. When I grew up, three more things were added to the list of things that could give me the same feeling and excitement, but we'll talk about them later.

In my surprised I noticed that girls were interested in me too; I liked it. Like any other teenager, I had my bad days too. One time, I thought I was deeply in love with a girl, but later noticed that she was interested in my friend, who wanted to do more stuff to her when they were alone! I used to think kissing a girl was a very serious offence to them; at least, that was what they tried to make us boys believe. But later, when I entered my thirteenth year, I noticed that, in fact, they were just pretending to be offended. So I decided to show more affection. Ironically, when I tried to be more intimate by putting my arms around their shoulder, they complained and pushed me back. Yet when I was polite and respectful they were even madder at me. I was confused.

I used to think, *what's wrong with them? Why do they do that? Girls are very complicated creatures!* Or maybe it was me who didn't know how to approach them at all. After few sadly-ending attempts at romance, I decided to leave the girls to my best friends (who were all older than me) and walk away. I thought girls were not clear about how they expected me to treat them, while they also got angry at me if I was not able to understand what they expected from me, even when they were not clear about what they wanted! I was like Mr. Spock in *Star Trek*. Logic was very important to me, and if I couldn't find logic in human behavior, I didn't want to have anything to do with them—the supernatural was an exception. However, despite all my logical conclusions, for some weird and pointless reasons, I still longed to be with girls. So after a year or so, I tried again and again, even though I didn't know why I wanted to be with them after all the pain I'd experienced. On one occasion, I caught the girl I thought I loved with my best friend, and the feeling was so awful that, for the next few days, I experienced this constant pain in my stomach, like I was about to throw up at any moment. I would ask the same question, over and over again, "Why do they do that?!"

The good thing was that I always had my anchor to go back to, and it helped me pull myself back together again—mystism and the supernatural! It was still the number one driving force in my life, especially when I understood the fact that I couldn't trust a girlfriend or even a best friend at all. Spiritualism never got angry at me, never betrayed me, and never hurt me. Oh my sweet sweet spiritualism—always there in thousands of forms, colors, and varieties; always filled with mysteries and excitements. I was almost 100 percent sure that my relationship with the mysticism would never end for any reason.

An older friend of mine in high school once said, "All you see in those weird books is not comparable to the mystery of girls, so why not be with girls instead of living in those imaginary worlds? Friendship with benefits! Girls are as mysterious as the stuff you like."

My answer was, "I don't know. Maybe because I just feel there is no end to this mystical universe, but there's an end to every girl; when you get her, you reach the end of that mystical experience."

I guess I was wise for a thirteen-year-old!

The child grew. Sometimes we wish we would never grow up, but it is inevitable. And this inevitability has its own twists and turns.

Illusion of Revolution

ALL PEOPLE, WHETHER YOUNG OR old, men or women, rich or poor, theists or atheists, scientists or non-scientists, are looking for something in life through which they can define their own existence. It is written in our DNA. It is born with us. We are all searching for something that seems to be lost or hidden from us. Even if we are in a state of denial, there is still the denial in us seeking more evidence to hold on to more denial. And there are enough facts in life to keep us going in any direction we may chose to walk, even walking in denial.

Do you believe in God? There is a lot of evidences to support or prove His existence. You don't believe in God? There are plenty of theories to prove He doesn't exist. Your spiritual or materialistic outlook may depend on where you were born, where you grew up, how you grew up, what your family beliefs were, what your culture set is, which school you went to, what religion you were born into, what your gender dictates to you, and what your five senses tell you to believe. Eventually, and as a result, these common circumstances tell you how to perceive and classify your further experiences. Even if your mindset is to "think universal," which simply means, "I don't belong to any "ism," you still believe in an "ism" in itself (like New Age spiritualists who claim to be followers of no "ism" while they call themselves a "spiritualist".

Of course, there are many other reasons for you to be who you are now. Everything is connected, and everything is purposeful. As meaningless as this might seem or as meaningful as it can be, it's an accepted fact that what you see and hear will undeniably affect your thoughts. You become what you see and hear. And, as you might also agree, your thoughts could give birth to your actions. Even reading these lines will probably have an effect; that's the reason behind all media productions, whether a movie, a song, a painting, a poem, or a book—shaping minds.

The whole world is somehow connected, just like James Cameron's imaginary planet of Pandora (in the movie, "Avatar"), in which even the smallest insects (as well as all other creatures) had this deep and beautiful connection with the whole planet, especially when something was threatening the very existence of the planet itself. What a movie!

There is a necessity behind the existence of every living thing, and even every lifeless object, that ever came into this world—whether it's a piece of stone or a virus. That is why I believe there's a search engine inside all of us, written in codes within our DNA which forces us to look for our meaning or our purpose in life. Of course, it doesn't mean that we all will find our purpose or, if we do, that we will understand and embrace it. It's there, and it drives us. It keeps us alive, in a sense. You may or may not be aware of it, and you may or may not accept it, but it's there. You can disagree with me, which is not a surprise because you have the right to believe otherwise. A friend of mine believes there's no meaning and purpose in life, and he lives accordingly. We are very good friends!

The same force—the search for meaning and purpose—was working in me since my early years of walking on this beautiful planet. But as I said before, this force was being shaped by my environment, and there was little I could do about it until I began to make that search a priority in my life, which happened around my twelfth birthday. You may say, "Twelve? How could you prioritize things in your life as a twelve-year-old?" I always knew what I longed for in life. You know what you long for, even from your childhood. I'm not talking about your dream job or education. There's something in your DNA that becomes prominent in your personality as you grow, and every adult around you can see and recognize it. The same element may finally become your passion, sooner or later. For me it happened sooner, and I'm happy about it. I decided to follow spiritualism, and my whole life was centered around and built upon it. We all have the right to choose. All the environments human beings are born into or live in are there to push us toward our passions, and our passions can become our destinies. Many forces in the universe are also there to guide our steps if we believe in our choice power and watch for the signs, the signs that a higher power has already set up on our way. I personally never ever blame anyone for the consequences of my own mistakes or even the things that happen to me, and I hope you do not either.

When I was about thirteen and half years old my uncle returned to Iran from Austria after finishing his education, earning a doctorate in Political Science. He had brought some souvenirs for his nieces and nephews, as the custom was in those days. Interestingly, among all the shiny stuff or t-Shirts that he gifted to other kids in the family, he gave me a cassette tape, a recording of a mixture of different American and European music styles. That tape truly changed my outlook in some areas, and it was the beginning of a chain reaction that continued to affect my life, even until today; it introduced me to the power of "messageful" music. This tape showed me that there were people who used music as a means to communicate their thoughts and ideas with people about the world we live in, and some of these ideas were very mystical. That tape inspired me to go deeper in my search for the mystery of life.

Before the Islamic Revolution in Iran, my country was one of the very few developed countries in the Middle East in terms of freedom, tourism, and night life. We also had accredited passports for travelling to hundreds of countries without restriction, and we even had a currency that you could spend in North America without the need to exchange it to dollars. We also were the greatest military power in the Middle East (just like these days as the government of Iran claims, and you've probably heard on the news about it).

Back in those days, music was as important as it is now in the lives of teens. Popular British and American music were on radio stations all day long, as well as Iranian songs. But I really didn't like the popular Persian music that was on TV and radio day and night. I could never understand that kind of music; it was just not for me. So when my uncle gave me that tape, it opened up a door to me to a new world. For the first couple of months, I listened to it for hours every day, seven days a week. To me, it was amazing how some singers or bands used music to share their ideas about life, social problems, the young generation's issues, good and evil, and even God and the devil!

What was in my DNA joined powers with the music styles of the early '70s, and all of a sudden, I found myself listening to the weirdest bands and singers on the face of the earth. Some of them are still playing today, some have disbanded, and some are dead. Since receiving that tape as a gift, my whole life was divided into two parts—school and listening to music.

Of course, it took me three to four years to grasp the picture behind the story-telling part of the music of the '70s. By the time I reached the age of seventeen, I knew of almost every living band on the face of the earth.

On the edge of time in those days, we were the generation of *The Wall* by Pink Floyd. That album came out at the exact right time; the revolution in Iran had just started. By that time, I had a pretty good understanding of British music, but *The Wall* was something I could have never imagined. It was truly unique, and it really shaped my social and political views and what I became in the space of a few months. The worldwide impact of *The Wall* was so vast that even schools in England were shut down for a while. Today, the young generations, even after more than 30 years, still love this musical masterpiece. At that time, almost everyone and everything in our lives seemed to be a brick in a wall that was being built around us; we all learned that through *The Wall*. We all know that young generations hate walls, limitations, and dictatorship—under any name. Walls should be torn down, whether they are built in the name of democracy, religion, or the proletariat. And music proved itself able to convey that message, as we later saw in Germany through the tearing down of the wall in Berlin.

Of course, in music, Pink Floyd was not the first band I gave away my heart to. My first love was a very well-known German progressive rock band called Eloy. I was sold out to them because of their unique work in the album *"Inside"*. They captured my soul for many years. I was so crazy about them that I spent hours and hours a day listening to them, and mostly to *Inside*. Even though the singer, Frank Bornemann, had a funny German accent, there was still something about their music that I couldn't resist.

During that time, many other good bands came and went, but only a handful remained to be my favorites. I liked these bands so much that I began to translate and study their lyrics—bands like Eloy; Pink Floyd; Genesis; Jethro Tull; Barkley James Harvest; King Crimson; Emerson, Lake and Palmer; Yes, Bob Marley, Black Sabbath, Led Zeppelin, Fleetwood Mac (with one of the bestselling albums of all time, *Rumours*), Camel, and (my all-time favorite, which wasn't really appreciated as it should have been) Allan Parsons Project. These are just few names among many, and others were added as I grew, including U2, Leonard Cohen, Dire Straits, The Cure, Depeche Mode, and so on. All of these bands prepared me for something I wasn't yet aware of.

Meanwhile, I continued my journey with the supernatural, and as I grew, I began to read more books on the subject. I could have graduated high school early in my sixteenth year, but I became badly sick for a whole year, and as a result, I missed school. So with a year's delay, on my seventeenth birthday, I was finally graduated. My graduation happened just prior to the beginning of the demonstrations that were followed by the Islamic Revolution in the winter of 1979—the year of *The Wall*.

Because of the musical revolution that had happened to me, I was politically ripe and ready to embrace new ideas and to fight the bad guys! A governing system was introduced to me through some friends, an idea that could be for everyone and could bring equal rights to all—Socialism.

It was then that I first heard the term *democracy*. What a term! For many centuries individuals and groups of people had sacrificed their lives to see the beauty of this word manifested in their societies—like human rights, freedom of speech and belief, and equality. Some dreamed about it; others took an action to see it fulfilled; while others died for it. Freedom has its own price. If you want it, you have to make sacrifices for it. But you also have to be ready to sacrifice your own rights and freedom for the sake of fulfilling the ideal for others. The Irony of freedom is that if you want it, you have to be ready to be imprisoned for it, to suffer for it, to be tortured for its cause! I began to think about these things.

Marina Nemat, wrote in her blog, *"The word 'democracy' comes from the Greek 'demos' meaning "people" and 'kratos' meaning "rule". But as the wheels of history moved along, it became evident that the rule of the people can actually lead to a terrible disregard of the rights of minorities. So in the modern world, democracy is defined by civil and political rights."* (www.marinanemat.com/essays_democracy)

Democracy is one of the most sacred words in the vocabulary of human beings in every ethnicity and culture. It is more than a word. It is an ideal, a progressive ideal, rather than an estate. *Democracy* is always against the use of absolute totalitarian power, while those who come to power in a democratic way begin to do the same ugly things like the group before them, but now in the name of the majority. The magical number of 51 might ring a bell in your mind (obviously, I'm not talking about Area 51), because that's all democracy is about. Whoever has the number 51 is in power. The irony of democracy is that sometimes only one vote can redirect or completely change the course of history for a nation. But what happens to the rest? They have to comply with that which is not a majority, but a half plus one. This number in countries like Canada might be even much lower than 51—minority majority!

You may say, "That's not the definition of *democracy*. *Democracy* is protecting the rights of others, especially the minorities, and respecting and tolerating other's opinions, and considering the human rights constitution as the highest value of humankind, like freedom of speech and belief."

You are right. But I'm not talking about what it means; I'm talking about those who come to power through democracy and then turn their backs on those ideals and their people, not because they are jerks, but because of the nature of politics—like what happened in my country, Iran. Is it the politics, or is there something else in the nature of human beings that causes even the best ideals to fail? I would say, "Human nature."

In 1979 millions of us, in Iran, fought for freedom and democracy (with almost no insight to what democracy meant), but what happened was that even with 98 percent of the votes for what we thought we wanted, we still got it wrong! I don't mean that we were cheated by politicians who came to power by promises of defending the cause of the poor and needy and the guarantees of freedom of speech and belief. They were just like the rest of us, thinking their political or religious system was able to fulfill those promises. We trusted them; that's all we can do in every political system, and then cross our fingers and hope they won't fail us.

Of course, I know that all of us, in one way or another, are in a complaining minority group—like Christians, Sikhs, Muslims, Jews, Baha'is, immigrants, refugees, blacks, Democrats, Republicans, socialists, communists, and so forth. It's funny that we all think of ourselves as minorities who want to be in power but only through our own belief systems or ideas. But it seems that there's always another group in control, right? Why does it seem that the Democracy is always in danger? Maybe someone has to do something about it and who better than us? After all, our own concept of democracy is far better than theirs, right? We want our group to be in power because, obviously, as Michael Jackson sang, "They don't really care about us."

Why do all the beautiful words in the world lose their weight and definition when they are used by another person or group rather than by our own group? Please don't get me wrong; I'm not against democracy. Obviously, it's all humanity is left with as an ideal! But to be honest, I still believe that the problem is not with *the system,* but with *us* as human beings.

Now back to my story. As naive as I was, in less than a month after the Islamic Revolution succeeded in Iran on February 11th 1979, as someone who was always interested in the wellness of others, I fell into the trap of Socialism and joined a party with communist ideals. This party was apparently fighting for democracy, except for the fact that the word *everyone* meant "the proletariat" to them, and the word *democracy* was replaced with *socialism!* After passing a compact, short-term course by some appointed, nameless individuals, I was awakened to a new horizon in the field of evolution. I suddenly believed, according to the Party's Manifest, that there was no God and that all the mysticism I used to read about was just my ignorance or lack of knowledge and science. In just couple weeks, all of my knowledge in the supernatural turned to a basis for defending the cause of evolutionary theory and the philosophy of Karl Marx. Mission accomplished; I was brain washed.

I immediately started my duty as the new brainwasher in the Party's branch in an area in Tehran, from Kennedy Blvd. to Freedom Square (how ironic is that?), that fairly covers one tenth or more of the Capital. It was a huge area and a huge responsibility for a seventeen-year-old—teaching hundreds of other young people, who thought the answer to their inner vacuum at the beginning of the Islamic Republic was found in joining a materialist/communist party and challenging the newly established regime. But soon we all tasted the bitterness of disappointment; a division happened in the Party, and again we became the minority, even in what we believed was the solution to the world's problems. How sad!

Around the same time, my father, through his influence in the Shah's military, found me a job at the Ministry of Defense in June 1979, when I had just turned to eighteen. Even though the Revolution had already taken place, the military and the military men still had some power. It was both funny and exciting to work there, for I knew the building like the back of my hand. I had grown up there. All the walls and curtains were filled with memories of my childhood. In fact, it had been almost six years since my last visit to the building. An old era had ended, and a new journey was going to start; it was a very revolutionary step in my life. It was also around that time when I tried my first cigarette and smoked my first joint. Apparently the walls were being "torn down." I was introduced to something which I called "Gettinghighism"!

Shiraz

I WAS STILL TEACHING EVOLUTION and basic materialism principles to some of the new socialist members of the Party when I began to work at the Ministry of Defense. But after the division in the Party, it wasn't like it had been previously. As I mentioned, we became the minority again; nothing was really what I expected from that "ism." Plus, the Islamic regime had already begun to identify the members of the opposition parties. Many were arrested and a mass execution of tens of thousands of people related to the opposition groups began in every corner of the country in the name of protecting Islam. The activities of opposition groups were somehow pulled into the underground. Because of my father's position and influence, I did not go through the ideology check when the Ministry of Defense checked my application for employment (as was the custom of the Islamic regime). But personally, I decided to take less part in the Party's activities. Not long after, I discovered some shocking news!

One day the person who was in charge of our underground unit told me that we were supposed to be equipped soon. When I asked him what he meant by *equipped,* he replied "Russian guns, for all of us!" That day was the last day they saw me, not because I was afraid (which I was), but because I generally did not believe in guns. I didn't believe they could solve any problem. They tend to add to the problems. In fact, guns are part of the main problem. We create them in the name of protecting ourselves, our loved ones and our countries (or the free world) while we speak of peace; then we decide to actually use them against every possible threat. But what happens when the guns are not selling? We create imaginary threats in order to keep the money flowing in our country's weapon factories and create more advanced weapons in case of new, unknown threats, in order to keep the balance. This is ridiculous. In other words, we create wars to protect us from war. We create evil in the name of protecting freedom. What a humorous generation.

When I turned 18, finding a prestigious job was not the only exciting thing that happened to me. I also got high on marijuana few times; I liked it very much, especially with music. Marijuana opened a new horizon into my knowledge of the supernatural (I was free from the stuff the Party had put into my brain.) I liked it so much that, after a short period of time, it turned into a daily habit for me, even at work. The only problem was the fact that I had to touch down the ground after an hour or so. But hey, it could still give me another ride, right? Lady marijuana was the only thing that could momentarily satisfy the emptiness inside me during that season; the hungry monster had just been awakened, and it wanted more. I had never imagined myself getting into such stuff so easily and so quickly. I guess that is the same problem with all of us who have tried this goddess; we never believed she could possess us.

I began to smoke weed as a personal choice. It wasn't under the influence of any individual or the rock music or even my involvement in supernatural stuff. I did it as a choice. One morning I woke up and decided I was going to start smoking cigarettes and weed at the same time. Within a week, I added hashish and opium to the list.

At the same year and after a terrible motorcycle accident that resulted in a broken leg and a few other injuries, I was hospitalized at home for two months. During that period of time, some changes happened at the Ministry, and a few people were replaced in my department. My father had retired sometime before that. Those who had hired me and were my father's friends were replaced, too. When I went back to work, with two canes under my arms, I was informed about the changes and told to prepare myself for a transfer. I was commissioned to work in another city, Shiraz.

Shiraz, the city of poetry, good wine, romance, and the great poets Hafez and Saadi, is the nearest city to the ancient Persepolis, or as we call it, *"Takht-e Jamshid,"* the capital of the Persian Empire in times of Darius the Great, where Alexander the Great finally defeated Iran (after losing the battle a couple times) and destroyed Persepolis.

I thought to myself, *I'm not even nineteen yet, and I am walking around with these canes. Now I have to pack my stuff and move to a city where thousands of war refugees are recently placed!* Yes, war refugees. The war between Iran and Iraq had already begun, and Shiraz was full of refugees. It was just a year after the success of the Islamic Revolution when Iraqi armies invaded our soil, thinking that Iran was in a fragile political and military condition. That was what Saddam Hussein thought, but he was wrong; he paid the price later.

Iranians—no matter what situation they live in, no matter how oppressed they are, no matter what tyranny is ruling over them, no matter how angry they are at their ruling authorities—when it comes to defending their land against foreign powers, become so united that they even swallow up their anger and join hands in defending their country. Messing with anything that has to do with the wholeness of Iran or its borders will awaken a furious sleeping giant in each and every Iranian, no matter what.

This war was also an opportunity for the new Islamic regime to deepen its roots in the structure of administrative and financial institutions in every possible area. And that's why a rumor was circulating for quite a while that the war was planned by politicians so that not only could a huge amount of money flow into weapon-building factories and their share-holders' pockets, but also so that the new Iranian government could have time to root deeply into every level of society. This war gave them eight years to do that, an eight years that turned into an excuse to intensely quiet every opposition against the regime in the name of treason at the time of war. The war took eight horrible years to come to an end. Tens of thousands of families made sacrifices from both sides. Many became blind, deaf, lame, crippled, and impotent. Thousands went to captivity, and over a million lost their lives in both countries. Three years before the war was over, I saw many of these miseries with my own eyes because I was finally compelled to enroll in military service; it was mandatory. We will get to that part soon.

———

There is no explanation for wars. I could not understand it then, and I never will. We all know what wars could do to our world, to our country, to our people, and worst, to the future of our children (even the unborn ones) and all humankind. But we still find ways to justify it, whether in the name of freedom or democracy or even religion! Many enriched themselves in these wars, like politicians, religious leaders, bankers, realtors, businessmen, and weapon-builders around the world.

Before the war began in Iran, one U.S. dollar was about 70 Rials, but later on, by the end of the war, it reached 5,000 rials, and that was just the beginning. Right now, a dollar is equal to 12,000 riyals (in 2011), and because of the world wide economic crises my prediction is that it will continue to soar even up to 20,000 by 2012!

Since this book is a spiritual account of a man's life journey, and war is just a cold bloodshed story, I won't be sharing much about those years I spent in front line. It could be another whole story.

So I was transferred to Shiraz during the first year of the war with Iraq, when I had just started to smoke weed! But this was not the worst part. It was just the beginning of a fall down into a bottomless pit, where the dark forces of hell were waiting for me to start their mission in my life.

———

There were four of us, four employees from the same department, who were all transferred to Shiraz. We were all young, but I was the youngest. The others were between twenty-two and twenty-five years old, but they were all sissies! Believe me; they were not mature at all. They all needed someone to run after them and clean up the mess they made every day. They never washed their dishes or even their cloths; mommy was supposed to do it for them! I hated that. The only things they thought about were sleeping with hookers and talking to their moms on the phone.

One of them, who was also the largest of the group in size (we used to call him Teddy Bear), couldn't go to sleep without crying a little bit. I had to talk to him about his bright future and his cute future wife until he would go to sleep. The other two always teased him and mimicked him, "Oh, I want my mom. Where's my milk? Give me a goodnight kiss mommy," and stuff like that. His name was Kiarash. He was very easy to trick. He reminded me of Little John in the Robin Hood story. He was very protective, though, and ready to beat up anyone who was in disagreement with us in any matter, even though he was a sissy.

The oldest one was Amir. He was the smart one. He could seduce every girl in the town into bed. Sometimes I envied him! In fact, there was a hidden competition between Amir and me in some areas. We both wanted to win the other two in our favor. Kiarash was closer to him, while Saeed was close to me. Saeed was smarter than Kiarash and had his own ways of doing things. Sometimes he didn't even listen to any of us. He was into anything that you could imagine, but in all things just for fun. There was nothing special about him except he was a very funny guy.

We decided to rent a big house with four rooms to live together. A new city with thousands of war refugees wasn't a safe place at all! It was better to stick together. Plus, Shiraz was famous for its criminal gangs and underground homemade vodka factories and wine production. The latter was one of the most sold-out products in the city, and many of the smugglers were also involved in robbery and selling drugs. The second most sold product was Hashish. Among us four, I was the only one who used hashish on a daily basis. Saeed smoked too, but only once in a while for fun.

A month or two after we moved to Shiraz, I made a close friendship with my boss's personal driver, a private with the name Morteza. He was the one who bought me some hashish for the first time in Shiraz. After I hung out with Morteza a couple times, one day he told me he wanted to introduce me to some of his friends—a group of young rebels who wanted to leave the social city life and live in a deserted place. It was an interesting idea, so I decided to meet with these weirdoes.

A week later, I met them in a park in downtown Shiraz. They were so cool that I fell in love with them almost immediately. All of them were into spiritualism and rock music, and they were all ready to die for each other! The next hour they blew me up with a golden Afghan hashish roll. It was the heaviest stuff I'd ever smoked. I was so doped that for about half an hour I even forgot where I was and who these people were!

However, the night turned horrible when the Revolutionary Guards suddenly surrounded us, yelling, "Freeze, don't move!" (They had found us because of the smell of hashish.) We ran in every direction. I couldn't even imagine what it would be like to be arrested as an employee of the Ministry of Defense, caught in gang activities and drugs! I ran like hell. I hit my right knee to a rock and fell but got up immediately and even though the pain was unbearable I kept running like crazy. I don't remember how I got home that night. But what I had experienced with those guys was so exciting that the next morning I asked Morteza to talk to the guys about me being part of the group; I wanted in. They had been friends since their early teen years. He told me that he had just had a talk with them and that they were very much interested in friendship with me as well.

But because they were a gang (even though they were not seriously involved in robbery or that kind of stuff), he reminded me that there were some requirements. He said that what most of them had seen in me the night before was very cool, but their biggest condition was, "He should not be a sissy." I thought to myself, *Ha, that's an easy one. It's true that I am an introvert, but not a sissy or a geek like most introverts.* For some reason, I had managed to develop a strong wise character, which carried a presence wherever I went. Unlike the stereotypes of the Hollywood culture, in which all who are into the supernatural and sci-fi stuff are called geeks or nerds, I wasn't one. I wasn't on that course because I was a freak; it was because I felt my destiny was waiting for me at a crossroads somewhere along that path.

By one week into our friendship, I felt like I had known them from the day I was born. We read the same books, listened to the same music, had the same creative Sci-Fi hallucinations, and had the chemistry that could hook us up for good. There were six of them, and if they would agree on me joining the gang, I would be the seventh. Bijan the seventh!

They accepted me but not as the seventh member. Plus my job and some other responsibilities I had toward my flat-mates and my family back in Tehran wouldn't let me be a 24/7 member of this cool gang, but the fact that they had accepted me to hang around with them was so pleasant to me.

However, Afshin (the one who later became my best buddy) told me that I couldn't be the seventh. They told me about a guy who was completely different from the rest of them and said that he was part of the gang, but not really part of it. When I heard this, I became a little bit disappointed, or a better word would be, *jealous!* His name was Masoud, and he wasn't a punk like them. In fact, he was a gentleman. He wasn't smoking pot like we were, only once in a while! I thought *What? Come on!* It was a disgrace to the gang. I was mad at the guys and Masoud both. They told me not to be worry about him because he was cool like the rest of us. After that, I really wanted to meet him. I said to myself, "My charm will finish him."

I'll get back to him later.

Wilhelm, Carlos, and the Six

SOME PEOPLE SAY, "GANGS ARE not for the brave, but for the coward." Being part of a gang doesn't solve any conflicts; it's just a way of expressing our frustrations, but there are better ways.

Although I was still working for the Ministry, I had this strong desire to leave everything behind and live with these guys. Finally, I had found what I was looking for—not just one, but a group of people who shared in my interests. They had all the qualities I've been looking for in friends. I couldn't have been happier. They introduced me to some other cool rock bands and great writers; I did the same for them. All we did was smoke pot, drink wine and engage in long conversations on meta-physics and sorcery—and ultimately about God, the purpose of creation, and our destiny, if there was any.

Since none of their parents would allow them to get together in their houses (because of the huge amount of marijuana consumption), I decided to invite them to my place to hang out, as a base. In less than a month, my other three friends joined us in a state of "heightened awareness," as I used to call it! Amir, Saeed, and Kiarash all joined in, and the more they hallucinated, the more my rule over them was granted. I know; I was mean!

During these every night gatherings, I was also introduced to the biggest mafia family in Shiraz, the Dehnamakis. They were in control of almost every crime in the city. They were in all kinds of illegal activities, like selling heroin, opium, hashish, home-made or smuggled vodkas and whiskies, as well as prostitution, robberies, and any other kind of organized crime. Their name brought fear to everyone, but they were cool to me. They were involved in some other things as well, things that I'd rather not mention here. Some reader discretion would be needed if I did. Trust me; you don't want to know!

So my place turned into a cave of mobs of all kinds. It was very interesting that even the oldest of them, who had been a junky for thirty years, still respected me deeply. Even though I was only nineteen, they still had that kind of respect for me.

One night there were fifteen of us, including my flat-mates and my gang of mystics, "the Six." After drinking some black label Johnny Walker and rolling at least ten to fifteen red Colombian rolls, one of the Dehnamakis who was around twenty seven years old, and most likely the next and youngest Godfather of the household, told me that he liked me so much as his new, cool friend that he wanted to cut his arm deep with his hand-made knife just to prove his friendship to me, a sign of brotherhood. I just looked at him in shock for a while, and after a long pause I said, "OK." I thought he was joking and that now everybody would burst into a laugh. But nobody laughed. There was a heavy silence while he pulled a beautiful and very expensive hand-made knife out of his pocket, clicked it open, and put it on his arm. In a fraction of a second, he cut his arm deep. There was no impression of pain on his face! He made a cut as wide as 2 inches. The knife was so sharp that it took few seconds for the blood to flow out. I tried to look cool; I was very excited but not at all scared. Then he took his own shawl, wiped the blood, and wrapped it around the wound.

Then he turned to me and asked, "Will you be my brother by having one?" I was confused for a second, but I came to my senses immediately. If that was the way he wanted to show his friendship and loyalty to me, the only proper response was to say yes. I lifted up my sleeve and offered him my arm.

He smiled and said, "I'll give you a small one." He changed the position of the knife and put it all in the palm of his hand and made a fist. I couldn't even see the tip of the knife. In the fastest move I had ever seen in my life, he made a vertical move over my arm and just touched the surface with the tip of the knife. I didn't feel any pain, nothing.

I asked, "That's it?"

He said "Yes, that's it. Thanks."

Then I turned around and looked at the wound. It was as small as a cat scratch, but deep into the flesh. After about five seconds, the blood flowed out like a fountain, and then I felt the burn.

Suddenly everybody began to whistle and shout. They clapped and welcomed me to the family, even though I wasn't very enthusiastic about joining the Dehnamakis! Then Mohammad, the one who had stabbed me, said, "Now on, your enemy is my enemy, and your friends are my friends. I will regard you as my own family and defend you to my death. Whoever gives you a bad look I will pull out his guts with this knife, and his mother will mourn over him days and nights!"

I looked at him and said, "Thanks man. But there's no need for that."

He looked into my eyes and said, "No one can do anything to my family members and go unpunished."

I decided not to say anything anymore. I just nodded.

Later on that night, my new friends (the Six) told me that it was a great honor and that I did right to accept the challenge; otherwise, something bad could have happened.

As time continued, our house became a base for all kinds of people, even prostitutes. Strangers began to show up at our door, bringing messages from the Dehnamakis, asking for a short time shelter. It was getting out of hand. The worst time was when our family members wanted to give us a visit. None of us wanted to be seen by the Dehnamakis or other gangs while walking around the city with our moms and dads shopping in public places.

I began to get tired of every night partying with mobs, and I wanted my privacy back—my reading time, my listening to music time, and my mystical conversations with my favorite guys, the Six.

—

One day, Amir's mom called him and told him that she had found a very good girl for him and that he needed to go back to Tehran to visit her. She also sent him the girl's picture, and he fell in love with her just by looking at her picture; she was pretty! Long story short, within two months they got married and moved to Shiraz. They stayed with the three of us—Saeed, Kiarash, and me.

It was obvious we couldn't live together that way, and since Amir had more influence on Kiarash, he made him bring up the subject to me and Saeed; he asked us to leave. The house contract was under my name, so he couldn't just ask me to leave. But when I thought about it, I saw an opportunity to get rid of the mobs and the troubles I had with them. A few days later, I told the story to "the Six." Afshin told me that his father asked him to work on one of his farms outside of Shiraz. His father was not very happy that his son was just wasting his life smoking pot, reading weird books, shoplifting, and dishonoring the family. They were a rich family with a good reputation, but Afshin didn't want to have anything to do with his dad's wealth. This farm was the most exciting thing that had ever happened to them. It was a farm, which meant they were now able to plant marijuana and a vineyard, turning that farm into a paradise of 24/7 heightened awareness! I decided to move in with them on to this farm.

Unfortunately, I couldn't be there all the time because I had my job from 8 a.m. to 4 p.m. at the Ministry. But I could ride on a minibus right after 4 p.m. and get there around 5 p.m. The same minibus could get me back to the city around 6 a.m., so I had thirteen hours to enjoy life to its fullest! What about sleeping?! I would only sleep for two to three hours because I didn't want to miss any moment of enlightenment with those guys—drinking wine, smoking the best Colombian marijuana, and sharing about the supernatural.

Most nights we would go to sleep around 3 or 4 a.m. The guys didn't have to wake up early. Weekends were so cool because we could all wake up early and go for a hike or climb the nearby mountains to spend a little time in awe of nature and practice some Yoga, Zen, or something of the like. We would get back around 9 a.m. and have our breakfast, if any, and then each find our own cozy spot in the field or under a tree or inside our cabin filled with books up to the roof.

We usually got together again when we were hungry. Most of the time, we had nothing to eat except a piece of bread and spoiled cheese. Sometimes we would go for a hunt, but not a real one. We were looking for sparrows, dead birds, or any other eatable dead animals by the roadside. Disgusting? Yeah, it was, but we had decided to live our lives as a rebellion against the society in which human beings were nothing but some cattle being guided by some politicians who were hungry for absolute power and were, themselves, nothing but unenlightened beings who looked down at others as servants, as if they were masters of the universe. Stupid! Rather, we were on a spiritual journey to find the ultimate truth; everything else in this world was meaningless to us (between you and me, I still somehow believe this statement).

One day, Afshin's girlfriend's brother-in-law, who was somebody in the United Nations office in New York (better not to mention his name here), came to visit the family in Shiraz. He was a cool guy with long hair and a long beard like the Sufis; he was a spiritual person, himself. He gave us a visit at the farm and was very surprised at how simply we were living our lives. Living a simple life, reading books on mysticism, and smoking pot!

I still don't know whether he was teasing us by saying good things about us or he was just mocking us. We didn't care. We were what we wanted to be. So in addition to more than a thousand marijuana seeds, he also gave us a book written by someone who claimed his teachings were from an old Native-Mexican sorcerer called Don Juan Matus. The writer's name was Carlos Castaneda.

The book was the third book written by Castaneda—*Journey to Ixtlan*. We immediately fell in love with his story. By that time, even though I was deeply into mysticism, I still had a great respect for a man whom I used to believe (and somehow still do believe) had an undeniable influence on the history of humankind at the late 19th century and beginning of 20th century. He was a German philosopher who was a one-of–a-kind, and if Jesus hadn't shown up to divide the time into BC and AD, he would have done it, as he himself had claimed. Yes, I'm talking about Friedrich Wilhelm Nietzsche.

I had a great respect for him and had read all his books, each more than 10 times. My favorites were *Thus Spoke Zarathustra* and *Beyond Good and Evil*. Nietzsche was the first philosopher I gave away my philosophical virginity to. His influence stayed with me for decades. Of course, this doesn't mean that I still believe in his thought system; I just have a great amount of respect for him for his brave stand against the whole traditional mindset of his time. I always dreamed about going back in time and talking to him about his influence on postmodern philosophy and telling him about the age of technology. For some reasons I always felt that he was a very lonely person, but a visionary too futuristic for his own time. He wasn't truly understood and appreciated. Some people blamed him and his idea of the Mega Human (Overman/Superman) for the occurrence of the Second World War, just because a lunatic by the name Adolf Hitler had interests in his writing. This didn't seem fair to me. Sometimes I strongly felt that I was the only person on the face of the earth and in all of history who could partially understand Nietzsche's point of view, and his loneliness.

Years later, I came to believe that neither *"the will to live,"* as Schopenhauer says, nor *"the will to power,"* as Nietzsche says, are the main will of humankind that causes us to continue the misery called "life." Rather, there's only one will that was and is leading us to wake up every morning and is moving us forward—*the will to hope*. We live, as self-conscious beings, in hope of finding a meaning and purpose for existence. And we will, if only we manage to keep this hope alive. Those who fall are usually those who lose their hopes. But even hope, like everything else, needs to be nourished and watered to grow and stay strong. That's where faith steps in. I'm not talking about faith in its religious form, but faith as believing in what you are hoping for, something that, deep in your heart, you know will become a reality. The most important point about hope is that it is only manifested as long as we have faith in what we hope for.

—

Being introduced to the teachings of Don Juan through Carlos Castaneda was a challenge for me because the things he was sharing were very close to my deepest true desires and passions, even though I was fascinated with Nietzsche. I had studied many books on sorcery. Some of them even shared about the ingredients you could mix up to summon demons and angels. Others were about the origins of evil spirits and how one was able to use them for one's benefit. I remember a book that I found in my cousin's library when I was only fifteen. It was a handwritten book filled with formulas taken from verses of the Quran, the Bible, and Buddhism, which were put together to show a person how to gain power over people or how to summon spirits. At that time, I even followed some of the suggestions; I began to feel and see the presence of the spirits around me and began to see horrible nightmares. I was so scared that I took the book and put it back in my cousin's library (I had stolen it). That was few years before I fell in love with Nietzsche.

After going through some other books by Castaneda, I gradually decided to put Nietzsche aside for a while and dive into the unknown world of a Yaqui Indian-Mexican sorcerer. At first I was afraid to practice the techniques, because of my past terrifying experiences, but step–by–step I regained my confidence, especially now that I was with "the Six." It was my innermost desire of all time to live a life like Castaneda and to have a mentor like Don Juan. Their story proved to me that what I was searching for was, in fact, a reality or at least something that could happen.

Thus, Carlos Castaneda was added to the list of my favorite people, which in those days was a short list, including Roman Rolland, Jean Jack Russo, Roman Garry, Nietzsche, Rumi, Hafez, Sohrab Sepehri, Ahmad Shamlou, and Forough Farrokhzad (the last three were the insightful and infamous contemporary Iranian poets who are not with us anymore).

Afshin, who was closer to me among "the Six," was very much into Don Juan. We usually had arguments regarding whether Castaneda's account was real or based on mushrooms! I wanted to accept its reality, but those bad experiences wouldn't let me dive into this new ocean freely, even though I wanted it badly. Afshin and I mostly spent hours in talking about the existence of God and whether, if he even existed, he was able to intervene in the actual history of humankind or the whole universe.

Our experience of God was different from each other; all of us had different ideas about him. Some of us believed in him as a higher being or awareness that is accountable to another higher power. Some thought of him as a watchmaker who put together the first elements and built this universe and then sat down and watched it work—tick tock, tick tock—just to enjoy his talent. Yet another believed he was just a consuming power with an insatiable hunger for more knowledge, meaning he was exploring himself in the realm of the material; wherever there was life (self-conscious life), he was there to absorb the awareness out of any living creature. In this theory, awareness was like food to him. This awareness (or let's say knowledge) was hidden inside the molecules of all material. One of us believed that God somehow was the source of the big bang just to explore his own being and to know his abilities and limitations better by absorbing the outcome of all the cosmic activities. We all had our own thoughts on God, like all other New Age followers.

(Here I need to mention that I have chosen to give fictional names to some characters in this book, especially the characters in the gang. I'd rather refer to the rest of the guys in our gang as the Six. It sounds more mysterious. They should remain as mysterious as they were, even though they were as real as you and me, and maybe more real than some of us.)

Among us there was another definition of God as an absolute blind power that was trying to get to a redemption point by going through a creating and destroying cycle until he could find a way to illumination, a nirvana in search of the ultimate nirvana. This process could have been eternally repeated for as long as it might take. I have no idea what this could mean, but it was one of the guy's ideas. Yet another one's opinion was that God could have been all the above with one difference; he was selecting and picking the higher forms of life, since the universe came to existence, in order to call them up to a higher level of existence form (which, of course, is not exactly what Hinduism says). The chosen ones would never come back to this life again; they would enter a higher sophisticated sphere, and there would be seven of them. The higher beings would pass other levels until they reached the seventh state, where God is. But even then, they wouldn't become gods or like God or even one with God. They would just co-exist with the other seventh level beings until all the material in the universe was consumed and turned to pure spiritual force. But why he would do that, we didn't have any answer. Sometimes it was just fun to talk about God. And though we didn't have answers, almost all of us believed in a higher force, a powerful, living awareness beyond our understanding.

Among us there was only one who was against the concept of God. We called him "old man." He was literally much older than all of us. He was very wise, but all his brilliant ideas were usually blossomed when he was at his highest possible "heightened awareness" state with lady marijuana! He had lived a very tough life. His father had left the family when he was only seven. He had gone through a lot. He had to start working from the age of seven while going to school at the same time, but ended up quitting school in mid-junior high. His family included his mom and five more siblings, each one year younger than the other. He reasoned, how could he possibly believe in God, in whatever form he was? Who cared? God didn't care about him and his family, so why should he care about God? It was a statement we couldn't argue with.

For him, only one thing was important: his friends, us. He literally said that once to all of us. He said it when he was sober, and that was what really scared us all. He said he would kill for us. Everybody said something as a reaction to his naked and straight statement, things like "Yeah, that's what I'm talking about," or "Yes, you're my man," or "Let's roll another one to this," and so on. But his statement really frightened us. We'd never seen or heard him talking like that! That was the only time he exposed his feelings about the group.

He was also the only one who never cared about walking around completely naked. When he wasn't around, you could always find him walking among the small marijuana farm or lying down on the grass or sitting and talking to a plant, naked. He loved being naked! Nakedness meant freedom to him. He reminded me of Don Genaro (Don Juan's funny friend) in Castaneda's account.

Deep in my seeking heart, I liked what Don Juan brought to the table. It was a mixture of all we believed. Carlos Castaneda was like a blender; he brought us all together. But in fact, we all fell in love with the authoritative and fascinating characters of Don Juan and Don Genaro.

As a result, we gradually began to practice Don Juan's techniques. We soon achieved some of the results Castaneda was sharing. Of course, at the beginning we, as many others, doubted the authenticity of Castaneda's account. But as soon as we began to practice the techniques, even twenty years after his first book came out, we experienced the supernatural results, and therefore, we believed they were authentic and were part of a shamanic system. The things that took Castaneda many years to learn, we had accomplished in less than a couple of months together just by sharpening our senses and concentrating on the techniques.

It was then when we decided to plant all the new red Colombian seeds right in the middle of the field where we had sown grain on the command of Afshin's father. The grain was tall enough to cover the baby weeds. We began to sell them and benefited a good amount of cash from them when they reached about 8 feet. We also planted a vineyard right in front it; yes, Shiraz without wine is meaningless! Paradise had come to our farm.

But sooner or later, we all had to face the fact that while on earth, no paradise is meant to last forever.

Marmar

AMONG IRANIANS THERE'S A SAYING about Shiraz. They say, "Shiraz, city of love, wine, and fun." And so far, I had experienced the wine and the fun part.

Now I am going to tell you the story of Marmar, which goes back to the first few weeks after our transfer. She was my direct boss at work, and she was also the administrative director and the colonel's right hand at our division. The nature of my work required me to be in direct contact with her many times a day, every day.

During the day and in order to get permissions or signatures for different pieces of paper work, I had to go to her office, and while she was going through the papers (to make sure they lacked nothing) we began a simple conversation about Tehran. She had graduated from Tehran University. She loved the city and its ever-crowded market places and old bazaar. She liked the northern part of Tehran where the city and the mountain become one; we call it "Darband." She was very romantic. She loved poetry, romance writings, and spontaneous love stories. But at work she was like a commander-in-chief. Everybody was afraid of her. She was very strict and straightforward, accepting no mistakes.

I don't even remember what made us talk about all those things. I just remember that after a week or two into our friendship, I began to write some poems for her, picturing her in those joyful places she liked in Tehran. After a while, a fountain of poetic talent began to flow out of me. One morning when I woke up, the first thought that came to my mind was to take one of those poems to her for the first time, something just to make her happy and to put a smile on her face just to begin the day with. Then I changed my mind and wrote her a new one. I wrote her four lines using the exact words she generally used in her sentences regarding her college days in Tehran. That morning I left the house earlier than other days (I was still living in my apartment with my colleagues). When I entered the building, only the cleaning guy was there. I sneaked to her office, left the poem on her desk, and closed the door before she got there.

Fifteen minutes later, my phone rang. It was her. She asked me to go to her office. Suddenly I thought, *Oh my goodness, what a stupid thing I have done,* and I began to curse myself. When I entered her room, she told me to close the door behind me. There was no smile on her face. She asked me to take a chair and sit down. I was nervous. I sat down and took a deep breath and opened my mouth to apologize for what I had done. She immediately said, "Hold on, let me start!"

And then she smiled, looking directly into my eyes, and began to tell me how wonderful the poem was, how happy she was, and how deeply she appreciated my kind gesture in bringing her a beautiful piece of poetry. She said I made her day!

I was relieved and filled with joy.

"Did you really like it?" I asked.

"Of course I liked it. In fact, I loved it, and I wonder how I'd never come across this poem before? You know how badly I'm into poems," she said.

I symbolically wiped my forehead and said, "I'm glad you liked it. I wrote it for you."

"What?! What do you mean you wrote it?! For me?" she asked, while leaning forward looking into my eyes with excitement. "Why would you write me a poem?" she asked with a pretty smile on her face.

"Just to make you happy," and I added, "You are more beautiful when you smile."

She began to blush and changed position on her chair. I told her that it was not just one poem, but that they were many, and if she liked, I could bring her one every morning. She loved the idea, but told me not to leave them on the desk. She was right; it wasn't a wise idea. I assured her I wouldn't and left her office with a new, exciting emotion I had never experienced until that moment. I thought I was in love. I was.

—

Her real name was Mary. She had a master's degree in Psychology, and she was thirteen years older than me! But I didn't care as long as I could make her happy and put a smile on her face. Who cared? I thought, *So what that I'm just nineteen; she doesn't seem to be bothered by the fact. The only problem is that I still don't know if she is seeing someone. It doesn't matter though; she likes me!* I said to myself, *We can sit together and talk about all the spiritual things in the world, books, songs, films, poems, and who knows what, forever!* But I was still afraid to ask if she was single.

So the job I hated turned into the most beautiful thing in my life. I began to show up early at work, wearing clothes that made me look older and more mature. I even began to show up in suits, but not ties. Wearing a tie was banned, especially in government offices. They were the signs of having western mind, which could easily be interpreted as being against the Islamic Republic. Even wearing short sleeves was not permitted at work. Some people were even arrested for wearing them in public places! That was during the first few years of the Revolution, and almost everything was a sign of being against the Revolution. It sounds ridiculous, but I'm not joking. Everything was somehow not permitted. It drives me crazy when I think about those days. But in fact, there was a time when even having a chess board at home was illegal and punishable, like music, fashion, hair styles, jeans, jackets with any logo on them, and hundreds of other silly things. I myself was arrested a few times, along with a couple of my friends, just because we were listening to music in the car! Sometimes I had to go through a lot of hardship to get the latest music from the bands I liked, and I had to pay five times more than the actual price just to listen to Pink Floyd, for example. And this was bad since, as I told you before, I was addicted to music.

The regime was so in fear of anti-Revolution activities that they literally closed all doors to anything that could even smell like the West; even perfumes were considered cultural invasion. All these things were happening in the name of "cultural cleansing." Cleansing from what? From bad smell? As a result, everything was smuggled into the country. There were smugglers everywhere, for everything, from music tapes (there were no CDs then) to hair products and colorful shirts and t-shirts. And by *everything*, I mean *everything!* So even wearing suite could put me in trouble, but I didn't care.

Mary had told me once that her father used to call her Marmar when he was still alive. So, as soon as I heard that, I began to use that name in my poems. Yes, I was a smart boy! In fact, that's what all men do. They try to find what women like and use those little things to make them fall in love with men. I know that guys will hate me for revealing this winning secret, but it's true. Even five-year-old boys know that!

One day, almost three month into our relationship (I liked to call it that, anyway), when I walked into her office to get her sign a document (which I had made up just to go and see her), I heard her talking on the phone. She said, "OK sweetheart, I'll ask daddy to take you there. Don't worry; mommy knows how to do it." *What the heck?* Not only was she not single, but she was married with kids—kids who were old enough to talk on the phone! *But she didn't even wear a ring! Cheater! She was cheating on me?! How could she?!*

I was just a kid.

I stood there, at the door, with eyes like a gold fish and the fake document in my hand. I didn't know what to do or say. It was like I was born without a tongue or without any nervous system to command my legs to move back to my office. I don't remember how long I was there staring at her, ten seconds or ten hours! I couldn't even think. Thank God she finally said something, "Give it to me," pointing to the document.

"It's fake" I said, with a voice that sounded like the noise a frog makes at midnight.

"What? What's fake?!" she asked.

"The paper," I reluctantly replied.

She asked if anything was wrong.

"No. Nothing's wrong," I answered coldly. Then I changed my mind and said, "Yes, I mean yes... Are you married?"

"Yes," she answered.

"Do you have a child?" I asked.

"Not one. I have two, a boy and a girl. Why?" She didn't seem to be bothered.

"Do you love him? I mean, do you love your husband? Do you love him?" I asked like a jealous boy.

"Of course I love him. What's wrong with you?" she sounded confused.

"What's wrong with me? What's wrong with you? Why didn't you tell me you are married?" I almost yelled at her.

"I don't know. I considered it a fact, maybe? Would you please tell me why you are acting like this?"

I just couldn't stand there and take it anymore; I threw the paper on her desk and yelled again, "Cheater, you betrayed me."

I didn't wait to see her reaction when I called her a cheater. She deserved it. She did a horrible thing to me. I was young, but I wasn't a fool to let someone do such a thing to me. What I mean is that she was mature enough to know that I was falling in love with her. She shouldn't have let that happen. That wasn't fair. Really, that wasn't fair. But it didn't matter anymore. It was over now. I ran to the washroom, rolled up a joint, and walked outside from the back door. I smoked the whole roll by myself, a roll strong enough for five people.

I came back to my desk half an hour later. I just sneaked in. I had asked Morteza, the colonel's driver, to take my place for a while. I couldn't just leave without a good excuse; after all, it was a military branch I was working in. She called few times, but I had Morteza tell her I was not there. Finally she came to my office and, in front of three other employees, asked me to accompany her to her office to discuss a document.

I knew she was trying to talk to me again, but I didn't want to give in to her game. She knew what she was doing to me; that was what I was angry about and not the fact that she was married.

But I had to obey her as my boss, especially in front of my colleagues. So I told her I would be there in a minute. That would give me some time to calm myself down. I went to her office five minutes later. She asked me to close the door; I disagreed. She asked me to sit; I refused. Again she asked, "What's the matter with you, Bijan?"

When I heard her saying my name, I almost forgot half of the story and asked her a question, "What's his name?"

She replied, "Hamid."

Then I said, "Why aren't you wearing your wedding ring?"

She looked at me and said, "I've put on weight recently, so now the ring is a little bit small for my finger. I didn't have time to fix it." We both smiled, but I tried to look serious.

I behaved like nothing important had happened, and I kept asking about her family, her kids, their names, their age, Hamid's profession, and so forth. She smiled and answered all my questions patiently. Then she gazed at me for a long time (at least it was a long time for me) and then asked, "Are we still friends?"

I didn't know how to answer her question. I mean, of course I still liked her and didn't want to lose her as a friend, but I was still mad at her. Our long conversation in her office could raise suspicion, so I just said, "Of course we are, why not?" Then I scratched my head and said, "Sorry for calling you a cheater. I'm really sorry. You probably know how I feel about you."

She looked down at the fake document I had dropped on her desk and tried to pretend she didn't hear my last sentence, "It's OK. I understand."

I asked her if I could leave then. Still looking down at the paper she said, "Yes." On the way out, I reminded her that the document was fake and that she didn't need to sign it. We both laughed.

She was the biggest thing that had ever happened to me since my discovery of rock and roll and drugs—beside my thirst for the unknown, and my friendship with the Six! The fact that I had to see her every day from 8 a.m. to 4 p.m. was not a good thing for me, especially knowing now that she was married and had two kids. It was a constant pain, but for some unexplainable reason, it was a good pain. I was addicted to seeing her, and if one day, for any reason, she couldn't show up at work, whether she was on a vacation with the family or taking a day off to do her banking or shopping, I would go crazy and had to see her after work. I was smart enough to come up with an excuse; she knew that and let me see her in a shopping center or elsewhere.

Something was telling me that she had the same feeling for me because if, during the day, for any given reason, there wasn't a document for her to sign or anything else I could use as an excuse to go to her office and see her, she would show up at my office door with an excuse just to see me. Sometimes she'd just call me and ask me to go to her office to discuss a work matter, but it was all an excuse. Of course, she kept denying her feelings and pretended it was not because she missed me, but I knew it was. Since I didn't want to hurt her feelings and not to leave her with a guilty conscience, I always pretended I wasn't aware of her game, because I loved her. Isn't that a normal thing that you don't want to hurt the person you're in love with? Mostly! How could I just put a guilty burden on her?

One day, while we were talking in her office (mostly about my poems or the books we were interested in), she gave me a long look and asked, "Why are you so late?"

"What do you mean by 'I'm late'?" I asked.

"You know what I mean." The tone in her voice was sad.

I tried to ignore what she meant, "I wasn't late today," I said.

She got mad at me and almost yelled "Bijan, I'm serious," and stared at me with anticipation in her eyes. These moments were very rare, and I didn't want them to fly away by just giving her a short answer. Love is also playful.

I kept ignoring the fact that I knew what she was talking about until she finally looked down to the papers on her desk and said, "You can go now, and please ignore what I just said."

I smiled at her and said, "As you wish, madam!"

That day, after I left her office I didn't go back there again. In fact, I didn't dare to face her the whole day because I was afraid to tell her that I knew she had feelings for me, too; that wasn't fair. She had finally admitted her feelings for me, but deep in my heart I came to this understanding that she was in pain. I knew that she was really in love with her husband and her kids by the way she always talked about them. I was still very young and inexperienced in true love. I used to think you could love more than one person at a time, for not everyone had all the qualities you were looking for in a person. I mean you enjoy sharing your music interest with someone and your literature observations with someone else. One person can give you peace, while the other one can give you excitement. In the presence of one you feel challenged, while you submit to the other one totally. You always look for a very special person who can be all the above for you, but through life you come to the conclusion that the qualities you look for in a person can be found in more than one individual. I just thought I could never find that special person; *we always need to sacrifice one for the other.*

But in fact, what we need is to sacrifice our own desires, our likes, and dislikes, in order to be with one of the few. We need to learn how to compromise some of our goals or our demands so that we can finally choose one over the others. And I know now that it is not easy to do so. Sometimes we miss the person who is the closest to our ideal just because we are waiting for someone else to show up, a better choice to help us fulfill our destiny. In the old days, not everyone knew this reality, but it seems that the age of data somehow has changed our perspective. The internet and media have enabled us all to share knowledge and common experiences at the speed of light.

A while ago, my niece, who is only ten years old, was talking to me about the boys in her class and the fact that she liked one of them. I tried to play an educated uncle and began to share my insight with her on basic relationship skills and about what guys and girls like. I was trying to use a very simple language to explain to her the principles of such friendships, especially at that age. To my surprise, she cut my words and began to tell me that she already knew all these game rules. She told me that even a five-year-old girl would know them, and she gave me a speech about how boys and girls should approach and treat each other. She spoke to me using a very sophisticated vocabulary.

After she finished sharing her own insight with me, she gave me a hug, kissed me, and said, "You know what uncle B (that's how she calls me)? Boys are such babies, but it's OK. We let them be." I guess she felt that I was shocked at her speech, because of the look on my face, so she added, "I love you uncle B; thanks for your help," and she went back to her room, leaving me with the wonder of the age of data and the differences between my childhood and these modern age kids like my niece. She already knew that she had to put up with the boy's childish attitude in order to keep running the friendship, and that's what I call conscious compromise. Today many in our young generation know this reality that love means sacrifice, or I better say compromise, and they seem to accept it as a fact. That's why my niece said, "And we let them be (babies)!" That's what I tried to do in my relationship with Marmar; I let her think she was innocent in what was between us. But deep inside, I carried a wounded heart. I wasn't doing the right thing!

I need to challenge you to think about my situation for a while. Just try to walk in my shoes for one minute. I was a nineteen-year-old young man in love with my married boss, who was thirteen years older than me. I was also searching for the ultimate truth of the universe by getting involved in sorcery, and I was in the company of a gang of robbers and junkie philosophers who wanted to create a better world by doing nothing except smoking weed and having fruitless debates on what they thought was the best for the world. I had a very sensitive job at the Ministry of Defense, and I was increasingly indulging in drugs and prescribed pills. I was away from my family, and I was afraid of people finding out about my addiction and secret love—not to mention that I used to be a communist, and I was living in the Islamic Republic of Iran. I was in serious danger of being arrested for all these. If you are able to put all of these together and be me for few minutes, you will be able to walk more easily with me to the end of this story.

For some reason, my relationship with Marmar became deeper and more complicated instead of becoming weaker. I suggested that she read some books that had great influence on me; she loved them. To be honest with you, I believe reading these books changed her life and her outlook in a way.

Sometimes we played the characters and gave each other lines from a specific passage, pretending we were the characters, male and female. She had had some experience on stage while she was in Tehran University. Although we were just exchanging sentences from a book, sometimes she was so persuasive that I began to clap for her! I truly admired her for her talent in acting. Most of our quotations were from two novels by the 19th century writer and philosopher Romain Rolland, *Jean-Christophe* and *the Enchanted Soul*.

We knew almost all of the conversations and topics of these two books by heart (I guess there are 19 volumes to them altogether). In fact, it was through the book *Jean-Christophe* that I came to know Nietzsche. Later on, I found out that Romain Rolland was influenced by Nietzsche, too. Rolland also had a great influence on the infamous psychoanalyst Sigmund Freud. They seemed to be good friends and kept writing to each other even until the death of Freud in 1939.

So, day after day, Marmar and I became more and more addicted to each others. I had this terrible pain in my stomach all the time, whether I was with her in her office or in my own office or even with my friends drugging and drinking. It didn't matter where I was or what I was doing; there was a storm inside me. I was suffering. The pain was so horrible that I just wanted to die. It was there all the time, whether I was in bed or awake, whether I was shopping or driving, whether I was drinking or high on opium, whether I was with others or with her, alone in her office. There was a hell inside of me, a real hell, I mean. But at the same time, I didn't want to get rid of that pain either. One thing that I couldn't understand was the fact that, even when I pictured myself with her all alone in some lost island somewhere in the world, enjoying all we could enjoy, I still had that horrible pain in my stomach. A friend of mine once told me that, "Love is painful, whether you are with your loved one or not. It's a longing, an addiction which, without that pain, will lose its magic!" He was right.

My pain got worst when she told me that she wanted to introduce me to her family. That was the weirdest thing she ever said since I had met her.

"Are you out of your mind?" I almost yelled at her!

"Bijan, calm down. And please close the door," she said gently.

I closed the door and asked her again, "Are you out of your mind?" but this time I whispered.

"I just want you to meet my family, my husband, and my kids, that's all!" She tried to be as persuasive as she could be.

"There's no way I come to your place to meet Hamid. No way. And I have no idea why you want this to happen!" I added.

"Come on, Bijan. I've already told them about you. They are excited to meet you!" she insisted.

"What are you talking about?" I almost lost my temper and yelled again.

"Bijan, please, it's going to be alright; don't worry. I just want to reduce this tension, this pain; this is bad for both of us, and it's not healthy! You know what I'm talking about." I could relate to her point, but still didn't want to meet with Hamid.

It was the first time that she was admitting the pain. So I asked her, "Mary, what are you talking about? You mean you're in pain too?"

She turned her face toward the window and began to play with her pen. I knew she was happy too. It was just a test for her to see if I was in pain, just like her. She tried to cover it up by dramatically looking at some non-existing far away spot, but it was too late. I had figured it out. She couldn't deny it. We both were pretending we were just friends, good friends, best friends, but in fact, deep inside, it was hurting us. I don't know if it was the guilt or if it was the fact that we knew we would never be able to be with each other that caused the pain, or maybe it was both.

We didn't need to talk about it anymore. We knew what we were going through, and it somehow gave us a sense of satisfaction. I just told her I would think about it and then left her office.

The only thing that prevented me from exploding was some happy pills and a piece of opium. She was right. To reduce this tension, for both of us, the only way was to get closer to her family and feel friendly so that I could get used to the situation. Brilliant idea! After all, she had studied psychology. Did it work? We'll see later.

Candidates

WHEN I THINK ABOUT THOSE days and the emotional and mental pressure I was experiencing, I feel a deep sympathy for the young Bijan. Sometimes I just can't believe it was me who suffered that much. None of the guys I knew who were around my age had experienced what I was going through. Of course, there were those who began a spiritual journey in their young age, but not when they were nine years old while being in a class with thirteen- and fourteen-year-old guys. There also may have been some nineteen-year-olds in love with someone, but not with someone thirteen years older than them who was married with two kids. Again there might have been many people involved in drugs and gangs, but they didn't also work for the Ministry of Defense, or even if they do (which I doubt), they were not practicing Ancient Indian-Mexican sorcery. And if by some miracle, there were people who were in all of these situations, they certainly were not living in Iran, Islamic Republic of Iran, in which even listening to music was a crime! (Or were they?)

"The Six" didn't know about my relationship with Marmar. If they had known, they would have been teasing me and making sexual jokes about us, and I didn't have the nerve to bear that, too. So I had to keep it a secret. But it was damaging me inside, so I finally decided to share it with Afshin.

When I finished telling him the story, he just nodded while playing with his thin, long brown beard. He didn't say a word for quite a while. After a long silence, he finally said something profound, "I understand."

I had thought that if I told him the story he would jump and run to others and tell them a funny story about me being in love with an elderly woman (as I knew their vocabulary) who was in a wheelchair and had no teeth and who had asked me to kiss her lips, and they would all begin to laugh at me, making gestures of how we would make out, and so forth!

But he didn't do that; he just said, "I understand." I asked him if he was going to tell others and make fun of me. He said, "No, why would I do that? You're already in a ridiculous situation. Why would I make it worst for you?" and then he smiled playfully. I liked him very much.

There was something about him that made me try to compete with him in the group, but it was a healthy competition. He was smart, but fragile. He was always trying to show that he was the leader of the group, but after I joined them, he felt threatened. One thing he didn't know was that I wasn't as tough as they thought and my practical leadership skill wasn't that good. Knowing about my situation could have been a privilege to him, but I hoped he wouldn't sell me out; after all, we were very close. Something in his eyes made me believe there was something he wanted to share with me, too. I was right.

After a minute of silence, he began to tell me about this girl he was in love with. He was badly in love with her. She was going to come to Shiraz to give a visit to her family and friends. She planned to stay there for a while.

He didn't tell me much about her, maybe just because he thought I would do the same I thought he would do to me, making fun of him. He told me that the guys already knew her and that she was sort of a group member, but she was mostly away from Shiraz.

You know, the problem with "the Six" was that none of them had any love experience; maybe they had some from childhood, but not in their teen years or even later, as long as I was with them. I guess I was the only one with some experience in that field. So the assumption for them was that girls were only trouble-makers and that they would waste your time with shallow stuff and cheap conversations. All they wanted was your 100 percent undivided attention. They were a danger to the existence of the group.

They all liked Afshin's girlfriend, though, but they also teased him about her when she was not around. At the same time, there was something about his girlfriend that made them respect her as well. When she was there, as I learned later, she was treated as one of their own. She was into spiritualism too; she smoked joint, was cool, was very attractive, was straight forward, and was fun to be around. That's all I heard about her.

For some reasons, I wasn't able to picture her in my mind, and I didn't want to. In fact, I didn't care, because I was too busy with my own story, and I didn't want to believe that an eighteen-year-old girl could have been so cool. Besides, she couldn't be all they said about her. She was too good to be true. Even her name was not a very common name, Saye (*saw'yeh*), which in Farsi means Shadow or Shade. Her name could have been an ironic metaphor for Afshin. I already didn't like her before I even met her. I had no idea why!

So even though I knew Afshin wouldn't tell others about Mary, I still asked him to keep that between us. He assured me he would and then said, "How about another orange trip now?" and he handed me a roll after he fired it up.

—

Previously I mentioned Masoud, the one who seemed to be the seventh member of the group before I heard about Saye. After participating in and observing the group for almost a year and a half, from mid-1980 to near the end of 1982, I noticed something very interesting about the survival of our group. These people had been together for many years. They were very close to getting into the huge mafia of drugs forever. They were just one step from being found lifeless in a dark ally. Addiction and drug dealing were both dangerous enough to put them to death, especially in the Islamic Republic, where the sentence for having one gram of opium was equal to that for murdering someone. I even knew people who were arrested for listening to music or for being at a party, and their parents never saw them again.

So what was the element that separated the destiny of this group from the other gangs I knew? What was keeping them from going to the point of no return? What was the secret that was keeping them alive, with their heads still on their bodies? It was the dominant and influential presence of a person, someone who played a mysterious role in the lives of these rebellious but so knowledgeable guys, and that person was none other than our own Masoud! However, the Six didn't know how important his role was; he didn't know it either, and I still doubt if he even knows it now after thirty years.

Masoud was a very interesting individual! He wasn't a very handsome guy, to be honest, but he had a kind of charisma, a kind of charm that could put you out of the competition quickly unless he considered you a worthy opponent. He owned an admirable insanity that was just woven into his character. I had never seen a person as original as him, and I never saw one after him. He had a weird and to-the-point sarcasm that always

so honestly but rudely expressed his point, adeptly convincing you
was right. He had interesting opinions about things, whether it was music,
love, literature, mysticism, God, women, or even drugs. His opinions were
so unique that I will reserve the right for him to write about them. He
was the balance stone to the group. He had the ability to push them to
both edges. He was able to force them to do things we definitely knew
were harmful, but no one could make him do the same, except for me on
a few occasions.

We managed to preserve our friendship, even after many years passed. I
remember once he sent me a handwritten letter that was written backward,
the whole two pages. On another occasion, he wrote me another letter,
but before mailing it, he ripped it into pieces, small pieces, making me go
through two hours of trouble to put the puzzle back together. He was an
interesting guy.

We all wanted to feel important and different. So within the borders
of our group, we were capable of being ourselves without the fear of being
judged or misjudged. I believe feeling important is a healthy and good
thing for our youth in such a web-in-web world—the world of loneliness,
artificial love, and identity crisis; the artificial but addictive world of
adventurous video and fantasy games and friendships on Facebook,
MySpace, Twitter, and the multitude of dating websites. Not everything
we, as human beings, are searching for is found on the internet. Rather, the
internet isolates us. And sometimes the answer to this isolation is found in
joining a group—some people refer to them as gangs.

In our world, nothing seems to be real anymore. Reality is what our
youth need to get in touch with again. This false adventurous video game
world can only move their fingers, not their whole existence. I'm not against
internet or technology; I just believe that there is value in grouping (even
if some like to call it gangs) that can give life to the youth's progress—
something that we used to call a bitter reality, experiencing, experimenting,
getting involved, tasting, trying, rejecting, accepting, challenging, and
finally paying a price for what is valuable. Humanity's engaging soul has
stopped moving forward for quite a while. That's why even a two-hour
trip to a remote area is so exciting for the kids these days. A couple hours
camping by the lake gives them goose bumps. Of course, they should still
be allowed to take their PSPs or iPhones with them; otherwise, don't even
bother suggesting a camping trip to them!

I realize that this is what we are hearing from almost every teacher
from the older generation of writers/speakers, and we think they say such

things just because they are not into technology or because they belong to Generation-X. It might be true, in some cases, but we need to know that what they say is not just an idea to bring bankruptcy to computer or game factories. No, they say what they believe because it's true. I encourage the kids around me to taste, try, and pay a little price to get some firsthand experience from the things around them, not just absorbing data. Data is good for analyzing the facts after you touch, taste, and experience something. Go ahead and tell me I'm wrong or old fashioned, but that's why people, like Paulo Coelho, are popular and their books are on the bestseller lists—they are introducing to us the old fashioned way of doing things all over again. And it's simply called "experiencing."

Maybe you prefer those brahmas sitting somewhere in a temple, repeating a verse or mantra. Spiritualism, as it has been known for thousands of years in the East, was only introduced to the western searching souls less than a hundred years ago. What was a journey of a lifetime has been turned into a saying or an expression in the intellectual mind of Americans who know nothing of the history or the richness of the experience that led to that saying. In the West, most intellectuals speak to each other using ancient sayings of Indian gurus, Chinese philosophers, ancient Persian poets, Japanese Haiku writers, or even Native American masters of secret knowledge, people like Don Juan.

These days, intellectuality is no longer something based on your own experiments, but based on some data you collect from Wikipedia, something you didn't go through any hardship to learn and own yourself. It's just there for everyone, whether you are a so-called philosopher or a salesman, whether you are an imbecile or a person with an IQ over 140, whether you are a terrorist or a charity organizer, whether you are an eight-year-old or a fifty-year-old. Everything is in Wikipedia! I'm not saying that having easy access to knowledge is bad, and I don't believe the fruit of the knowledge of good and evil was evil itself. What I mean is, "Do something worthy of gaining that knowledge, go through some challenges, use your muscles, and pay a price." I'm not talking about an "Are you smarter than a fifth grader?" show! Just do something adventurous. After all, it is called "life" and not "staying alive!" We used to search, look, try, test, taste, make mistakes, learn, and apply. At least we used to learn from our mistakes. But what a young girl or boy knows now is just what they get from the internet and TV, just data, and it is a kind of data that they can't even analyze, apparently, because they're too busy or lazy to analyze; however, they can easily quote someone on the topic.

Another benefit of belonging to a group is that you learn to trust others, and when you trust others, it is easier for you to admit your mistakes and easier to accept correction. That's what we learned in our gang; we learned to trust each other, even if we didn't know whether or not the other person was good at what we trusted him for.

On occasions, for instance, we would sit in the car (one of us used to have a Volkswagen for a short period of time), turn the lights off in a pitch dark night, and trust the driver to give us a ride on a narrow mountain road. In another scary situation, I remember sitting on the back of a bike, on the edge of our cabin's roof, letting one of "the Six" give me a ride. Sometimes we just walked on the edge of the roofs of the high rise buildings, in order to overcome our fear of heights, while listening to some crazy music like Judas Priest's song "Breaking the Law." I guess we were one-of-a-kind in the whole land of Iran! Insanity! Or you may call it stupidity. Yes, I agree. This is wrong, and I strongly suggest you should never do such things under any condition, but what I do mean is that we need to experience life with all of our beings, not just get whatever we want from Wikipedia! You don't have to (and should not) do what we did, because we were the rebels. To experience life you just need to come out of your comfort zone, just a little.

In all this, the gang needed Masoud to keep the balance. Of course, sooner or later all gangs are destined to be disbanded, but having an element called Masoud was definitely a great help for "the Six" and enabled them to survive for a while.

If Saye, as Afshin told me, was planning to stay in Shiraz, she and Masoud were the candidates for the role of the seventh—a position I wanted badly.

Shadow or Shade

MUSIC, OUR SPIRITUAL JOURNEYS, THE combination of prescribed drugs with the so-called goddesses of hallucination, and finally Don Juan's teaching had brought us so close to each other that the only danger we felt was the danger of losing each other. And that was why everybody was cautious not to say or do anything against Saye while she was there with us as Afshin's girlfriend. None of us wanted to provoke her to do anything that would or could end up taking Afshin away from us; she was a present and clear danger! After all, we believed that women were capable of doing things beyond any man's logic, and that was why most of the greatest intellectuals in the history of the world did not marry (as we used to think). But it was clear to us that this creature was able to make or force a man to cut his ear off (as in Van Gogh's case). We just didn't want to lose our own Afshin or any other member of the gang, for that matter. Who knew what Saye was capable of?

In fact, she was a very cool girl. She was almost into everything we liked. Of course, girls are interested in some other stuff too, but generally she was fun to be around. Like any other member of the group, she had a sharp, stinging sarcasm that could be like a dagger, piercing right into your heart. She was worthy of being in the gang. She was a one-of-a-kind, too.

For me, looking at her when she was smoking Golden Afghan Hashish while talking about the teachings of Don Juan and her mystical observations was a very new experience. As far as I remember, she was just a year younger than Afshin and me, meaning she was only eighteen at that time.

Afshin and Saye were a cool couple. They didn't have those challenges other couples usually have, or at least their challenges were of a different kind. I usually don't ask people questions about their private lives, even if they are close friends, until it's somehow related to me. So I never asked them about their relationship. But there were times when Afshin would ask me questions about Mary and our odd friendship, and I knew that, by asking about Mary, he was saying he wanted me to ask him about Saye. These were the only occasions when I allowed myself to ask how their relationship was going.

I guess sometimes he just wanted to talk to me about her because he didn't feel comfortable talking to the Six. I believe Masoud and I were the only ones Afshin used to talk to about Saye. Besides, I think he somehow felt I had more insight into a mature relationship with a female, which I didn't. He also knew that I wouldn't laugh at him or tease him about their relationship. Others would always make funny dirty jokes about them, but only when Saye was not around. They didn't want to awaken the sorceress. Masoud, on the other hand, had a deeper wisdom about girls, which he himself was not capable of applying to his own relationships with girls, but it was very helpful at times. I already mentioned how weird he was in every aspect!

Afshin had already told me about some of the problems they had in their relationship, even before I met her. So I had an idea.

My friendship with Mary was on a different level. It was a tense and intellectual relationship (and more romantic). Don't get me wrong if I also use the term *sacred!* By using that word, I'm not saying that what we had was right or holy; no, not at all. I do not suggest that kind of relationship to anyone. In fact, I'm warning those who are in this kind of relationship, and I beg them to somehow deal with it sooner than I did because it won't produce a happy ending at all. Not only may it bring sadness and despair to your own life, but it can also destroy other people's lives, whether they are part of the relationship or not.

As I mentioned before, up to that point, they had nothing in common with Mary and me, except what is common to all women and all men, the differences of Venus and Mars! There are many things that we as men have not understood correctly about women, and I believe we never will. But I also believe this is not because women are more complicated (or even as some men claim, too shallow), but just because they follow a different logical path in what they pursue at the moment. Something that makes them so happy or excited on one occasion can be the most boring thing ever on another occasion. I also believe that, as much as men might misunderstand women, there are things that women misunderstand regarding men. The challenge for both is to admit this fact, for most conflicts rise from this denied reality that we are different.. I personally believe that men are much more complicated than women in terms of logic. We tend to complicate things, and we usually get upset when women come up with a simple answer to the problem at hand. Women see things in a different light; they can find short cuts to the answers. But in general, all human beings need attention, security, acceptance, and respect. All other things fall into right place if we understand and admit those needs.

Afshin told me how he really loved Saye, but it was cool not to show it at all, especially since she was not there in Shiraz all the time. He felt it was easier for him not to make a big deal out of it. But it was already a big deal, because at this time he was preparing himself to have some more serious talks with her and with his own parents, particularly his father about the relationship.

His dad didn't like the situation Afshin was in, hanging out with a bunch of irresponsible guys, doing drugs, wasting his life with nonsense like magic and ancient knowledge, reading weird books, dealing with Jins, and completely denying his own responsibility in life, especially regarding the inheritance he was supposed to get. His father was not going to give him anything if he wanted to continue that lifestyle. After all, he had offered that farm to him (and the gang) in the hope that he would settle down and begin to work with his own hands, tasting the benefit of such business. And to be honest, he did. They all worked on the farm with excitement. They sowed grain and made some good money within the first year. But they also grew some of the best marijuana in central Iran and benefited a lot from that, too. And of course, there was the vineyard and the wine itself, which was mostly consumed by seven or eight of us every day, seven days a week.

Afshin began to think about his future. In fact, he came to the conclusion that with the Six he didn't have any chance of starting a life, having a family of his own, or even getting his inheritance. So a gap began to form in his relationship with the other members of the Six. They felt it too, but somehow they put the blame on Saye. They thought she was trying to steal Afshin from them. The very existence of the group was in danger. But what they didn't want to admit was the fact that they couldn't possibly continue this lifestyle until the end of the world; sooner or later they each had to make the same decision. Some of them were very poor, and some were from other neighboring towns and cities. This farm was their only hope of sticking together and surviving the cruel world—creating a new world without war or filthy rich people, without revolutions and separations, without invisible walls of selfishness, but filled with love and trust and honesty in relationship, an everlasting paradise.

I couldn't blame them. Different cultural groups or even different layers of society have had their own imaginary worlds, too—according to their pleasure and pain factors. But we all know that this is nothing but a dream. No group of people has ever been able to reach their goal of living in such a perfect society. Those who seemed to succeed are the ones who made an attempt to commit a collective suicide (like the ones we hear about now and then in some part of the world, on an island or in a remote area, under the influence of a crazy so-called charismatic leader).

Saye wasn't thinking about this kind of stuff. She had a free spirit. I guess she cared for friendship more than marriage. She wasn't even that selfish to let Afshin sacrifice his friendship with others just because of her. If there were any words concerning marriage and a more serious relationship like an engagement, they were more among the parents than the couple. I didn't know much about Saye's likes or dislikes. All I learned about her was through her short trips to Shiraz and some collective personal observation of her behavior in the group, as well as what Afshin told me. She had a very unique and strong presence; she always brought joy to the group.

But it wasn't my business to get involved in their relationship. After all, I had my own problems to take care of.

From a general point of view, Saye was tall and beautiful. She was 6 feet tall and very attractive, with a kind of laugh that was the most apparent evidence of her free spirit. Most girls back in those days would not laugh that way (except my own younger sister). She was one of the most feminist people I had ever known, in a true sense. She wasn't one of those girls who wanted to be more like men in society, but she preferred to be genuinely herself. She wasn't after gaining rights for women; she'd rather just be one without bargaining about it.

Except for the fact that she was a danger to the existence of the group, because of the potential of her stealing Afshin from them, she was accepted and was actually a respected member of the group, even though she wasn't there most of the time.

She would engage in all of the hot and tough conversations we had in the group, especially with Masoud. She discussed many controversial matters with the group, but mostly it was Afshin or Masoud who really engaged in these kinds of discussions with her. We had some short talks about Nietzsche, though. She used to think I was trying to pushing him down their throats. For some unknown reason, I was a little afraid of her; it was more like I felt danger whenever she was around! I didn't want to engage in deep conversations with her. But after a while, just before my days were up in Shiraz, I overcame my fears and had some exciting dialogues with her.

She brought a fresh breath to the group whenever she was around, especially after we got to know more about the teachings of Don Juan through Castaneda's books. In his latter works, he introduces us to some women who were also part of the team. They were trained by Don Juan and his friends, who were called benefactors and were also his team members before they jumped over the Eagle, a term they used to describe the estate of passing over into death while preserving their whole awareness. By doing that, they would seemingly trick the Eagle (which was also vacuuming the life out of every living conscious being in the universe in order to add to his own knowledge by swallowing up their awareness) and continue life as a conscious awareness without a body by becoming one with what they called Infinity. Obviously, this was a privilege provided for those who had the chance to master their awareness.

It is impossible to explain in a line something that took Castaneda his whole life to understand. He couldn't finish the race himself and wasn't able to jump over the Eagle at the end of his journey, maybe because there was no such a thing as jumping over death! I guess he just wanted to leave a legacy so he decided to establish Cleargreen Incorporated to promote the idea he called Tensegrity, a form of unity with the whole existence he concluded from all his years of apprenticeship and centuries of ancient Yaqui shamanism. Indeed, Castaneda was a pioneer of New Age spiritualism, which began around second half of the 20th century and took the world like a storm.

Anyway, these women brought a new understanding to Castaneda's perception of Don Juan's teachings—something he wouldn't be able to achieve by himself. Many years later, I read somewhere that in his last years of life Castaneda lived with three women, as his apprentices, who were also walking on the same path. It is said that all three disappeared into thin air mysteriously a day after Castaneda's death. Saye played a specific role in my understanding of life in those days, even though she wasn't fully aware of it. I'm not sure if others looked at her that way, even Afshin himself. But I respected her very much for that.

Afshin still thought he could somehow keep his dreams alive by persuading his father to let them all work on the farm and share the profit. He also thought he could keep that balance by bringing Saye into the picture and promising his dad that he would marry her, even though she was not exactly the kind of girl his dad wanted to bring into his family as a bride. But I guess he was persuaded by Afshin's mom to accept her as she was so that, through her, Afshin could be granted a future.

I'm not really sure how they expected all these things to work, but as you know, life has a very strange sense of humor. Even today, there are still so many people around us who think they can change the surrounding realities (their problems) by clinging to some other momentarily satisfactory solutions just to get rid of the problem at hand. It's alright if you don't agree with me on this (you practically can't argue with me because I'm in a book). Let us just be honest and admit that we cannot just get rid of our problems by jumping over them in the hope that we will enter another zone in which we will handle things in a different way with different abilities and skills. We all know things won't work that way. Of course, there are times when outwardly things seem to work that way, but just outwardly.

I did not know much about Saye's opinions and views on all of these things, but I remember that once Afshin told me that Saye never thought official marriage could be a guarantee for a couple to love each other and that she never believed in marriage as a stronghold against betrayal or treachery. He agreed with her, but the traditional family view had to be met to receive an inheritance. I wasn't there to see the finale with my own eyes, although I know the end. But for now it is enough to tell you that Saye will come onto the scene again.

In those days, something was reaching its climax in the lives of all of us. It wasn't necessarily a sad or a happy ending. Not everything in this world is supposed to end happily or sadly ever after. It's not the end that matters; it's the transformation that counts. Something was happening, and pain was an essential part of it; something was moving toward some kind of death, and something else was supposed to be born out of its ashes.

Preparation

SINCE I DECIDED TO MOVE in with "the six" there were times when I missed the minibus to the farm, and I had to stay in town. In such cases, I always stayed with two guards at the dormitory of my work place. One of these two guys was a very fanatic Muslim. Sometimes during my stay, we talked about politics and social matters. He didn't like my views. Although I didn't believe in communism any more, my outlook regarding social issues was always based on equality, human rights, and freedom of speech and belief. He didn't like those ideas at all (probably because he was not able to understand anything other than Islamic Law). I pitied him. Plus he would always say bad things about city boys who would come to Shiraz to defile Shirazi girls. I knew where his arguments came from, but I wasn't one of those typical city guys he was referring to, because I was in this highly sophisticated relationship with Marmar. Anyway, the point is, he didn't like me at all.

Meanwhile, my relationship with Mary was getting tense. By tense I mean worse. We didn't want to talk about it because we both didn't want to admit it. But it was really going nowhere. After I listened to her advice and visited her family, everything seemed to change. Her husband sensed something, but he was a real gentleman, and he didn't mention anything to her. It wasn't a pleasant night for him or me, but I guess we both did it because of our love and respect for Marmar. Her kids loved me, though. The idea seemed to work, but it had a side effect on me.

After that night in their home, I began to think about her kids and the lovely nest they had. The fact that her husband knew our secret seemed not to bother her, but it made me realize that I was damaging their marriage and family. When her kids called me uncle Bijan, I realized how stupid I was and how precious and innocent they were. I began to see myself as a monster—a consuming virus that did not care about anything else except his unsatisfied craves. I began to question my ideas, my "ideals." Who was I really? What was I doing? What was the result of all those books I had read? How could I speak of justice and social equality while I was destroying someone else's family? What was I thinking?

Within next few days after that night, something in me began to crack. I hated myself more and more. But it was just the beginning. In order to escape the situation, I increased the dose of everything I was consuming; I mean *everything*—at least ten rolls a day, plus a very remarkable amount of opium, along with 15 different strong pills. Some of them were very dangerous to take together. I wasn't able to think clearly anymore. The pain in my stomach (which was obviously guilt) had returned, and this time it was unbearable. I couldn't sleep well. There were many nights when I went without sleeping. My mental condition caused me to behave strangely, and I couldn't hide it anymore. Everybody noticed my strange behavior. Afshin felt it necessary to talk to me. Others in the group felt the same, but did not say anything. Afshin took me aside one night and began to ask questions.

"Bijan, what's wrong with you?"

"Nothing, I'm cool."

"Oh come on man, you're not cool; you're totally spoiled!"

"I'm cool, I'm fine. I'm just a little bit tired."

"Hey, I'm not doing well myself, but you my friend, you are beyond reach!"

"Isn't that what we try to achieve, being unreachable?! Isn't that what Castaneda was learning? To be out of reach?"

"The hell with Castaneda's teachings! We're supposed to get over things, not get stuck in them."

"Why should I get over things when I'm going nowhere? Where are we going, Afshin? To what destination? I'm tired, man, tired. I can't continue this. I'm destroying people's lives; we're not supposed to do that," I said.

"Come on, we're just defending ourselves against the tyranny of the world. We didn't want to come to this damn world, did we? That's all. We are the good guys. Don't let anything you do put the blame on you. We're not destroying anyone's life. We're here in this farm just to protect ourselves; otherwise those monsters outside would tear us apart. We're just trying to survive.

"No, Afshin, don't deceive yourself," I replied, "We are destroying lives, first ours and then others' we claim to love. We pretend to be cool, but we aren't. Maybe *we* are the monsters, and we're just using our intelligence to justify what we do. Show me one good thing we've done, just one."

He thought for a second and said, "I think we're much better people compared to the gun dealers. What they do is awful. Millions of people are dying because they want to sell their guns just to get richer. We have nothing in common with them. They are the monsters Roger Waters spoke about. They are the wall makers; we're just trying not to be trapped in those walls."

I didn't agree with him, he didn't give me an example of what good we were doing, so I went on, "Come on man, we're doing the same thing. We sell Marijuana, opium and Hashish to young people. A cocaine dealer can say the same thing to justify himself. At least he doesn't claim to have ancient knowledge, nor does he consider himself an intellectual. We ain't nothing, we're in sh**."

"Oh shut up, we're not," he tried to defend his belief system. "I'm going to have a good life. In a couple of years from now, I won't live like this anymore. I don't know about these guys, but I'm going to have a cool life soon, you'll see".

"Yeah, you are. Keep saying that to yourself," I replied. "We're just rubbish, we do rubbish, and until we find a way out, we will reap rubbish."

"What the hell are you talking about? Something's really wrong with you." He got really mad at me, "Is it all about that woman in your work place? I should have known. She's dangerous, man. She's playing with you. I'll go and waste her. Don't let her play games with you. She's just having fun; she laughs at you! I thought you were smarter than that. I mean, you are. You just need to pull it back altogether again."

"No. It's not just her. Nothing in my life seems to be in the right place. Nothing. Yeah, I like her, but it's not all about her. It's everything. There's nothing left in me to drive me forward. Not a damn thing." I was almost crying.

"You can stay here with us," he seemed concerned. "I've already talked to my father. He agreed to let us stay and work on the farm. Saye might also join us. You have to quit your job at that damn War Ministry and move in completely with us. It'll be alright."

I wanted to yell at him and say, "You are stupid! How much longer do you want to think like a baby? You ignore all realities, and that's how you're destroying your life and the lives around you—by being irresponsible, indifferent, numb!" But I controlled myself. I knew he was concerned about me. I didn't have any strength left in me to argue anymore. So I said, "I can't just quit. There's a war outside, and if I quit, then I have to join the military. They're counting my civic service as military service; you know that. Plus, you just said that you're going to have your own life in the near future. I understand what you're trying to do." He just stared at me without saying a word. I continued, "I just know I'm not feeling good. This void, this hellish vacuum, is killing me inside. I can't think clearly. I can't think at all! But thanks for nothing, man," I teased him. "I love you. I know everything's gonna be alright. Let's go back in and have fun."

I didn't tell him that I really liked the idea of quitting my job and joining this crazy gang forever, even though I knew it was just a childish thought. That was another mistake—the idea of living together forever on this farm and smoking up all the weed in the world. But still, no matter how silly the idea was, it was better than grabbing a gun and killing people in that ridiculous war. I knew Afshin's intention was good; he was just being nice to me. Most people in such circumstances say such things to calm down the other person—things they don't believe deep inside. I didn't want to hurt his feeling by telling him how stupid his idea was. He simply thought he could continue this idiotic life and even bring Saye into it! But at least he was trying.

I wanted to die. There was no other way except to end this nonsense life. What a sweet thought—death, end of everything, eternal peace, becoming nothing. But I couldn't tell him what I was thinking about. At least by thinking of death I could calm myself down for a while. It was funny, because it was exactly what Nietzsche says. I don't precisely remember the phrasing, but he was right. The idea of committing suicide was able to postpone the actual attempt. It was like pouring water on fire. In fact, I had been thinking about it for a couple of weeks, and the idea itself was a pacifier to all my miseries. To me it was like a blank check. It was there; I just needed to sign it whenever I thought the time was right. It was really a peaceful thought. But as we all know, whatever you focus on, sooner or later you will do.

Russian Roulette

ONE MORNING, IN THE SPRING of 1982, around 10 a.m., my phone rang. It was Mary. She told me there were two gentlemen in her office who wanted to talk to me. I told her I would be there in a minute. It was not a strange thing. Sometimes our clients would go to her and complain about the delay in their paper work. I thought it was the same situation.

When I entered her office, I saw two goliaths (one fat, one tall) standing there waiting for me. As soon as I entered the room, one of them grabbed me from behind, and the other one put hand cuffs on me. It happened so quickly that I couldn't show any reaction. Mary jumped up from her chair and yelled at them, "What are you doing? Let go of him!" The one who put the hand cuffs on me held his right hand against her face and said, "Please, sit down. It's a matter of national security!"

I thought, *What? National security? What are they talking about?*

I heard her saying, "What? National security? It's ridiculous! I'm calling the Colonel."

"We can't tell you anything; it's against the protocol," he said.

They didn't wait another second. They took me out and threw me in the car. I heard the car's doors click. I came to myself after the click. It was real. I had been arrested by a government intelligence service!

"What have I done, may I ask?" I said in a soft tone.

"We cannot discuss the matter before the interrogation," he replied.

"But I don't understand. I haven't done anything wrong," I insisted.

"Please sit back and keep quiet," he said.

I took a look outside. Everybody at our building pushed to the front door to see what was going on. It was embarrassing. I looked the other way.

They took me to a place I already knew. We had passed this building a couple of times before with some friends. They had told me about it. It was the headquarters of Military Intelligence. Shiraz wasn't a very large city, so it wasn't difficult to know what was where.

They put me in a dark and cold cell. They kept me there for hours. Somebody brought me some food. It was stinky. I was hungry, but I didn't want to eat that garbage. So I began to make noises, "Hello! Anybody there? I'm hungry; get someone to buy me a sandwich! I'll pay for it." Then I laughed at what I just said. What was I thinking? I began to shout, "Hey, I'm sick, get me out of here. I haven't done anything wrong. I want to see your boss."

After about 10 to 15 minutes of yelling, finally somebody showed up at the door of the cell and asked me to keep quiet; otherwise they would put me in one of the underground cells.

Oops, I thought, *better to be quiet than to be sent to those dungeons! No one knew what was going on in there.* So I told the guard that I was hungry and that I couldn't eat that food, and to justify myself, I added, "I have stomach flu and can't eat this. Do you have something else to eat?"

He silently looked at me for a while and then left without saying a word. I thought, *"What a cruel and cold look. If I catch you outside, I'll know what to do with you."* But he was back within a few minutes with a bowl of soup and a piece of bread. He slipped it in through a small door at the bottom of the cell door. I thanked him. I felt embarrassed. First I was hesitant to try the soup, but it smelled so good that I finally gave it try. It was very good, and the bread was fresh. I liked it.

After I finished the soup, I began to make noises again, kicking the door and yelling, "Get me out of here! Hello! Anybody there?" And I kept kicking against the door. I thought to myself, *Come on man, what are you doing? They can just shoot you in the head and dump your body somewhere out of the city.* But I didn't have anything to lose! It would be nice if they would shoot me. I would die a hero. Death, sweet death! This way, my wish would come true without any further troubles. But on the other hand, I thought to myself that they could keep me there for months and torture me if I made them mad. I was kind of curious as to why they had even arrested me in the first place! I had a hunch, but wasn't sure.

Finally, after about four hours, the same guy who brought me the soup opened the door and took me to a room. I took a quick look around and saw a signed paper on the desk, "Judge Hashemian." I was in a judge's room. Two guys came in, both fat and in their mid-fifties. One of them sat behind the desk, and the other one stood beside him. He was the one who had put the hand cuffs on me. Later on I found out that he was the chief inspector of the Military Intelligence base in Shiraz.

The Judge began to speak, "Why were you making that much noise? We were out for lunch."

I said, "Excuse me? You were out for lunch? You put me in that cell and went for lunch? I yelled because I have stomach flu. I couldn't eat that food. You didn't want to eat it either. That's why you went out for lunch!"

He laughed. Then he threw a book in front of me, asking, "Is this yours?"

"No, it isn't," I said, while slipping the book back.

"You didn't even look at the title. How could you say 'no'?" he asked.

"Because I know my books," I replied, "I can tell you if it is mine or not even from ten feet away!"

"Please take a closer look, young man; your name is on the book!" he said.

I sat straight and grabbed the book. He was right; my name was on the book, but it wasn't my handwriting. I told him it wasn't my writing and that anyone could have done that. "Anybody can put your name, as a judge, on a paper and claim it's yours."

"How do you know I'm a judge?" he asked with curiosity.

"Your name is on that paper right in front of you, Judge Hashemian," I pointed to the document.

He looked surprised, "Of course. And I also signed your arrest warrant. I can also let you go if you cooperate."

"Why did you issue an arrest warrant?" I asked. "Just because somebody put my name on a book?"

"No, because of the content of the book. It's a book by Karl Marx." He sounded very serious this time.

I didn't tell them that, in fact, I had read the book a couple of years ago and I knew very well who Karl Marx was. "But I told you, it's not even my book." I passed it back to him again.

"We also had a report from someone who knows you," he continued.

"Do I know him, too?" I teased him.

"You are smart. Are you interrogating me?" He leaned forward.

"Maybe I should, because you are interrogating the wrong person." I couldn't believe I was talking like that!

Suddenly the other guy (the chief inspector) walked toward me and said, "Watch your behavior. Maybe you should explain to us why we found this book in your desk drawer last night."

"Maybe you should tell me who informed you that there was a book in my drawer? Apparently it's not a good book because it's the cause of this conversation. I'm telling you the truth, it wasn't there yesterday afternoon when I left the office," I replied.

"How do we know you're telling us the truth?" said the Judge.

"Because yesterday afternoon around 3 o'clock I was sent to the city hall to get some papers signed by the Mayor, and it took so long that I had to call my boss and ask him to have someone else to do my job at the office," I explained. "And if you give enough attention to this so-called evidence, you will see someone else's name at the end of the last page of the book. I saw the name in a quick examination of the book. How come you didn't see it? He is the one who sat behind my desk yesterday afternoon. You can check this with my boss. The guy I'm talking about is a guard who happens to dislike me very much. Plus, these two handwritings are the same, but it's not mine, so it should be his."

The judge turned to the chief inspector and asked him to check the matter with my boss. He left the room to make a call.

"You should become an inspector," the Judge said, smiling.

"I'm so tired of life that I don't want to be anything."

"What's your problem young man?"

"Nothing."

"One thing's for sure, you have attitude!"

"Sorry Judge, but I'm really ill. Can I go home now?"

"Not that fast. Where's your home, by the way?"

I thought, *Oops! This is going the wrong way. If they find out where and with whom I live then everybody will be in trouble, considering the amount of Marijuana plants, Hashish, and opium bags.* I had to quickly come up with another convincing lie.

"With friends." I replied. "My flat-mate got married a couple months ago, and I had to leave the apartment to him and his bride. I'm looking for a new place, but so far nothing's available. I stay with friends."

"Where? We need the address," he sounded serious again.

The chief inspector came back to the room. They looked at each other. The Inspector nodded. They had the name. I was happy, not because he was in trouble now, but because I thought maybe the Judge was right, and I could make a good inspector!

"Inspector," the Judge said, "Please take him to his friend's place and do a quick search. Here's the warrant." Then he pointed to the door, meaning I had to leave.

I asked the Judge if he already knew where I was living. He replied, "We know how to do our job, young man. And yes, we already knew where you live; the warrant is signed already."

My heartbeat increased. That was not good at all. I was afraid to death. We were finished!

After we left the building, I did my best to persuade the Inspector not to take me to my friend's place. I told him that they had nothing to do with this, and that if he searched their place, they wouldn't let me stay there anymore. I tried to awaken his sense of sympathy, but nothing worked. I was worried for everyone. I didn't care about myself; I was planning to waste myself, after all. I was thinking of Afshin's dream.

The night before, they had been talking about uprooting the Marijuana trees and taking them to a friend's barn to dry them. There were about 100 grown trees. I found myself wishing they had already done that. I wasn't worried about the bags of Hashish and Opium, because they were always buried under the ground, somewhere in the field.

We got there around 4:30 p.m.—six guys with automatic guns in three cars. I felt sick in my stomach. We didn't have a parking lot in front of the cabin, so from the place they parked the cars to the room we lived in was about one minute walking.

Immediately I noticed that the guys had already finished uprooting the plants. The Six had seen us parking the cars from afar. Quickly they hid everything that could possibly be considered illegal. They were smart.

The guys with the guns entered and asked everybody to leave the cabin and wait outside. One guy remained outside with us. I assured my friends that everything was alright and that it was a regular procedure because of my job (I couldn't tell them what was really happening because of the guard who was standing beside us).

They searched every corner. All they found was hundreds of books. Pointing at the books, I reminded the inspector of what I said earlier about knowing my books. He shook his head in affirmation. They went through all books one by one. Good thing we didn't have any communist books.

The inspector took everyone aside, one by one, and asked them some questions about me. I was very confident that these guys knew how to answer him. It's very assuring when you know you can trust someone with your life. They were perfect in this area. Many years have passed, and I still miss that special thing about them.

After an hour or so, the Inspector was handed a piece of paper by one of the guards. "There's nothing to be worried about," I told myself. "I'm pretty sure there's nothing there to connect me to communism."

He began to walk toward me. He showed me the paper and asked, "Is this your writing?"

"I think so." I took a closer look at the letter.

"Who is Marmar?" he asked.

Something hit me so strong that I almost lost my focus and began to shiver at hearing her name. My brain stopped working. Everything around me went black. He noticed. "Who is Marmar?" he asked again.

In just a second, thousands of thoughts stormed my brain. *What is this letter? When did I write it? What if they find out about our relationship? What have I done? I just destroyed a family. What do I do now, what do I do? Stupid Bijan! If they'd find out about our friendship they will stone her to death!* Even a relationship as pure as ours could be considered an act of adultery!

I pictured the worst in my mind. It's funny how quickly our brains can react to such things and try to analyze every possible way out in less than a second. I told myself, *Come on Bijan, say something, say something!* My heartbeat rate was so high that I felt my heart was about to explode, and the sound of it was so loud that I thought the Inspector already heard it. My face was so pale that the Inspector told me to sit down. "Who is Marmar?" he said again.

"A friend," I replied, with almost no sound in my voice. "She is a friend. It's just a letter. Please give it back to me. It's a personal thing." And the picture of people surrounding her with stones in their hands shouting, "prostitute, adulteress, die, die" kept getting bright and brighter in my mind. A heavy burden on my chest was making me almost cry.

"Is she living in Shiraz? Who is she?" he kept asking.

"I beg you, please give it back; it's just a stupid letter," I was trembling.

"I just want to know who she is. Don't worry," he assured me.

"She's just a girl I like. I already told you. She has no idea I like her."

"Just tell me who she is and we're done. But remember, don't lie, alright?"

I knew if I would lie to him, it could end up in another disaster, a much worse situation. I wasn't sure about the content of the letter or which letter it was. (I had written her many romantic letters, which I never gave her to read, except for the poems.)

"She is a co-worker."

"And?" he didn't seem to give up.

"And nothing! I just like her and wrote her some letters that were never intended to be given to her. I guess I wrote this a year ago. We have nothing to do with each other; please believe me. She doesn't even know I like her!"

I couldn't bear the pressure anymore. Although we were standing in open field, I felt like there was no oxygen in the air to breathe. I couldn't let a stupid letter destroy her career and family life.

To my surprise, the Inspector gently handed me the letter and said, "It's OK now; don't worry. No one will know about her, I promise. You seem to be a nice guy, but you have to be careful who you associate with. How long have you known these guys?" he pointed to my friends.

I thought, *My goodness, not again! Now the Six?* I had put everyone's life in danger. I never ever imagined one action could create such a destructive chain reaction. And now he was asking about the Six!

"I asked how long you have known these guys?" he insisted again.

I thought, *If I show him weakness, he will continue to ask more questions, and it will get worse.*

"I've known them for about a year and a half now. They have been very nice to me. I can swear to them. They helped me a lot since I came to Shiraz. You are Shirazi, right? Shirazis are very hospitable, you know."

He stared at me for a while. I knew he was trying to figure out whether I was lying or telling him the truth. I always knew that those who join the intelligence services must be very suspicious people in nature. That's not good for their health! Suspicious people not only distrust others around them all the time, but also do a crime against their own selves. I'm not just talking about inspectors or cops or secret service agents, but suspicious people in general. It is a sickness that follows you every second of your life. People run away from you. You won't have close friends. You may end up having no friends at all. Suspicious people are the loneliest people on the earth.

He offered me a handshake and said goodbye. I exhaled. It was over. I'm sure you can imagine how I felt the moment I shook his hand.

Soon after they left, I explained everything to the guys, apologized for the inconvenience, and explained to them that the Inspector had already known the place where I was living. They said that they understood and that I didn't need to explain anything.

That day was the toughest and the most stressful day of my life, especially with all the recent pressures I'd been going through. Insomnia, pills, all the drugs, Marmar's case, the void in me, the meaninglessness of everything in life, and finally all the damage I could have brought on all my loved ones around me. I was responsible. Enough of this stupid Russian roulette game; I made my decision, "I'm gonna do it!" I kept hearing a dark luring voice in my head, "Just enjoy the moment and have fun, for tomorrow you'll be gone!"

———

Early in the morning, earlier than any other day, I walked into an old tea house called Abdullah, which means "Allah's slave" (kind of ironic, right?). It was just a two minute walk from my work place. It was ironic; I was sitting there in a place called "Allah's slave." All my life I had thought I was searching for God, the ultimate truth, but it seemed that he never cared. After all, how could I expect God to care for me? Did I care for a bacteria or even an ant? Why would I? Then I thought, *Am I really a slave? A God's slave; maybe I am my own slave or the devil's slave!* But it didn't matter anymore; I had made my decision. I was staring at the small container in my hand, which contained 50 strong sleeping pills, diazepam 10m. It was enough to put me to sleep forever, twice, making sure I would never wake up again. It was easy to get that stuff on the streets after the war, especially in Shiraz. I was calm. I thought about all the special people I had met during my 20 years of life. I wasn't feeling like a twenty-year-old at all. I had the mind of a person in his late forties. All those philosophical and mystical books had made me sound much older. I had figured out that knowledge could only add more pain to life and that ignorance was bliss! But there would be no more pain from now on—just floating out there, somewhere in nowhere land! I thought, *Who knows, I might be back in the form of a coyote or a snake. They are smart animals.* I didn't believe in reincarnation, though. I was just teasing myself before I was no more.

I had already ordered some fried eggs (half-done) with some black tea. I was really hungry. It was the first time in the last couple months that I had my appetite back. It was interesting; I could have ordered a cow for breakfast. I wasn't feeling bad at all. I had been thinking about this moment for several weeks by then. I couldn't wait for my food to arrive. The tea house was crowded and filled with smoke. I looked at the pills in the container, and with no hesitation, I poured them all into my mouth at once. They were bitter. My food came, and I ate it all with passion, salt, and pepper. The food and the tea tasted so good. In fact, everything around me felt so cozy and warm. I had had a good time the previous night with the Six back at the farm. People in the tea house seemed not worried about life. Most of them were old. I felt I was old, too, and tired. To make sure the pills work, I ordered another plate of eggs, and after finishing it, I gave a good tip to the young kid who was serving me at the table. I thought about his future, and in my heart, I wished him no pain. What a stupid wish!

I walked out of the tea house and lighted my last cigarette. In five minutes I was behind my desk, looking out the window. Even the weather was good—sunny, and refreshing. I had already left a poem for Marmar. After twenty minutes, I began to feel so light and happy that I burst into laughter without control. Thirty minutes later, I couldn't even walk straight. My phone rang, and I knew it was her. I left the phone to ring. I walked toward her office with a funny smile on my face. She immediately felt that something was wrong, but didn't take it that seriously. She thanked me for the poem and asked me to take a seat. She seemed serious about what she wanted to tell me, but my laughs made her uncomfortable. She told me to go and come back later when my laughter was over. She was apparently offended, but I couldn't stop laughing. I told her I loved her, and then I left the room. She ran after me and called me by my last name twice. Everybody turned around to see what was going on. I didn't care. I just kept walking toward the entrance door. I was walking on the clouds, and there were butterflies in the air.

Die Hard Twice

A FRIEND OF MINE USED to proudly say that he was smarter than God because he was cheating him constantly by changing the course of his life every now and then to get what he wanted. Funny guy! We can't cheat God. We're not even able to cheat others for a long time. We all have a purpose to fulfill. For some people, the concept of God is always accompanied with destiny and fate. But some of us know that these two are not the same; one involves humankind's free will, and the other doesn't. I used to partially believe in fate, but now I believe in destiny. You will know why.

I woke up in an unfamiliar room filled with very old stuff; even the furniture was probably one hundred years old. I was lying on a hard bed. It was like a table, a short one, and close to the floor. I was covered with a white sheet up to my neck. I could hardly move my body parts. I thought *Oh my God, no way! Is this my hell?* I had always pictured hell as a place filled with the things you always hated or feared in life; I hated old rooms with old furniture; they are creepy! I hated the room. A huge sadness came upon me.

My ears were buzzing. I felt like a thousand-pound piece of boneless meat. I had a terrible headache and felt sick in my stomach. *Am I really dead? If not, then where am I, and what's happened to me? Where is this creepy place? How long have I been here?* I tried to say a word, but it was like my mouth was glued. I heard footsteps. I was afraid to see who would open the door. The door opened, and there was Morteza, the Colonel's driver. So I wasn't dead! But where was I?

69

"Hey man! How are you?" Morteza asked.

"Where am I? Where's this place?" I said. I almost had no voice.

He giggled, "You are in my place, my parents', actually."

"What happened?" I asked.

"I am the one who should ask you that question," he said, "You were so high on something that when I came in to work you were laughing like crazy in the middle of the main hallway near the entrance. You were making fun of people, but in fact you made a fool of yourself. The only thing I could do was to grab you and throw you in the car and bring you here. You've been sleeping for four days now." Then he added, "What did you take?"

I tried to remember what had happened, but everything was blurry. All I remembered was the eggs, the tea house, and my last words to Mary. I felt sick in my stomach and was about to throw up. I felt so weak. If he was right, those eggs were the last thing I had had for four days. I had been fasting!

"What did you take? Whatever it was, it was very strong stuff."

"Fifty Diazepam 10m," I replied.

"Wow, man! Fifty 10m?! You broke the record! My friend's girlfriend took only 20 of them last year, and she tripped to the other world and never came back! And you only slept for four days!" After a short pause he continued, "Of course after all those drugs we take daily, it's not a surprise. Did you see Don Juan on the other side?!" and he laughed hysterically. Then he took a deep breath and said, "Why did you do that?!"

"It's a long story." I was not in the mood to explain the whys. I asked, "What time is it?"

"It's 2, afternoon. Why? You want to go somewhere? Do you have a date or something?" He laughed again.

"Yeah, I need to go to the office. I have things to do." A foggy idea had just come into my mind, but I wasn't sure what it clearly was; it was just a dim picture. Plus, I really wanted to get out of that creepy room. It smelled like death. And I had just come back from the dead. I needed some fresh air.

He helped me stand up and put my shoes and jacket on. Then he went upstairs and came back with some food and water. Even the food looked like dead people's food. I had no idea what it was, but I couldn't eat it. I just had some water. Everything in that house was cold and dead. Or maybe it was me who was dead inside.

He told me it wasn't wise for him to take me to the office, but he would drop me somewhere close by. I agreed. I had no strength left in me to argue. He took me to the car. It was like a long journey. I breathed heavily.

"Do the guys know about me?!" I asked him out of curiosity.

"Yeah, I told them what happened. They wanted to come and see you, but you know my parents; they hate the guys!" he replied.

"Yeah, I know."

"So... honestly, did you want to kill yourself?"

"It's not important anymore, but yep."

"But why?"

"Come on, Morteza. I'm not in the mood. But thanks for taking care of me."

He was shy and never able to take any kind of complement. He laughed and said, "No problemo, brother. I couldn't stand there and watch you disgrace yourself in front of everyone, especially in front of the clients." I thanked him again. I didn't want to engage in conversations. My mind was preoccupied with something else; a plan was forming there.

He dropped me off somewhere near the office and took the other way. He was heading to the office too, but didn't want anyone to see us together; after all, he was the Colonel's driver.

When I got there, I was out of breath. Mary saw me coming in from a distance and ran toward me, but she slowed down when she saw that the hallway was filled with people. She tried to talk to me, but I ignored her and passed her by. I went directly to the Colonel's office. He was in his own executive washroom. I stepped inside and closed the door behind me. The key was on the door. So I took it, locked the door, and put the key in my pocket. The Colonel was still in the washroom. I went to his desk and searched the drawers to see if he kept a gun somewhere. There was none. There on the desk I saw a letter opener. I grabbed it. It was as sharp as a knife. It was more like a dagger, traditionally hand-made. Now I knew what I was supposed to do.

During my two years of life in Shiraz, I had learned and heard many things about the Colonel. You may be surprised, but he was a very influential person in the city. From businessmen to MPs, from Ayatollahs to the heart of Shirazi mafia, from underground vodka and wine-making factory owners and smugglers to the operators of prostitution business—they all knew him, and he was respected highly because of his uncountable wealth and his influence in Tehran among authorities. I personally hated him, but never cared about him. While he was still in his executive washroom, I thought to myself, *It is because of individuals like him that so many people in Shiraz are in pain, especially the youth.* He was one of the biggest and strongest bricks in the Wall. Roger Waters was right. We all were part of that wall. Even Mary was. I was. The Six were. All of us were.

But there were people like the Colonel who caused the most damages. He was like an unseen Godfather to many gangs and mafia groups. And he knew exactly what he was doing. He was also in the real estate business, especially after the war when thousands of war refugees had to move to Shiraz; many of them were rich enough to buy houses and lands in Shiraz. After the Islamic regime came to power, they executed many rich people or anyone who had a tide with the Shah's regime (literally thousands). Many opportunists came to power, and as a result, they took over and owned the empty houses and palaces. Our own Colonel, through his connections, turned these places to whore houses, or he sold or rented them all to rich, hopeless war refugees. He turned the other places into lust houses for Mullahs (something like that secret place of gathering in Stanley Kubrick's masterpiece *Eyes Wide Shut*). He was a Mason. In the Shah's time, there were many of them in every position, literally almost everywhere in the government.

He was really something. His power was even greater than many generals and mullahs. He was a very close friend of Shiraz's own Ayatollah Dastgheyb, who was the handpicked representative of Ayatollah Khomeini, the founder and Supreme Leader of the Islamic Republic! So you can imagine what kind of power he had.

"What if I kill him right now, right in his office?" I said to myself. "It could be a great service to humankind."

The phone had been ringing now for a while. Knocking on the door became stronger and louder. I heard the voices from outside, "Colonel, Sir, are you alright? Please open the door," Some of the employees went out to watch what was going on inside from behind the windows. I locked the windows too and closed the curtains. He came out of the washroom. He stood at the door of the washroom, confused and baffled for few seconds, and when he saw the letter opener in my hand, he ran toward the door, but I was smarter, even in my weakest condition.

While he was still hopelessly trying to open the door, he said, "What are you doing here?" He was frightened and pale.

"Nothing special, Sir! I just wanted to see you and have a chat," I said sarcastically.

"Why did you lock the door? Give me the key," he stretched out his hand toward me.

I gently shook my head and told him to sit down, while showing him the letter opener.

"You're out of your mind, kid. You better give me the key before it's too late. Come on, give me the key." He was really afraid.

"Yeah, it might be so bad for me, you know, they might even hang me for this. But hey, I just came back from being dead. I was almost dead for four days, so I have nothing to lose, Mr. Colonel, Sir! Please sit down." I didn't know how that courage or boldness came over me, but I liked me.

Then I told him I just wanted to ask him few questions. I knew I didn't have much time. Since he was well known for his wise advice to those under his supervision, I asked him how he could live on every day knowing he was one of the most disgusting people in Shiraz and maybe in the whole world.

"I say it again, you are out of your mind, and you have no idea what I can do to you. You better come to your senses and give me the key. Otherwise, I will have to deal with you. Have you heard about military disobedience during the war?

I cut his speech and said, "Listen Mister, I don't give a damn about what you're saying, OK? I can kill you right now and then kill myself, too, before anyone can break in to rescue you. So I don't care; you got it? I DO NOT CARE!

He looked at me silently for a few seconds, and then he went back to his desk and sat on his chair.

"What do you want?" he asked.

"Answer my question. How do you live? How can you even walk around and breathe? Do you still have any conscience? How do you deal with yourself every day?

The phone kept ringing. He pointed to it gently, meaning that it was better to answer the call. I nodded. He answered the phone and told his assistant that everything was alright and that he was coming out soon. Then he turned to me while hanging up the phone, "I have noticed you before. You are more mature than those idiots who came here with you from Tehran. I told my assistant you were smart." He paused to see my reaction, but when he saw my motionless face, he continued, "These are the questions that an old man asks himself, not a young man like you."

"Cut it Colonel! You know what I'm talking about. Prostitution, parties for mullahs, mafia. We both know we don't have the whole day.

Plus I'm not asking these questions of myself, but of you, *so answer me,"* I yelled again.

"Alright, I don't exactly know what you're talking about and why you are asking me those questions, but if you mean how all the five billion habitants of the earth are dealing with life or their mistakes and weaknesses, I can give you a hint." He continued, "Life is tough, and to live you have to be tough. If you don't kill to survive, you'll be killed. You should have known that by now. Sometimes life is more than just surviving; it becomes about power and winning. Those who complain about life are usually either the weakest, who would do the same to others if they had the chance, or those who are ashamed of who they are, but try to blame others for their own mistakes. Look at the hunger in Africa! People put it on imperialism, but I tell you the truth. They are nothing but a lazy people who are fighting their own people, tribe against tribe, killing each other like animals, and then they blame everything on rich countries! Your question is not about me; it's about human beings and their nature. We're all the same, some less, some more. Now give me the key, and I promise not to file a law suit against you.

"We're not done, yet. I didn't ask you about Africans. You don't think I'm stupid, do you?!" I said. But while he was speaking, I noticed that what he was telling me was exactly the same things I was telling Afshin the other day. Wasn't he the mirror picture of my own self in the future, if I would choose to live?! Then I thought maybe he was just buying some time before the Air Force guards arrived (one of their bases was right across the street from our building). Maybe. But who cared. Since the door and the windows were locked, only one of us would walk out, in case the guards attempted to break in, or maybe neither of us! I was ready to put an end to his life and then to mine as well.

I thought, *Maybe, after all, he was just like me when he was younger? Or maybe he was smarter than I thought. Maybe what he is doing is right. Maybe living with that mindset is not a bad thing at all.* But one thing I was sure of—he was afraid; I could see it in his face.

He was in his mid-sixties. He was a short guy, half-bald. He would always come in from the back door and leave the same way. He was probably scared or ashamed or both. Surely he was clever and was trying to confuse me, but he didn't know I was already confused. I saw myself in him, only forty years later. It was for this reason that I wanted to kill myself—fear of becoming like him. I was good for nothing except to become someone like him. I had the potential to become a much worse monster. I didn't want to be like him, but I knew that if I would continue to live, I would become a monster much uglier than him. I pitied him.

I thought, *I will be a very dangerous threat to people around me.* I thought about all the young people I had and could have poisoned and brainwashed. I could turn into someone worse than Hitler or Stalin. I had the potential, if I just wanted to.

He continued, "Listen, son, I'm not sure about what pushed you to the edge. I know something's wrong in your life, but believe me, you will get over it. I'm informed that you are in literature and philosophy. Mrs. S. (Mary) has told me about you. Sometimes knowledge works against us. I used to read a lot, just like you. But life's not in the books. You have to live life to know what life is about. Maybe you just need some time. You're still young. Give yourself a chance. Now be wise and give me the key."

He was sweating! I was right that he was scared to death. He was weak. For a second I was falling for his trick. He sounded like a spiritual and wise man, but he was lying. All of a sudden I felt a fiery anger toward all the philosophers and spiritual leaders in all of history; they all could have been like him, liars. I had been deceived all my life. Even the wickedest people could say the most beautiful words. He was a sick criminal who couldn't find a way out of his misery, just like the rest, so he gave in to corruption, like a medicine, like an addiction, like an intentional forgetfulness. He was far more miserable than I thought. I picked myself over him. At lease I wanted to kill myself, but he had lived and became a monster. I stared at him for a while with pity. I said to myself, *Bijan, let him go. He's a victim too, a victim of a corrupt system called life.*

I told him to call his assistant and tell him that he was coming out soon. I told him I would walk right behind him, and if anyone did anything stupid, I would stab him from behind. He nodded. He made the call and asked them to clear out the way. When I opened the door, in a quick move, I pushed him out and locked the door again. I heard noises outside; everybody was concerned about him, asking if he was OK. I sat on the floor. I didn't want to become like him, a monster. In a very quick move, I cut both of my wrists deeply with that letter opener. I could hear shouts and knocking on the door. Contrary to my experience at the tea house, this time I didn't feel good at all; a hostile force was pulling me down into a dark abyss, a never-ending nothingness. I gave up. Everything around me went black.

—

When I woke up, I found myself in a military hospital. "Damn! I'm still alive," I whispered. I was handcuffed to the side of the bed. Apparently I had lost lots of blood before they broke the door for I didn't remember how I got to the Hospital. It wasn't fair. I just couldn't bear being alive anymore. I began to cry. A deep sadness, along with an unbearable pain, embraced my whole being.

I wept like a fatherless child. In that moment, I hated God.

———

The next day I was informed that my father was there to take me back to Tehran. Apparently the Colonel hadn't filed a lawsuit. I guess, after what happened between us, he knew it wasn't worth it. He didn't want to lose his reputation. Plus, by not filing any complaint, he showed everyone how gracious he was. Not bad for him.

My father had to sign some papers to release me from the hospital, and then he had to take me to my work place and sign some other papers so that they would let him take me to Tehran. He had to assure them that he would take me to the authorities in Tehran within three days. When he came to my room in hospital, he took me in his arms and cried; no words were exchanged. But I could read in his eyes, "Don't worry, son. Whatever happened, it's over now."

We went to my work place. I could hardly walk. The Colonel didn't find it necessary to see me, even though my father asked him to let me apologize to him. He allowed my father to see him, though. I waited in Mary's office. We didn't say a word. Something had changed. I didn't feel the same about her. I guess psychologically or mentally something had happened to me. I wasn't able to talk. I wasn't even feeling anything. I had lost my identity. I didn't know who I was. I didn't even care. Amnesia?! Maybe, but in a different way. I remembered almost everything, but at the same time, I felt no connection to anything, neither people nor environment.

We feel things because we make connections. We care because things are important to us. As soon as we lose our connection to the world, we lose our feelings and identity. That was what had happened to me. I knew everyone, I remembered everything, but I felt nothing about anything. I guess my soul, brain, spirit, or whatever I used to call it had shut down all my senses. I was there, but I wasn't.

Mary was talking to me, but I didn't even care to listen. I was watching her talking and crying, but I couldn't understand what she was saying. It was like she was speaking in Martian language through another time and space dimension. Probably she never ever thought that she was one of the main reasons I committed suicide. I only saw her one more time, about ten years later, when I took a trip to Shiraz on a vacation. In that final meeting I spent less than five minutes in her office. We didn't have much to share anymore. She seemed happy. I guess what had happened between us helped her and her husband to appreciate each other better.

My father came in with papers, thanked Mary, walked me to the car, helped me in, and drove away.

—

We had to go to the farm to get my stuff. Morteza, the Colonel's driver, came with us to show my dad the way. The gang knew what had happened. I'm sure they were proud of me for what I had done at the Colonel's office. But that was not something I boasted about. For them, on the other hand, it was an act of bravery—a confrontation with the system that was stronger and louder than many intellectual debates. I didn't feel that way. I didn't feel anything.

They came to greet me and my dad. Only two of them were brave enough to talk to me. Afshin offered for me to stay there with them for a few weeks. Silly Afshin! My father told him I needed to be at home for now. They hugged me one by one and wished me wellness. Habib, the only atheist among us (the always naked one), was smiling subtly as if he knew something none of us knew. They assured me that everything was going to be alright. After they said that, a song from Bob Marley, "No Woman, No Cry," entered my head, especially the part that repeats "everything's gonna be alright"; it kept playing in my head for hours!

The Six helped my dad put my stuff in the trunk, and we were off.

All the way back to Tehran, I was staring at the road. My dad tried to open up a conversation with me a few times, but I couldn't talk; there was nothing to say. Nothing mattered.

When we got home, everybody ran out to embrace me and welcome me. They didn't know about my nervous breakdown, but when they saw me, they thought I had gone insane forever. My mom cried. I went in and sat down on the couch. I walked like a robot. They put my luggage in the den. Our new house had only two rooms, one for my parents and the other one for my sisters. For the next several months, that couch turned into my only resting place.

Three days after we got back home, as my father promised the Colonel, he took me to the authorities at the Ministry so that, after some inspections and other medical exams, they could take the proper action on my case.

Before we went, my father asked me to bring him the release papers the Colonel had signed in Shiraz. I went to the den and opened my luggage; right under my clothes, I found something, something that gave me a sudden hope again, something to live for, something desirable, something I needed badly at the time. The naked man had done it. That's why he was smiling when he was saying goodbye to me. There was a huge black bag of Red Colombian weed with an estimated worth of at least five thousand dollars right under my clothes. I was back in the game again. I smiled!

The Guru

THE MINISTRY SENT ME TO one of their hospitals and made me go through lots of medical and psychological tests. All the doctors agreed that I was mentally sick, and even though I was not a threat to anyone anymore, I still needed to be seen by a psychiatrist regularly. Only then would the Ministry be able to decide what to do with me, based on the psychiatrist's medical report.

Months passed. Every time I was about to meet with a doctor or go for a brain scan, I smoked a couple rolls to make them believe I was sick, a harmless insane, and it worked.

To be honest with you, ten days after I was back, I felt like I was getting better. I was able to communicate with the world around me. I began to have short conversations with my sisters. I began to thank my mom for the food and say some other little things, but no long talks.

From time to time, they would let me go out in the front yard to enjoy the late spring weather, and every time, I had a small dose of weed to boost my senses up.

After a month or two, I went back to my favorite books again, Castaneda's narration of this marvelous old Indian sorcerer, Don Juan Matus. This time, I wasn't trying to find a solution for the problems of the world like poverty or war, nor did I try to find answers to my mysterious questions. Rather, I concentrated on the journey itself. I thought, *Well, if the strange state I entered in during the last fifty to sixty days was because I was disconnected from the bitter reality of the cruel world* (and to be honest, I liked it), *then what if I just find a relatively suitable channel and put all my efforts to activate that channel in order to reach the Beyond instead of trying to find a remedy for the world calamities?!* That became my goal.

So in the next two months, I began to go deeper and deeper into *the other reality* Castaneda was talking about. I found it much easier now to grasp and apply Don Juan's teachings. I wondered why it had taken Castaneda that long to experience the reality of it all (if he ever did). Maybe it was because I didn't have any ego to block me from reaching to the point of letting go of myself. Something that took him years to understand took me only a couple of weeks, not only to understand, but also to exercise and experience the supernatural outcome of it.

There was a nature park in our neighborhood that became my home during the day through the whole summer. There were many quiet places in remote corners of this park. It was there that I experienced the presence of what Don Juan calls "an ally" for the first time; I saw it in the still waters! That place turned into my practice place. Unspeakable things happened there! I saw cloudy shape beings, man-like creatures in the still waters, and I traveled to some places that I have no words to explain. The interesting point is that in most occasions like these I wasn't even on any drugs while I was practicing Don Juan's techniques. I had no idea what I was entering into. It seemed like the breakdown process somehow had cracked and affected my mental perception of things around me.

It was during those days that I found some new friends in that park, and in no time, I began to share my knowledge with them. They were amazed! Soon they became my disciples, and I became their guru. The New Age movement was just finding its way among the younger generation. In fact, holding on to the philosophy of the New Age was the only alternative to the brutality and cruelty of the Islamic regime for those who still believed in some kind of spirituality. In just a few months I made a name for myself as a spiritual teacher and a mentalist.

As I mentioned before, at that time, it was a crime to listen to music, to walk with a girl in the street, to wear short sleeves, to have long hair (as a man), to walk a dog, or to go to a music institute or painting classes; sometimes even chewing gum could be an act of lawlessness. The problem was that anybody could be an agent; you never knew. The government provided the ground for everyone to spy on their neighbors; they promoted it with gifts and positions. You never knew who was spying on you. It could even be your own neighbor or classmate, your teacher or even your own friend. In Islam, anyone can consider himself an instrument of God to correct you, and if you don't listen, he can use force in the name of the Sharia to deal with you. It's ridiculous!

Everything was like the story of the world in the book *1984* by George Orwell. I tend to believe that Iranians who belong to that period of time still carry a suspicious behavioral pattern, no matter where they live now. If you know an Iranian, you may have already noticed that. We all used to think that somebody was watching us all the time (like the song from Michael Jackson, *Somebody's Watching Me*). It was a very scary feeling. Many of those who belonged to that era felt they could no longer trust people. I guess the authorities knew what they were doing; they were using this scheme to destroy any kind of trust among people.

These new guys in the park, who were my disciples, were nothing like The Six and Masoud, but they were thirsty for the supernatural and some mystical experience. To them, I was like Master Yoda in *Star Wars*. I had plenty of time and usually spent six to eight hours a day practicing Don Juan's techniques.

There are some people who totally reject any of Castaneda's reports. On the other hand, there are some who have exalted him to a god. What I say here is just what happened to me while I exercised and learned how to do the techniques, that's all. You may accuse me of spreading false theories, but that's not what I'm doing. I simply exercised and practiced some of the techniques mentioned in Castaneda's books, and I got the results. Does it mean anyone else can get the same results? No. Does it mean they are divine? No. Does it mean they convey any truth? No. Realities maybe, but truth, I don't think so. Were they beneficial? No. But it is important for me to mention these experiences because they happened and they were real (in terms of a non-ordinary reality). What I was experiencing took control of me in a way that it began to enslave me. When you are walking on the path of the supernatural, you will never know what is waiting for you on the way. You may easily open up yourself to forces so evil and so strong that you cannot even imagine. That's why I said they began to take control of me. Later on, they proved their destructive power to me through a series of horrible events that happened to me and someone else you already know. More on this later.

These new guys fell in love with me. Well, I too, began to fall in love with me again. I wasn't living the dirty life I used to live. Here I need to mention that in this memoir, I have left many of the terrible things I did in Shiraz unsaid for two reasons; one, I don't want to disgust you, and two, some people are not able to clear a bad image from their minds, like my mother. She still, after three decades, doesn't want to believe I was that bad, so some things are better left unsaid.

The more I exposed myself to these forces, the stronger and healthier I felt. Meanwhile, I noticed how desperate people were for the unknown and the supernatural. They were even ready to pay for it. There were people who offered me good money to tell them about their future. By that time, I somehow found out that I had an ability to read cards and summon spirits. I even learned to read the Chinese *I Ching* (a kind of fortune-telling using six or seven pieces of small carved sticks). These were my areas of specialty, and they drew people to me. In almost all big or small parties, there were people who wanted me to tell them about their future or to summon the spirits of their deceased loved ones, and I did it (or at least I thought I did).

Whether you believe it or not, I was able to open gaps between the worlds. I don't mean parallel worlds, for although I was practicing sorcery, I never believed there were endless numbers of parallel worlds slightly different from our own reality. What I experienced was totally different from parallel worlds, and personally, I don't believe in that theory of the endless parallel universes or the multi-verse theory. I know there are some scientists who believe and promote this theory based on new discoveries in String Theory, but that's not what I believe is going on in the supernatural or spiritual realm. Some people read too much sci-fi or watch too much SG-1. Of course, imagination is a good thing, but getting lost in imagination is not!

Unfortunately, while I was becoming popular and known as someone with psycho kicks, I began to indulge in pot, opium, LSD, pills, and syrups again, and later I got involved in cocaine and heroin (the latter was even cheaper than a pack of cigarettes). Something I liked about that nearby park was that there were so many undiscovered areas in it. I used those areas to plant more Marijuana seeds, and after a couple months, I was able to sell them for a very good price.

Meanwhile there was something about me that I wasn't able to understand. I was asking myself why I kept doing the same things that resulted in putting me right back in the same horrible situations, like the things I went through in Shiraz? I had no answer for that question. Some higher power, for some reason, had given me not one but two chances to live again. But why didn't I want to change, even after that mental breakdown? Even the doctors issued a letter to the Ministry indicating that I was mentally sick (I knew I wasn't). But it seemed there was something about me that caused the ultimate creative force of the universe to not want me to leave the earth until I had completed my purpose and gotten it right. But I was getting it all wrong.

Through practicing the sorcery techniques, I became familiar with the world of the spirits more and more. I used to believe that bad spirit were nothing but confused or wandering ghosts who were stuck in our world, the world of the living, and that they could be used for various purposes by people we call mediums. So I believed gifted people could catch these spirits or draw their attention to themselves and compel them to do things or make them tell us about people's secrets, mysteries, futures, or ancient knowledge! I was very proud of myself for being able to communicate with them because that was one of my dreams. To me it was a great achievement, and it was meant to connect me to the ultimate truth I had been looking for all my life. I was even able to make them obey me and do things like move objects, mess with people's minds by making them do what I wanted them to do. I used to think, *Why would they do that for me?* and I would reply, *Because I am special and gifted!* In fact, this is what all of us think when it comes to such stuff; we think the only reason they communicate with us is just because we are special. It is the biggest lie they want us to believe, and we love it.

What we were doing was so exciting that we began to have a weekly session just to summon spirits of our dead relatives and friends (and even famous dead people), and they would show up, telling us stuff we didn't even know! It was like a party for us. Some people never joined us because they thought maybe the spirits would come and never leave or jump on them and possess them.

One night we were asking for the grandpa's spirit to show up, but after a few questions and answers, we noticed it wasn't the grandpa. He was a very aggressive spirit. Doors were being slammed with loud and horrible sounds. Winds began to blow inside the room. Cracking noises were heard from every corner of the house. And we could sense his angry presence right at the backs of our necks! He didn't seem to want to leave. We finally decided to let go of hands and be separated for a while, but as soon as we held hands again and tried to summon other ghosts, there that same spirit was, making us uncomfortable. He eventually left, but it was a very scary experience.

Two years passed, and I became more and more involved in sorcery, black magic, and ghost games, and I indulged in drugs and sexual relationships. I even began to teach my transferable skills to my disciples. Two of them were very diligent and stayed with me for about three more years. Others left us because their first motive was weed, not the spiritual journey.

During that time, I was so soaked up in my supernatural abilities that I almost forgot why I began my search and what I was looking for in the first place. I almost gave away myself to every stream of the supernatural on my path, from Don Juan, to African Voodoo, from Sufism to Indian mystic paths, from Chinese I Ching to reading cards, and the worst of all, animal sacrifice to keep the spirits pleased and satisfied with me! I didn't want to bring this one up, but we did some bad stuff.

All who walk down this path will inevitably reach a point where they have to deal with some of these spirits whose ultimate intention is to possess and take control of people's bodies (some people call it signing a contract with the devil)—something beyond any explanation and absolutely horrible. In the next chapter, I will have an encounter with one of the most horrifying creatures in the history of mankind which exists almost in every culture but under different names. Keep the lights on while you are reading the next chapter!

Night Mara

ONE NIGHT, WHEN MY FAMILY and I were visiting my grandma in her very old house, one of my uncles told us about what had happened to him the night before. He said that he woke up around 3 o'clock in the morning sensing a disturbing presence in the room. The next moment, he felt a heavy, horrifying being crawling up on his body. He wasn't able to move, say a word, or even scream. It was the most disgusting, frightening, and hellish thing he had ever experienced, he told us. My grandma, very dispassionately, said that she knew the creature and that she had seen it a few times before in the den and around the kitchen late at nights.

This presence is very well-known in every culture, but it is called by different names. In Farsi we call it Bakhtak, referring to the Jin who lay on your chest at night to suck your soul out of you.

It mostly happens during the night sleep. Interestingly, it mostly shows up around 1:15 a.m. or 3:15 a.m. I don't know why, but most people I spoke to agreed about the time. They explained it with the same details—a horrifying presence crawling up on the person's body, taking away all their energy, sucking the soul of the victim, feeding on the soul, unexplainable like death, unfathomable, but ugly as Satan himself, even though you can't see its face at all. I read some articles about this paranormal activity, and I noticed that in old Irish stories it is called Night Mara. Some scholars believe the term Nightmare has been derived from the Irish name Night Mara. Thousands of individuals from around the world have been picked by paranormal investigators to be studied in regard to this phenomenon. They all expressed the same details—being paralyzed while being totally awake and aware of things around them, a tense and horrifying presence that absorbs their strength, a terrifying sense of choking, and no ability to

85

move or say a word are some of the signs. Some Christian scholars believe these are demons experimenting on humans in order to get ready for the time when they will be released to do a whole possession in a massive way during the end-times. There are even cases reported involving sexual content.

That night in my grandma's place, after my uncle finished his story, I proudly told him, "Send it to me; I know how to deal with such creatures," and I laughed. My youngest uncle said, "Ok, Mr. Jin, you heard Bijan; you can go to his place and leave us alone. This is his address," and then he said my home address out loud. My mother got mad at him and told him to stop, but he began to run around the house laughing and repeating our address a few more times. We all laughed.

I should have cried, for what happened that night was the beginning of a series of the most horrifying phenomenon I've ever experienced in my whole life.

Long story short, the thing showed up the very first night at our place. I woke up in the middle of the night and took a look at the red digital clock over my couch. It was 3:10 a.m. I rolled around few times, but finally lay on my back with my face toward the ceiling, a position that I usually don't feel comfortable with. For some reason, my five senses were sharper than usual. I was sleepy, but my body was alert. All of a sudden, I sensed a frightening presence in the room; something or someone was walking toward me. It was coming out of the den. With every step it took, I felt a heavier weight on me. I tried to move, but my body was like a piece of wood. I tried to say a word, but there was no sound in my screams; my teeth were locked.

A presence more horrifying than anything I had ever experienced in my whole life began to walk toward me like it was a zombie. I was completely awake. I could feel his every step on the floor with all my cells. Even though there was a small blue night light in the room, as the thing was getting closer to my feet, everything around me began to turn pitch dark, and something like an electric wave began to move through my body, starting from my toes up to my chest. It was crawling up on me like a thick black cloud. I'm not sure if it was scanning me or if it was trying to suck the soul out of me, or maybe both. The worst part was that I was awake the whole time, knowing that something demonic was happening to me. Although I couldn't see anything at the beginning, after few seconds, I saw a figure like a monk dressed in one of those old black overalls or something like Darth Vader from *Star Wars*, but a thousand times scarier.

I completely felt crippled, letting this creature do whatever it wanted to do with me, with no power to stop it. I thought I was the most miserable being on the earth. The amount of fear I was experiencing (or releasing) was a thousand times greater than watching the movie *Exorcist* at home, alone, at midnight, with no lights on.

For a second I thought to myself, *If this thing touches me, I will die!* So I gathered all my energy to make a noise. My heart was just coming out of my chest. So with all the energy left in me, using every cell in my body, I began to howl from between my teeth like a wolf. As soon as the first sound came out of my larynx, I found out that it was the only way to get rid of that ugly thing, so I focused more and howled more, screaming like a baby from between my teeth. Immediately, I heard some footsteps running toward me; the thing just disappeared into the thin air. I was relieved.

My parents rushed over to me, calling my name, trying to wake me up, not knowing that I was already awake. There was no way I could explain to them what had just happened to me. To them it seemed like I was just having a nightmare. After bringing me some water and making sure I was alright, they went back to bed. I was there all alone, frightened to death, unable to go to sleep until I saw the dawn when the beams of sunshine lighted the room.

The next day, I called my younger uncle and cursed him with all the swear words I knew. He was laughing hysterically, accusing me of having too much pot the night before. To revenge him, I began to utter his home address aloud on the phone so that *the thing* would go back to his place and have some fun with him as well. But that never happened.

From that night on, for almost six months, literally every night the creature was there over my bed, trying to soak up all my energy. Sometimes I just wanted to die before the night came. It didn't matter whether I took the strongest sleeping pills or smoked many rolls, I would still wake up, every night, at 1:15 or 3:15 a.m., and sometimes at both times. I tried to read books on the subject, but none of the written codes in ancient books or even modern psychology could come up with an answer to prevent the incident. No matter what I did, it was there every night, crawling on my chest, sucking life out of me. I became the topic of conversations among my relatives and friends. It didn't matter if I stayed the night over at my friend's or relative's house; it would still show up and scare everybody to death through my midnight screams. People didn't want me around at nights. I couldn't sleep well. Most times I had to stay up the whole night in fear and then go to sleep when the sun began to shine. I lost more than

20 pounds. I lost my concentration, lost my appetite, lost my social life, and began to lose my reputation. My whole day was spent in fear of the night. Even as I increased the dose of opium I was taking to avoid sleeping at nights, I would still struggle with thoughts like, *What if I go to sleep and this time no one comes to my rescue? What if he overcomes me this time? What if, what if, what if…*

I wasn't able to teach my disciples anymore. My meetings were not as successful as before. I had lost my reputation. Friends and relatives began to call me "mommy's boy," "chicken," "demon possessed," "Darth Vader's chick apprentice," and so on. I didn't care. What I cared was how to fight this monster back. So far nothing had worked except my midnight wolfish screams. By that time, I was almost twenty-three, and the most embarrassing part was that some nights I had to sleep in my parent's room under their bed! For whatever reason, those were the only nights when I was able to have some rest. But what twenty-three-year-old wants to sleep in the same room with his parents for the rest of his life?!

You may call me mentally problematic, a liar, an exaggerator, or paranoid. I don't care. Almost all of my family members and friends know about that period of my life. To assure you about the reality of this horrifying experience, I should admit something. Within those several months, some kind of bond was created between me and that creature. In fact, at the end of that period, I was able to hold on to my awareness so much that I actually began to fight him back to a degree in order to show him that I was not easily giving up. I wanted something out of that experience, too. In simple terms, it was not as frightening to me as it used to be, and the creature had figured it out. It was still unbearable, but after I resisted, somehow things changed; the creature began to submit to me gradually! When I was mad at someone, it was just enough to say their address out loud, and the very same night the creature was there, scaring the hell of them! The only time it didn't work was with my younger uncle, and I never knew why.

It was more like the creature and I had formed a kind of an alliance. The more I was able to fight it back (by not being afraid, as I was in the beginning) the more it began to listen to me and kick my enemies' butts.

It was then that I found out a truth about these creatures—they feed on fear! Fear is one of the most distinguished emotions human beings can release into the atmosphere around them. It's like they can smell it, and they love the smell of it. I would even say they lust after it, in a sense. I noticed that none of the other emotions we release are as strong and vivid as fear. You can feel the amount of energy you're releasing into the sphere around you when you're scared. You can feel your brain exploding, or even your heart, for that matter. Nothing can come even close to the density of fear, especially fear of the unknown in the dark.

So after about six months, I found out that I could use the creature the way I wanted, not only to scare people who were messing with me, but also to make them believe in my powers. So the more I sent the creature to people around me, the less it was messing with me.

I was not aware of the fact that I was just signing up for a dangerous game; the more I sent the creature to people, the hungrier it became! It wanted more, and if I, for any reason, stopped sending it to others to feed on, it would attack me more and heavier. In those days, I was translating one of the books written by Castaneda, in order to make some money (I never completed the work, though). As far as I remember, there was only one book from him translated into Farsi in those days, *Journey to Ixtlan,* which was his third book.

By that time, I had read seven books from him in English and had practiced almost all the techniques Don Juan and the other benefactors had been teaching Castaneda and their other disciples. I learned that controlling our fear in such cases (encountering the spirits) was one of the main techniques. Although the New Age movement had already started in America in the early 60s, I believe we were among the early frontiers in introducing Castaneda to the Iranian young generation in the early 1980s. What Castaneda represented was the beginning of a new mystic age for the young generation throughout the world. His ideas are still in function through internet courses, even after Castaneda's death in 1998.

One thing I truly regret about those days of Shamanism is the fact that, in order to be unreachable (as Don Juan taught Castaneda), I decided to gather all my childhood pictures and burn them all, along with some of my certificates of achievement! Who does that?! We can't hide behind being no one.

What I used to think I was achieving was just part of a game these dark forces usually play with you to mess with your mind. In fact, as long as you are in contact with them, they are the ones who control you, no matter how hard you try to convince yourself that it's you who is controlling them.

One night I woke up, and it was 1:05 a.m. I got up and went to the washroom. When I came back I sat on the couch for a couple minutes. Then despite all the fears, I decided to go to bed again. As soon as I closed my eyes, I heard the disgusting dragging footsteps on the carpet again.

It was getting close. I opened my eyes, and there it was, standing over my bed by my feet. One of the strangest elements of these encounters was that, no matter how many times I had experienced that fear, it was always as crippling as the first time. But this time something weird and unusual happened; I saw myself being lifted up from the couch with the white sheet on me. I was about three feet above the floor, levitating. And then, to my amazement, my body began to turn around 180 degrees horizontally, floating in the air, while facing upward, until my head was toward the den—the place I always felt the creature came from. Then I started moving toward the den, on the air, just like you see on some horror movies like *Exorcist*. I saw myself moving over the dining table, the furniture, and the coffee table. The closer I got to the den, the stronger the sense of reaching the end of my life became. I literally sensed a black whole behind me, absorbing all my energy. This time something was different from every other time. I knew I was going to die; the black hole was the death itself. It was many years later when I found out that almost the same thing happened to Paulo Coelho. That was one of the reasons I began to read his books.

I knew in seconds that I would be dead if I ended up in that den. Suddenly I came to my senses. The thought of being caught by such a disgusting, dark evil power in a black hole for eternity quickly compelled me to react. In a blink of an eye, I remembered my suicide attempts and how I was spared miraculously. I don't know exactly if it was my will to live or the mysterious force who had saved me before that gave me the power to resist the creature. However it happened, I decided to let go of the fear of that creature, the fear of death, or even the fear of the black hole, which was less than 6 feet away from me.

I made my decision; there was nothing to be afraid of. Fear was just a mental reaction to the unknown. I told myself I was safe. Everything happened so fast. I gained my confidence and began to rule the situation, over both the creature and the black hole. I concentrated more intensely. The whole world disappeared from before my eyes. There was only nothingness. I felt that something stronger and much higher than me or the creature or even the death itself was present there. It was so good to know that I was being watched by such an awesome being. I knew I had a purpose, and that purpose gave me a strong motive to ignore the fear, even the fear of death. After all, I had experienced death twice before! The moment I figured out I had power over the situation, something happened; I traveled through something like a tunnel with the speed of light. And then I found myself on the floor close to the den. I wasn't dreaming. It all had actually happened. I was sweating like a horse. The creature and the black hole were gone.

Over the next several weeks, I felt the presence of the crawling creature a few more times, but the episodes never lasted for more than few seconds. A reality had been revealed to me; despite all chemical activities during a frightening situation, I could be in control because I had learned that being afraid was a normal reaction to the unknown, but remaining in fear could be a decision. I decided not to fear that creature anymore. The assurance that the higher being gave me during my last experience with that creature proved my idea—there was a meaning, a purpose, a destiny in my life that I needed to fulfill. That was why I was still alive.

Somebody knew what he was doing!

A Shattered Shade

DURING THE FIVE YEARS AFTER I started to build up a reputation as a medium and a spiritual mentor, I noticed that my younger sister also had some abilities. But she was my little sister, and I didn't want her to get involved with the spirits. I was worried about her getting into drugs or sorcery. What if she was not ready for that? She was always interested in the supernatural. But at the same time, there was something about her that convinced me she wasn't meant to be in this at all. I'm mentioning her because, for a period of time, she manifested a great deal of power, especially as a medium. There were times when she didn't even need anyone's help to summon spirits, especially when doing the Vijay board. But luckily, she was just trying to have fun. It even got her a chance to marry someone who, according to the signs of spirits, was the Mr. Right, but everything went wrong (I mean right), and fortunately they didn't get married. Despite the signs, he wasn't the right person as the so-called spirit told us—something that made me think twice about the spirits' authenticity or even their true identity!

She married her true Mr. Right few years later, and they made a great couple. She never went back to summoning spirits again.

Another person who came into the picture in those years and who got involved in Castaneda's stuff was Saye, Afshin's girlfriend, who had moved to our neighborhood with her family—just about a two-minute walk from our apartment. She ended up becoming good friends with my sisters. Most of the time, I was out with my friends meeting odd people who claimed to be someone in the realm of supernatural, but they just ridiculed themselves by their claims; they were no one! Other times I was partying while consuming all kinds of obtainable drugs, including cocaine and heroin along with a huge amount of alcohol. At some of these parties, my friends would ask me to make fun of someone by sending my allies (spirits) to them to scare them while they were checking the closet to get their jacket. I still don't know how I was able to do that, but it worked every time, and we all laughed.

With Saye living in our neighborhood, it was easier for me to keep in touch with some of the guys from Shiraz, especially Afshin and Masoud. Afshin usually brought me a great amount of Marijuana as gift. He used to stay at our place during his stay in Tehran, which was usually about a week. My parents were not very happy about me still staying in touch with these guys, but they didn't want to make a big deal out of it. They knew I was doing some drugs, but didn't (and still don't) want to believe I was in deep sh**. Something they never wanted to admit was that I actually was a drug dealer.

Saye and I had been good friends, but had never really gotten to know each other on an intimate level. I had always admired her, but her friendship with my sisters prepared the way for us to get to know each other better.

Saye and I became closer. Most of the time, when I would come back home, Saye was there with my sisters. Sometimes Sherrie would go to Saye's place and leave a note for me to join them. After a while, I found out that Saye's older brother liked my sister, Sherrie, and that she felt the same way about him. Sherrie was always the life of our parties. In fact, she had started her recreational drug use a year before I did! For her, life had another meaning, which was living it to its fullest. Drinking, smoking pot and partying were her thing, and I stole my first roll from her jacket's pocket! (I should mention here that she's not into any drugs anymore and is busy with her two beautiful kids and her job as a skilled hair stylist, but still a "sparkling flame".)

Saye's brother had just come back from the UK. He was an interesting guy. He had experiences with some weird drugs that I had never even heard of. He was much deeper into the stuff than any of us. He used to be into the mystical stuff, too, but after a horrifying experience that happened to him and his girlfriend in a trance, while using some LSD, he decided he didn't want to have anything to do with the spirit realm forever.

The friendship between my sister and Saye's brother brought me and Saye closer to each other. Eventually, one night when Saye was staying over at our place, she told my sister that she loved me. I could swear to all the holy things in the world that I never even imagined she could have had that feeling for me. To me, she was too good to care about someone like me. Plus, she was Afshin's girlfriend. But one thing I didn't know was that prior to Saye's move to Tehran, she and Afshin had developed some relational problems, and things didn't work between them like they expected. Afshin didn't tell me anything about their challenges, but he told me he thought she liked someone else. I didn't have any clue that the person was me!

However, I didn't want her to like me. She was an ideal girl for me, yet I knew that as soon as I gave in to the situation my friendship with Afshin would be over. I didn't want that to happen at any cost. So I decided to change my schedule. I began to come home very late at night, hoping she would already be gone. Or when my sister wanted me to join them at Saye's place, I would come up with excuses for why I could not join them. But it was difficult to keep those excuses going on. It was beyond difficult to keep her out of my mind. She was a year younger than me, she was into all of the stuff that I was, she was hot, and she liked me; how could I not like her? She thought I was playing game with her, but I wasn't. She told me that she was not with Afshin anymore, but I felt like I couldn't allow myself to do such a thing to my best friend.

However, the more we were around each other, the more I grew some kind of feeling toward her. It had been almost six months since I had heard any news from Afshin. Saye told me that the farm had taken her place. She said she was replaced by a piece of land! It turned out that she was right; the last few times I saw Afshin, the only thing he was talking about was how the farm had become his first priority and how wealthy he had become through the farm. He actually asked the other guys to leave, and he hired some laborers to do the job. He was getting rich. His second interest was hunting. He had changed into one of those people we were always against—a feudal! I guess he took Saye for granted. It is easy to take something or someone for granted, and when we lose them, we blame the whole world for our loss, putting the fault on everyone else except ourselves. I called him few times, but he was too busy to talk to me.

Saye and I became closer after she told me she had already broken up with Afshin. In fact, she became part of our family and joined us at our weekly house parties. We began to officially date. We used to sit down and talked for hours about Buddhism, Hinduism, other Indian ancient paths, and Castaneda. We really enjoyed being together.

War was still going on, and the Ministry had already informed me that my civic service to the Ministry could not be counted as my military service. I only had one more year of work before I would have received my military completion card when I quit my job. Now I had to do the whole two and a half years of the mandatory military service. I kept delaying it for almost five years after I returned from Shiraz. There were military personnel everywhere in the streets, asking men for their military situation. If you didn't have the card, they would put you in a bus, which was more like a cage with metal bars, and take you straight to a military base. They issued heavy sentences to those who were running away from military service (fugitives) during the war. No one knew what would happen in a war. But as a man, I had to take some responsibility if I wanted to start a life with Saye.

Our relationship was not very romantic, but more intellectual and based on friendship and trust. Romanticism is nothing but pain. Romantic people fight over the silliest things just because they want 100 percent of the of the other one's attention. They keep hurting one another in the name of love. To them, love should be put to test every minute of every day. They live in a constant fear of losing the other one, and by doing that, someday, sooner than they imagine, they will eventually lose that person. They expect too much from each other, and since most of these expectations cannot be met, they are in a constant state of frustration. That's romanticism! But we were not like that. We didn't need to be worried about those things. Personally, my only concern was money and my military situation. I couldn't even find a job without completing my military service. We were a kind of *come what may* people. But "with true love comes true responsibility!"

Before I tell you about my next decision, I'd like to tell you a story about what practical magic can bring upon a person who thinks he or she is ready for a supernatural trip. This was the purpose behind adding this chapter to my book.

Since I told Saye about my ability to open up gaps between the worlds and control the forces, she told me that she had also begun to do the same. According to Don Juan, the focusing center of women is not their belly per se, but their womb. That was what Saye was doing, concentrating on her womb to open up a gap. That was dangerous if you really didn't know why you were doing that. The difference between my experiment and Saye's was that she did not really know why she was doing them or what she wanted to accomplish at the end. She told me that she had been practicing the technique for a quite a while and she was expecting something to happen soon. But expecting what? She had no idea! That made her vulnerable to the outcome. Meanwhile, she had some dreams, as well, in which she was able to see her hands, which was the first step of creating your double in your dreams—a double who was able to do all the things you were able to do in real life plus supernatural things that you, in the body, were not able to do. This was another technique that Don Juan taught Castaneda. What I'm sharing here is just what we experienced by practicing those techniques, nothing more and nothing less. Whether they were illusions or real is another subject, but we went through them, and I personally can't deny the things that actually happened, and I won't, because they are proofs to the existence of powers and forces far more evil than you and I could ever imagine.

It had been almost two days since the last time I had seen Saye. It was unusual. I called her home, and her mother answered the phone. She said that Saye was busy and couldn't come to the phone. I knew she was hiding something. I felt it in my guts. Something was wrong. I got out and ran all the way to her place. As I entered, I saw her parents standing at her door discussing something with a man who was dressed up in a suit and had stethoscope around his neck. From where I was standing, I could see Saye lying down on her bed, covered by a blanket up to her chest. She was so pale that I thought she was dead.

Her parents didn't want me to see her. In fact, they seemed to blame me for what had happened to her! I insisted and finally got the permission to go in and sit by her bed. She was in a terrible shock. She could hardly talk. Tear drops were falling from the corner of her eyes. She was frightened like she had seen a ghost. Her lips were shaking, but no words were coming out of her mouth. I thought, *Maybe that ugly creature gave her a visit.* She was shivering like a baby. I didn't make her tell me what had happened, but I knew it was about her practices—the concentration on her womb to open up a gap between the worlds. I also remembered that the moon was at its fullest two nights ago, which meant she was in her most powerful, but at the same time most vulnerable state during the month. I believe she had opened up a huge gap, or a gateway, to some forces that she wasn't equipped or ready to handle.

The doctor diagnosed her with a mental breakdown or a rare dangerous delusional attack. I didn't care what they thought; she wasn't delusional or insane. She had just had a visitation, but a bad one.

I wasn't allowed to see her for the next few days. Her parents still blamed me for what had happened to her. I knew that for sure. Eventually when, after a week, I got permission to be with her alone, she was still unable to communicate properly. She told me she wasn't crazy; she said she saw *them*. She looked nervous, was even afraid to talk about *them*. I assured her that I would stay with her as long as her parents would allow me. She didn't want to be alone. To keep her calm, they were giving her a high dose of sleeping pills. I asked if she was comfortable to tell me what had happened. She was worried that I wouldn't believe her either.

She took a deep breath and then pulled up her shirt and showed me her sides and around her chest and her hips on both sides. I was shocked. There were scratches, blue areas, and things like mouse bites all over her body. She said she couldn't explain what exactly happen to her. She continued, "It was a heavy and horrifying presence, but at the same time I also sensed they were many small and ugly creatures around me even though I couldn't see them. They all came out of a gap in the wall in front of me," she said. "They just kept coming out, attacking me. They surrounded my bed. They were all over me, soaking all my energy and I couldn't even move or scream; I was crippled."

She was shaking, holding my hands, begging me not to let them come back again. I told her I would stay there as long as she wanted. She told me she just wanted to do the practice of focusing on her womb when the moon was full. She never expected such a horrifying thing to happen to her. Then she told me that nobody believed her and that everybody thought she was insane. I understood what she was going through. I told her that I believed her and that she was going to be alright and that they would never ever again harm her. I stayed with her until she went to sleep. Before she slept, I kissed her on the forehead. She held on to my arm and whispered these words in my ear, "Carlos Castaneda has done the greatest crime of all times to the humanity by writing these books. He shouldn't have been given the right to publish them. I hate him!"

Maybe she was right. Or maybe not everyone was supposed to walk in this path. Maybe there was a reason that all those creatures, in any shape, were so aggressive and violent in encountering human beings. Maybe there was a war going on between these creatures and humankind. But why?! Perhaps we were destined to take part in this battle, perhaps not. And maybe we need to choose sides. Maybe we need to position ourselves under a protection before we got involved in this battle. But how would we know the answers to these questions unless we sought, looked for, and experienced the extraordinary? Maybe, according to some people, we are not supposed to engage in this battle at all. I thought, *Why do these creatures hate us and want to harm us?* I answered myself, *Perhaps we are better than them, or maybe we have something they don't have, and for that reason they hate us. Maybe they are cursed for their evil nature. But by who? Maybe by a higher force, a wiser and good force who knows things we cannot know or understand! Perhaps the main battle is between the ultimate good and ultimate evil, and we all need to choose sides.*

I was gently playing with her short hair while I was thinking all these thoughts!

Destiny vs. Karma

THE WAR WAS GETTING WORSE. The military needed more soldiers. I had watched many TV reports on how the enemy was killing our young soldiers. Cities, including Tehran, were being bombed. War refugees were everywhere. In every major city, there were tens of thousands of them. I always tried to avoid war news for I knew I supposed to be there, and I didn't want to go. As I mentioned before, my father was already retired, and I wasn't sure if he had the power to keep me in the city if I registered. My cousin had the same situation, but eventually he enrolled, and my father kept him in Tehran. I began to think that if my dad was able to do that for my cousin, then he was definitely able to do the same for me. So I shared my thoughts with Saye when she finally overcame the trauma of the incident, and then I shared it with my parents.

We all knew that, without going into military service, I didn't have a chance of finding a job, officially marrying, going to university, or even getting a passport and leaving Iran. It was a very complicated situation. Saye was feeling much better. It was almost the time to throw away the philosophy of *come what may* and be serious about life. It wasn't that I wasn't serious at all, but I had noticed that I was caring more about my spiritual journey than anything else in life. In that case, what was the difference between me and Afshin, who preferred the farm over Saye?

I thought it through.

One day I made my decision and bought a very thin gold ring and asked Saye to be my fiancé; she accepted. We didn't think of any ceremony. In fact, we didn't think we should have one, at least until I would finish my military service. Our love didn't need to be proven by ceremonies. But I should admit that she gave me a beautiful, expensive ring. I wasn't working in those days, and she was perfectly aware of my financial situation. I also didn't indulge in drugs anymore. I was more mature than I was in Shiraz. I was 25. She had already stopped using weed at all after what happened to her. She threw away all Castaneda's books with no regret. She was done with that stuff. Instead, she began to read poems, history, and art books. She seemed content.

I remember one time, after I gave her the ring, we were walking in north of Tehran, hand-in-hand, laughing freely. I had already decided to make things better by enrolling for military service. Our families knew about our decision (except her father). Both sides were not really happy about it. They thought we were not right for each other.

While we were having fun, walking down the Pahlavi Street, we saw two Basij patrols passing us by. We immediately knew they were going to stop us and ask us about our relationship, so we quickly separated and went our own ways. There were usually two kinds of patrols, one specifically for men and the other one for women. We were right; they had seen us. Their job was to look for inappropriate acts in the society, whether it was about people's clothing or opposite sexes walking together. They were called Ershad Gasht. They were supposed to educate you in the ways you should behave in the society, but in fact they had nothing to do with educating you; they would just arrest you and send you to temporary jails until you paid them some money to be released. Sometimes they would take you to a judge, and after a short ridiculous trial, they would sentence you to forty slashes. If you had money to buy your sentence, you were free to go. You would have to admit you were guilty, in writing, to be released. They had no mercy; if you argued with them, they would immediately put the sentence into action—forty slashes, no "why's"! Any further arguments could result in more punishment.

They arrested both of us. They put us in their vans, each with three guys and three unreasonably fanatic women all dressed in black *chador*, like a bunch of crows. It reminded me of the day I was arrested in Shiraz. The guy who seemed to be the leader asked me if I knew that the penalty for holding hands with an opposite sex you were not in lawful relationship with was whipping. I told him that we were kind of engaged and that our families knew about us. He said, "We have to call up the father to the station to make sure."

I said, "But her father is the only one who doesn't know about us yet. Her mother knows though, that's why I said 'kind of.' I'm looking for a job, and as soon as I get it, I will talk to her father too."

He looked at the other guys in the car and after a long silence, got out the car and went to the other patrol car and asked the leader of the women patrol to get out. They walked to a corner and began to talk. Their conversation looked more like an argument. He then came back to me and said, "It takes a little while; wait here."

Later on, Saye told me that the women were mocking her (and me) because of the size of the ring I had given to her. They also asked her to clean up her makeup and nail polishing before they let her go. They were really something.

That was the last time we went out together. We decided to spend the rest of my time at home. I had already signed up for military service, and I had only two weeks left before I officially started my three months training period.

It was the early summer of 1986 when I said goodbye to Saye and my friends and family. I was sent to a Navy base. That three months was the toughest time of my life up to that point. It was more like a state prison than a military training base.

The only thing that helped me go through all those tough trainings (I was physically very weak because of the constant use of drugs) was Saye. Her laugh, her voice, and her presence was with me all those days. We kept writing to each other almost every day on a regular basis. One day, almost halfway through my training, I received a letter from her in which she asked me if it was OK for her to have a short trip to Istanbul to accompany her niece so that her sister, who was an American citizen, could come to Turkey to pick her up and take her to America. She would have to stay there in Istanbul for a week until her sister could manage the paper work with the American embassy. I wrote her back, mentioning the fact that she didn't need my permission, and said she could go and wished her a fun trip.

While she was there, she wrote me two letters. In the last one she mentioned that she had met with one of Afshin's friends there. That was her last letter to me. One week passed. I knew she should have been back by then. I tried to call her, but her mom kept telling me she wasn't home. A month passed, I still had no news about her, and I seriously began to worry. Even my sisters had no news about her. Two more weeks passed. My training was over, and I had permission to go back to Tehran for only five days before they sent me to a Navy base in a war zone. I left the base at 4 a.m., took a bus, and arrived in Tehran around 5 p.m—almost thirteen hours on the road. I didn't tell anyone I was coming back. I went home, spent an hour with my family, took a shower, and went to Saye's place. Her father told me that she was at her sister's place. We had often spent two or three days a week there. I used to get them hashish or opium. So I took a taxi, and in ten minutes I was there. Her sister came to the door. She was very surprised and seemed to be caught off guard. She let me in and ran upstairs to let Saye know I was there. I waited in one of the rooms for quite a long time. It was one of those very old houses in an old uptown area of the city. It was decorated with all kinds of old and new furniture—strangely shaped lamp stands and weird paintings, and everything smelled like Indian spices. It was cold and dim, too, and very creepy. I knew something very serious had happened, but I thought that, whatever it was, we would be able to get over it. I was sure she was alright. I knew it had nothing to do with her health.

To be honest with you, I already knew what had happened; I sensed it, and I knew I was right. I had that terrible pain in my stomach again; I hadn't had that pain since five years before, after Marmar's case. I was about to throw up, but managed to control myself. After I spent a long 15 minutes waiting, she showed up, said hi, and sat in front of me on the floor without saying a word. We were there for about ten minutes until she began to cry deeply but quietly. She wasn't able to say a word. I wanted to tell her, "It's alright, Saye; whatever happened has happened and passed. Don't worry, it's alright, you don't need to tell me anything." But I couldn't. I knew she was in pain. Finally her sister came in and asked her to give us a minute. After she left, her sister told me that Saye had other opportunities better than I had offered her. She said I wasn't a good choice for her, and they didn't want her to mess up her life with me. She said that Saye would never be happy with me and that she had the chance to become someone, but with me she didn't have that chance.

I was surprised at her tone and vocabulary. She never ever had talked to me that way before. I knew she wasn't telling me the whole truth. I told her, "Saye never thinks that way except you put these thought in her mind; we do have a chance." But I was lying to myself; I didn't deserve her. Her sister was right. I was just a junkie, a drug dealer, no matter how intellectual I sounded to people as a spiritual teacher; I knew I was no one! But I also knew that Saye's case was all about the guy she met in Turkey, Afshin's friend. I should have expected that, the Karma. I did the same to Afshin, and now the same thing happened to me. I didn't want to get involved in details of the story, so I immediately got up and left the room. While I was on my way down the stairs, her sister ran after me and said,

"Bijan, the ring—please, give it back!" I looked at the ring, thought for a while and then without any attention to what she said I left the house; it wasn't yet over for me until I would have a chance to talk to Saye again.

Few days later we met. We had a short talk and I knew I had lost her. I gave her the ring.

I never saw Saye again until a decade later. Shortly after the day we met at her sister's, I heard she got married to the same person she had met in Istanbul. They lived happily after. I guess both studied Archaeology and worked in the same field for years. As far as I know, they have two grown up son and daughter. She found my sister on Facebook recently, after almost three decades, and I found her on my sister's friends list. We reconnected again. I told her I'd been writing my life story. She asked if she was in it. I said, "Yes, of course you're in it!" She sent me a smiley face in response. I'm glad that destiny forced us to make the right decision. Destiny is always right, even if what is happening to us seems unfair and is painful at the moment. A higher and wiser force is still watching over us.

—

I finished my military service after two and half years, late in the fall of 1988, right before Christmas. I survived many Mig-26 attacks, many bombings on our Navy base, a couple wolf attacks in wilderness, one grenade explosion three feet away from me, which caused the deformation of my friend's face right in front of my eyes, one plot of Iraqi prisoners to take over my weapons while I was guarding them, a few serious fights with my superior ranking officers, three arrests for possessing drugs, a few weeks of jail for not wanting to be engaged in a military attack to a Iraqi base near the border, and finally one horrible and deadly chemical poisoning. The latter sent me to the hospital for days. I was infected and became delusional, thinking everybody was trying to kill me. That was my military service in just one paragraph.

I'm not going to trouble you more with what happened to me during the war. I continued to teach the soldiers around me (who also became my disciples) about mysticism and the supernatural, while still using heavier drugs. We did lots of dangerous things together and were punished many times by our superiors. We were even thrown in military jails for our rebellious behavior. I was always the smart leader, whether we helped people in times of bombings or when we burned the military files just for a laugh. Those stories could all be the subject of an entire other book.

After I was released in mid-December 1988, the same time that the end of the war was announced, I got my passport. On January 1, 1989, I was on a flight to Tokyo, Japan. I had decided to expand my spiritual search starting in Japan. That's where I experienced the turning point of my whole life. Destiny was waiting for me in Tokyo in an area called Shibuya.

Big in Japan

Japan—land of the Samurais, Geishas, Sake, Sushi, and technology. But there was much more to it, too. I never imagined Tokyo being so crowded. It was fascinating. In 1989, Tokyo was like one of those futuristic cities you would only see in Hollywood movies. Monorail Sky-trains, huge billboards, giant TV screens at every corner, colorful racing motorbikes, and cars I had never seen. It was exciting to see young people in full leather jackets with rainbow-colored hair! The things that most people in 1989 only saw in fashion magazines and the music industry, the Japanese young people were living! They were enjoying the fullness of their freedom, without drugs, as far as I noticed.

I never got tired of walking in Harajuku, Shibuya, and almost every other area of the city. There were millions of people walking in streets, even at the quietest time of the day, during working hours. Restaurants, coffee shops, Sushi booths, and game shops were always filled with people. It was the most animated society I'd ever seen or even heard of.

Everybody had a walkman. All of the young people in the trains and buses wore headphones, listening to music (which by the way indicated how lonely they were). Remember, I'm talking about late '80s. Later I made friends with many Americans and Europeans who were also as amazed as I was about Tokyo! I haven't yet seen so many people in the streets or in trains and buses wearing earphones, even though I travelled to many other countries afterward. Of course, in the late '80s there were only small tape players that people carried around; not even those round CD players were popular yet. In those days, the main competition in the field of music players was only between Japanese electronics companies like Sony,

Toshiba, Akai, and others; it's not like today, when everybody's striving to have an iPod, iPhone, or iPad.

Travelling with drugs was much easier in those days, especially from Iran. Although Japan was a drug-resistant country at the time (meaning the government had a serious control over the sea and air borders), I managed to pass a great amount of opium and weed through to Tokyo, enough for a year's supply. And since I had found a black market job at a huge beer and whisky delivery company, I had the chance to try out nearly 4000 kinds of alcoholic drinks. I had a relatively good salary, $17 an hour in 1989. Literally every night I was wasted on weed and Japanese Sake. I almost forgot why I went to Japan; my spiritual journey turned to 24/7 drunkenness and drug consumption once again.

My boss, Usui San, was so excited to introduce me to his friends in every pub in the city. He was a very nice man. Every evening before we finished at work, he would prepare me a very special drink just to warm me up for the big round. He had an endless circle of friends. Most of them were managing or operating Japanese traditional bars, the kind that only men would go to, where beautiful women would sit at your table to serve you drinks. They were not those bad places you might think. The girls' job was to sit beside you, serve you with Sake, and just talk with you. They were mostly educated and surprisingly aware of the things going on around the world. Usui San, like all other Japanese, liked to sing karaoke. He was very eager to teach me how to sing in Japanese, and guess what, I was good at it! He liked my voice so much that I had to perform in every pub we went to. His favorite was a song called *Tokyo Sabaku*, which means Desert of Tokyo. To be honest, I was very good in singing that song. Most Japanese I met during my stay in Japan told me I was very "Jozu" in my Japanese, meaning "skilled" or "expert." In fact, many Japanese friends used to tell me that if they would close their eyes and listen to me, they could not believe I wasn't Japanese because of my accent, or in fact because I had no accent! But that was more than twenty years ago, and I only remember a few words today. Yes, you are right; I need to start practicing my Japanese again!

I really enjoyed being popular among my Japanese friends, so I began to think, *What if I just stay here and live a fun and quiet life in Japan? What if I marry a Japanese girl and live happily after all?* I loved it there, and I eventually began to search for ways of renewing my visa or legally residing in Japan. Japan was (and is) a very expensive country to live in, but a foreign worker could get higher wages and higher respect, like in my own case. I could have had everything I wanted. For me, Japan was an ideal place to live and have fun, but still I felt a void in me that apparently nothing in this world was able to fill, and it was eating my soul away from within.

It was hard to admit, but I truly hated myself and my pretentious intellectuality. There was nothing in my lifestyle that could possibly fit my ideals. After my attempt to commit suicide, I had made an unspoken vow to myself that I would never let myself become like the Colonel—a coldhearted man who knew that what he was doing was wrong, but his lust for life so dominated his whole existence that he couldn't stop being who (what) he was and doing what he did. But I didn't know how in the world was I able to prevent that from happening.

An everyday life of drinking and smoking to the last breathe and then passing out at the door of my apartment was a temporary escape from my problem of lost identity and purposelessness. A line from Robert Smith's song (lead singer of *the Cure*), "A Thousand Hours," was in my head all the time; "For how much longer can I howl into this wind, for how much longer can I cry like this?"

In those days, I was also informed about my dad's unfortunate bankruptcy. He had invested all of his savings in a company that was doing all kinds of businesses, from chicken and cattle husbandry to agriculture, from import to export, from real estate to stocks. After the war, Iran went into a very heavy financial recession. Everything was so expensive, and the cost of living was so high that almost everyone in the family had at least two jobs and worked hard just to survive. In most families that lived under the poverty line, even children had to work as gum or flower sellers in the streets. Others sold chocolate and candy, even at the age five. We all know that the middle class of society, when it comes to recession, always goes through the toughest time because they had already and painfully managed to keep themselves up to a standard of living that is almost impossible to reverse. When we taste the luxury of living in the middle class of society, it will be much harder to go back to the old days and previous lifestyle. This is a fact for every middle class in every culture.

Fortunately we were not a poor family, and my parents, through the sacrifices they both had made, had managed to build a good life for us. We had a very nice house in a very expensive area of uptown Tehran—and a piece of farm, plus some shares in a taxi service company and other small investments here and there. But during the war, things began to change. Because of bombings, all of the house prices dropped drastically. The selling and buying market of farms stopped, and people did not use car rentals anymore. My dad was retired, and his benefit was not enough to manage a household. The Government could not hold on to its promises of bringing the oil money to our tables, as they had claimed at the beginning of the Islamic regime (we all knew they were lying, even from the beginning). Thus my dad had to work harder in old age. Even my youngest sister had to work hard so that she could pay for her own expenses and help the family as well. And I also began sending them some cash from time to time from my income in Japan. Sherrie had already managed to leave Iran and was living in Switzerland in those days. She, too, made many sacrifices to send money to them occasionally.

But even with all that was done, my dad was finally forced to sell the house to pay off his debts, and that was the beginning of a financial nightmare for them. When my parents found out about this huge company, they decided to sell everything else they had and invest it in the company. But as you may guess, they lost it all, not because the company was fraud, but because the government found out about these investment companies and the huge amount of money that was circling in the market through them. So the government decided to come up with an Islamic interpretation of Sharia law, which enabled them to file a case against those companies in the Revolutionary Court, a law that claimed that this kind of business is Haram (unlawful) for both the company and all the shareholders and that the government had the right to claim the money and the possessions of these companies in favor of the Islamic Government (which by that time was hundreds of millions of dollars). That was the end of life for tens of thousands of middle class citizens.

Just to clear your minds from any "why's and how's," I need to remind you that where Islam rules, you have no rights to object to anything because there is always an interpretation of the Sharia Law that can come right against you. In Iran, if you wanted to stay alive and not to be considered an infidel, you had to zip it up and swallow your right.

As a result, my sister, Sherrie, and I had to send more money to help the family survive. But it was impossible to do it every month; Japan was a very expensive country, and even though I had a relatively fair salary, still the expenses were way too high. More than half of my salary would go for the rent and bills for a small 86-square foot bachelor apartment (almost $1000), not to mention the other costs of life in Japan. Fortunately, I never spent any money on drinks; it was all paid by my boss, Usui San! I couldn't bear the bitter reality of my family collapsing. As a result, I indulged in alcohol to forget the situation.

I tried, many times, to use all my psychic powers and abilities to communicate with the so-called spirit world to somehow find some answers to my questions, maybe even come up with a solution for my dad's situation. But the more I tried, the more confused I became. In most communications, the spirits didn't (or seemed to be reluctant to) share their secrets with me especially about the existence of God because I believed that if his existence could be proven to me, then I would be able to live my life more easily and trust him that he was wise and loving enough to do justice on my behalf regardless of my expectations. But for some reason, those spirits never wanted to directly talk about God. In some cases, they mentioned Satan, but not much about God.

For whatever reason, I never got what I needed to hear about God. But maybe it's not a bad idea to give you some hints about these whatsoever creatures. During many years of search and study, I collected some general ideas regarding the nature of these creatures or whatever they were. The following became facts for me:

- There are definitely other distinct worlds or non-material realms where what we believe to be spirits reside.
- Most of these spirits seem to be very aggressive and violent.
- Apparently they could be summoned through some rituals while they could also appear to you on their own decision.
- Most spirits don't like to talk about God, but if they do, they'll tell you the things you've already heard or known through most dominant religions—nothing new.
- Spirits are able to introduce themselves as familiar or famous dead people's ghosts and deceive us. Thus, they are not truthful.
- They have some collective knowledge, which is mostly ancient rather than futuristic. In some cases, they seem to be able to predict things, but what they claim is more based on a cosmic calculation of the data circulating worldwide within their spiritual realm, just like what we as humans do—a deliberate guess based on information and data.
- They all have the ability and an unsatisfying thirst to possess human bodies if the person will give them permission, willingly or by ignorance (for example, through rituals or personalized supernatural and superstitious beliefs).

- They can enable you to do unusual stuff (physical or supernatural) if you allow them to use your mind and body. This way they can make you believe you have powers over them and others.
- They can do harm to you and others.
- They feed on fear. Scaring human beings is their best way to approach and control people. Through this method, they have been able to create a worldwide genre of horror stories that have been circulated within the history of humankind (like monsters, wandering ghosts, vampires, werewolves, demons, and so forth).
- Some of the things that are contributed to their powers are not real at all, but just illusions. They have the ability to mess with your mind and your perception under specific conditions.
- In some cultures, they are considered to be able to put a spell on you through what is called black magic or through some spiritual rituals. They can make you feel sick or make you eat things that can damage your body and mind. They seem to possess a vast knowledge of using the natural ingredients, like the herbs, plants, animals, insects, and so forth.
- Some of them seem to be harmless and helping spirits (but I personally had only couple of encounters with the harmless ones up until those days. Maybe they were (and are) always at work as guardians but they don't want to intervene in our decision making process.
- There seems to be a battle between these spiritual beings over human beings—some with good intentions, some with evil intentions! On occasions, it is seen that they are afraid or disappear at the mention of the names of God or some other religious figures with divine attributes.

Of course, there are more facts about these creatures or spirits that I learned in my fifteen years of formal search prior to learning the truth, but these were some of the main facts. I'm sure some of you have other items to add to this list. These are simply the ones I learned up to the age twenty-eight, when I finally had a mind-blowing encounter with something beyond all I had experienced up to that moment. I did my best to stay true to those experiences in this book. After that encounter, I gradually gained a new understanding about these beings, their purposes, their origins, and their functionality, and most important of all, I gained understanding about confronting them, if I were supposed to confront them again at some point.

I had tried everything I could to figure what was going on in this universe. I wanted to know the source of these so-called spirits so that I could find a meaning for life in general. But those spirits were only pointing to an evil force instead of the God I had always heard about. We used to sacrifice animals to the devil, and we thought we were doing an amazing job, but we didn't reap anything from what we sowed except more evil. Now, I believed, it was time to wrestle with God, if he was really there. If I believed in the devil, I needed to believe that God existed, too. I had personally experienced encounters with those spirits, and I knew they were out there. I could not deny their existence. Even the most atheist scholars admit there are things in this world that no one can explain. But whatever they are called, they didn't help me find my answers. My family was on the verge of falling apart financially, and I couldn't do anything about it. All my abilities and powers were worthless; they were of no use and couldn't do me any good when I needed them!

Close Encounter of the First Kind

WHEN YOU BELIEVE IN SOMETHING wholeheartedly, you don't need any complementary explanation to act upon your beliefs. And if you don't believe in something, no explanation will be able to change your mind until you decide to activate a switch called faith. The worst part is that some of us don't even know there's such a switch.

It was a crazy night of drinking. The company I was working for had this pleasant custom of throwing a party once every two months in a huge restaurant, hotel, or other luxurious place. Most Japanese companies do that. They do everything they can to increase the efficiency of their employees, and partying is one such incentive.

Parties would usually start right after the work hours at approximately 5:30 p.m. I would start drinking around 4 p.m. with the drink my boss offered me (Scotch whisky mixed with hot water, or two to three shots of sake). Then I would go to the party, and since I was the only foreign employee there, everyone would want to pour drinks for me, and I had to take them; otherwise I would be considered impolite. The good thing was that I didn't need to wait a long time for food; they were already on the tables, with a small candle burning under every dish. They would have all kinds of the best sushi and sashimi, juicy steaks, lobsters, shrimp, fried chicken, rice, soups, and tons of other vegetable and sea food dishes, along with all kinds of Japanese strong and light drinks, not to mention beers, whiskies, tequilas, and wine. And, of course, there was the most important part of the party—karaoke.

Sometimes before going to these kinds of parties, I would swallow a piece of butter so that I wouldn't get easily drunk. That's something I learned from crazy nights of drinking with the mobs back in Shiraz. And it always worked.

That particular night, I got so drunk that I do not remember anything from that night except a blurry picture of a verbal fight with the one we call God right in front of my apartment door. I just remember I was swearing at him, yelling at him, saying all kinds of bad things to him for bringing me into this world and leaving me (and millions of others) there alone to suffer and to figure out a nonsense thing called life. I reminded him of how many times I had asked him to help me, to give me an answer, to appear to me, to show himself to me, to say a word, and so on, but he had never done anything in response. I was on my knees, crying out. It was 2 or 3 in the morning, and I was kicking against the door and pounding the floor. The last thing I remember are these words I whispered to him in desperation and tears before I passed out in front of my apartment door: *"I'm exhausted and I'm tired. I hate myself and my life. If you are there, if you exist, if you created me, if you made me, if you care for me, and if there's a reason you brought me to this world ... please, for your own sake, kill me or save me."*

The next morning I woke up on the sidewalk by my apartment. I was right there in the middle of sidewalk. It was around 6:30 in the morning, and fortunately nobody was yet in street. I noticed I was lying on my mattress! There was a pillow under my head and a blanket over me, but I was in the middle of the sidewalk! The last words of the night before were still echoing in my ears, "kill me or save me, kill me or save me." I didn't remember a thing from the party, and I didn't remember how I ended up in the street on my mattress, half naked! I immediately took my stuff and ran into my apartment before the neighbors saw me; that's not something you want your neighbors to see. I was shocked to find myself in that situation—so embarrassed and ashamed of myself and my life. I felt my head was as big as the world itself. The headache was unbearable. I took four or five strong pain killers and swallowed up a small dose of opium, took a shower, and took a short nap. I woke up at 8:30 and ran to work. I didn't talk to anyone until 5:30 p.m. I really wanted to end my shameful and meaningless life. I could not understand how others kept living the way they did—so hopeless.

After work and on my way back home, I went to the bank and sent all the money I had to my parents. Then I took the subway and for some reason (I had no idea why), I got off at Shibuya station. I went up to the main street and walked for a while, then decided to go back home.

I was about to enter the subway station when I saw an Asian girl holding a black binder standing near the intersection talking to three Indian guys. Suddenly I felt a weird move in my stomach. A nonsense and ridiculous thought came to my mind: *You must talk to this girl.* I laughed at the idea. I turned around to walk toward the subway station, but I felt my feet were nailed to the ground. *You must talk to this girl,* I heard the voice say again. It wasn't a voice per se; it was more like an urge. I couldn't understand why I was feeling that way. She was cute and pretty, but so what? There were literally thousands of girls standing or walking in that area, and many of them were much prettier than her! I could not understand that strong chaos in my belly. It was ridiculous; I had a strange, but strong feeling about that girl.

She didn't look like Japanese girls. Her skin was darker; she was probably from Southeast Asia. What could possibly attract me to her? There were many Japanese couples sitting on benches or leaning against the walls, making out in the crowd. Most boys and girls would meet their dates in Shibuya area. Thousands of people were on the move, like a sea of moving, soulless creatures captured in an eternal photo frame. Every second a new wave of people appeared, and then they were gone. But she was still there, and so was I, thirty feet away from her. Everything else seemed to be blurry except her. I thought she was the centre of the whole world in that moment.

Whatever nailed me to the ground had a purpose. I was into signs enough to know that there was a reason for her to be there and for me to come to Shibuya that afternoon. We were destined to meet. I thought, *Maybe she is a lost soul like me, and we are supposed to save each other!* What a sweet thought. I said to myself, *But life is crueler than that. I'm over girls. Girls cannot be part of any redemption or even any revelation regarding the purpose of the universe.* I was caught in my thoughts for almost ten minutes; then I finally saw those guys shake hands with her and leave. She was still standing there, looking around proudly, like she had something no one else had ever had. I couldn't waste the time anymore. I almost ran to her.

"Hi."

"Hi," she replied with a smile. She didn't seem surprised.

"You are not Japanese, are you?" I asked.

She laughed so beautifully, "No, I'm not," she replied. "Why?"

"Nothing, just wanted to decide whether to speak with you in Japanese or English!"

I guess she noticed I was nervous, so she tried to make it easier for me by stretching her hand toward me saying her name, "I'm Cheryl." We shook hands.

"Hi, hello, I'm Bijan," I said. I guess I had the most ridiculous smile on my face when I introduced myself. I tried to be as cool as I could, but there was something about her that made me completely vulnerable. It was like she already knew everything about me; I felt naked before her.

"Nice to meet you," I said.

"You too," she replied.

"I need to be honest with you," I said.

"OK." She looked curious, but was alert!

"I was on my way back home when I saw you talking to those three guys and something nailed me to the floor," I said, "I knew I had to talk with you, but I have no clue what I'm supposed to say, if you know what I mean."

"I guess I know what you mean," she said, while showing me the back of her left hand and her gold ring, "But I'm engaged!"

When she said that, nothing changed in what I had been feeling. What I had felt about her was beyond all that. In fact, I didn't care when she said that she was engaged.

"Oh no, I didn't mean that," I tried to clear the misunderstanding. "I just felt like there is something we need to talk about, even though it may sound so weird and crazy."

She never stopped smiling while we were talking. She took a look around and then said, "OK, but you need to know that I only talk about one thing—God!"

The moment she said that, everything around me seemed to collapse; everything went black. I felt I was fainting. Really, everything seemed to fall apart in me with the speed of light. All those fancy, colorful neon lights in that crowded Shibuya area lost their glory and seemed small and worthless compared to the light I saw in her face. There was no way I could hide my excitement and awe in what was happening to me at that moment.

"That's all I need to hear about," I said with a trembling and excited voice. "Please tell me more about Him, I mean God"

She stared at me with a surprised look on her face for a while and then pointed to the only empty bench near us and said, "Let's sit."

I ran toward the bench before anybody could take it. I sat there while she was slowly walking toward me. I was so excited to talk to her that her every step seemed to take hours to me. She finally came and sat beside me.

"What can you possibly tell me about God that I haven't heard yet in my whole twenty-eight years?" I began the conversation. "I've been after him with all my heart. I've been to the desert in search for him. I've been to the highest mountains, to the darkest caves, to Sufi's gatherings, to Buddhist temples, to Mosques, to secret gatherings of Indian Gurus. I've read hundreds of books about him. I've searched within thousands of articles on creation, meta-physics, and the supernatural, and I have been practicing hundreds of methods to communicate with other worlds. I have been successful to a degree, but even those stupid spirits have no idea about him! What else can you tell me that I don't already know?" I opened up my whole heart to her in total trust, in no fear of embarrassment or of being ridiculed.

She listened to what I said attentively with the same smile on her face. She just looked at me with eyes as innocent as a two-year-old! She then said, "Wow, so honest and right to the point! I might not be a very good judge for that, but I think it wasn't you who was after God; it was God who was after you in all those places while you've been trying to run ahead of Him. Or maybe He was waiting for the right time. He had been preparing you for this day! He loves you and cares for you more than you can imagine. But we need to learn and experience this truth through life itself! I don't mean that He won't help us find the way, but He never forces us to believe Him."

"How could you say that He cared for me and He loved me?" I became defensive, but deep in my heart of hearts, I knew she could be right. There was no way to go against what she had just said except emotionally. Logically what she had said was true, for what she had said was what we as human beings do to train and educate our children. Even teachers, whether spiritual or otherwise, do the same thing to train and educate their students.

I wasn't that ignorant or illogical to fight her reasoning. It is useless to argue with someone you know is right just because you are desperate to win the conversation or don't want to admit you are wrong. I considered myself an honest person; at least I was honest with myself. And she was right. I always sensed the presence of a higher intelligent super power around me who not only created the whole universe, but also was in control of it.

But because of the many injustice we all see in the world, I wasn't able to relate such a creator to the unfairness, poverty, hatred, wars, killings, and all other absurd and nonsense things going on in the world. There was no way to relate a good God to all this. Plus, I didn't want to accept the fact that God was allowing me to go through many disgusting things in order to educate me—things that I was always ashamed of. *How could He stand there and watch me cutting my wrists or taking fifty sleeping pills to kill myself?* I thought.

"I know you can't believe what I just said, but it's true; I've been there. Trust me; I know what I'm talking about," she was playing with the pages of a book she was holding, the book that I first thought was a binder. I sensed a closeness to her that I wasn't able to understand. The attraction wasn't sexual at all! There was something beyond my comprehension.

"Please don't get me wrong, but how come I feel so close to you, Cheryl? I can't understand." I wasn't sure about asking her this question, but I felt she would understand me.

"Well, maybe it's because I know exactly where you come from. I've walked down that path before, and someone helped me find my way. I myself have been on this journey too, even though I thought I was a good person and observed religious duties to a degree."

"What religious duties? Where are you from, by the way?" I asked.

"I'm from Malaysia, and I used to be a Muslim," she replied.

"I was born in a Muslim family, but was never really into it," I said, "There was something about Islam that I could never communicate with. To me, there was no soul in it! It was only rituals. Did you feel the same?"

"Kind of. But there were more issues in Islam that didn't make sense to me," she admitted." But talking about what we used to be will not help us in finding who we are created to be."

I said, "I understand, because once I've made an extensive study on Islam; it seemed to me that, rather than commentaries and explanatory notes or observatory conclusions others added to it during the centuries, there wasn't any other new stuff to it. You can sum up everything in "be a good person, help the needy, and perform the rituals, and maybe God will have mercy on you." You know what I'm talking about?"

"Yes, I do. And the rest is just nothing but 'Do this, do that, don't do this, don't do that.' That's what I got. As you said, there is no soul in it," she said.

"I've gotten into drugs during my spiritual search, badly! I don't know why I'm saying this to you! Sorry, now you think I'm a junkie!" I felt embarrassed.

She laughed loudly, unlike shy Japanese girls. I liked it!

"Did I say something funny?" I asked.

"No, no. I'm sorry. I shouldn't have reacted like that. It was…I mean, just the way you said it was funny!" Then she added, "I have a friend you should meet. He can be more helpful to you," and she got up.

I didn't want to talk to anyone else; I wanted to keep talking with her till the end of the world. She was so friendly, kind, accepting, and honest. She didn't judge me when I said I was in drugs. She was full of life; I wanted what she had.

"Where are you going?" I asked.

She replied, "I'll be around. I think my friend can help you better. His name is Fernando." Then she called out to him and waved hands, "Fernando! Fernando! Over here!"

He was slim, kind of short, and blond. He had tattoos all over his arms. He walked toward me and said hi. We shook hands, and he gave me a half hug, "How you doing, brother?" he said. Cheryl introduced me to him, "This is Bijan. He wants to know more about God," then she smiled.

I liked him. He was cool. He wasn't wearing any t-shirt or shirt except a brown cowboy leather vest. He had torn jeans on, and was wearing a pair of Texan boots. He had a light beard and blue eyes that matched his appearance.

"I'm fine. How are you?" I replied.

"I'm cool. What's your name again?"

"Bijan, B-I-J-A-N." I repeated again. "J like in French language."

"Cool! I like it. Where are you from?" he asked.

"Iran."

"Is it near the UK?" He wasn't sure.

"No, that is Ireland. I'm from Iran, Persian Gulf."

"Oh, OK. I see."

"Where are you from? America?" I asked.

"Well, my mother is American, from California, but my dad is from Mexico City. They live in the States now."

Cheryl told him a little about my spiritual journey and my challenges with God. Then she said to him, "I thought you could be the right person to answer his questions." She continued, "He used to be in drugs." She didn't know I was still using some. In fact, I had some in my pocket at the moment.

"Wow!" Fernando said. "I've been into all the drugs you could imagine for ten years. I just got saved six months ago. He found me. JC's cool, man!"

I thought, *What did he mean by "being saved," and who is this JC?*

Cheryl left us alone to talk, but before she shook hands with me she said, "Hope to see you soon. Fernando will give you our address; if you'd like, you can give us a visit."

I said, "Sure, I would love to see you again."

Fernando asked me to sit down before anyone else took the bench. We sat down and talked about our experiences with drugs. He told me about his trips with Mescalito and all other kinds of mushrooms, weeds, heroin, cocaine, LSD, and so forth. I had already tried all of them except Mescalito. I only heard about it in Castaneda's books. I asked him about it. He said he knew Castaneda, and then he gave me some explanations about Mescalito (sometimes he referred to it as Peyote), but told me that taking the cactus was more like a personal experience and that it could be different to everyone.

I remembered the days in Shiraz again. In those days we used to mix some kind of medical syrups with some other pills and put them together with hashish oil. Not everybody could take that stuff. Sometimes we were left in other worlds for a day or two. We had different experiences. Some were as horrible as Castaneda's, some were milder. I never got to know the ingredients; it was the old man's formula, the naked Habib from the six!

Then I asked him what he meant by "saved" and who JC was? He said, "Jesus Christ, who else?"

"Jesus Christ, the prophet?" I asked in unbelief. "Are you guys talking about Him? I already know Him. He was a prophet sent by Allah, like Moses and Mohammad" (that was what Islam had taught us back in Iran). I continued, "I never thought you guys were so enthusiastic about someone whom I already know. He's mentioned all over the Quran—Holy Mary, His mother, and the fact that He talked in His cradle as soon as He was born (I was taught that, too). But He couldn't fulfill His mission because some corrupted religious people and politicians wanted to kill Him, so God took Him to Heaven, and later on He decided to send Mohammad as His last prophet. Yeah, yeah, I know all about Him. So you guys are Christians, missionaries! I thought you and Cheryl were talking about something different, like a mystical revelation or experience!"

In fact it was like a slap in my face when I found out he was talking about Jesus! I thought these people were more sophisticated than that. *Jesus?! Oh come on! So pretentious!*

"Hey, what's gotten a hold of you? It's not like what you said. It *is* different." He continued, "I was told that this is what Islam says about Jesus. It's not that He failed at His mission and that God took Him up to Heaven because of His failure! He actually accomplished what He came for. He was supposed to die for us on the cross. That was God's plan to save human race, before the beginning of the creation. It's not that God sent Mohammad to finish what Jesus wasn't able to do. I heard this has been going around in Muslim tradition for a long time, but it's not what really happened."

"Fernando, my search has nothing to do with religion. Religion is for the sheep," I said, "and I am not one! I can decide for myself. I have a brain and tools like logic and reasoning. I do believe that, if there's a God, he would reveal himself to those who are diligent enough to search for him, otherwise how could we know who is wiser and smarter among us? That's what God wants to know! Like what Carlos Castaneda says about jumping over the Eagle!"

He said, "What? You believe in that myth? Now I can't believe *you*, man! That stuff happened three decades ago and was woven together by a mere man, and you believed it? You believe in what a man says as a truth, but don't want to believe what was actually planned and done by God himself through the ages to save us?"

"What do you mean by 'save us'?" I asked again. "It's not about being saved; it's all about the journey of life and how much you grow in knowledge and wisdom and how much you become aware of the higher forces of life and how highly intelligent you can become, in mind and soul; then you will have the chance to get in touch with whatever you call God so that you can become like him, too. That's my understanding of existence and being saved." I had completely forgotten what I asked God the night before; kill me or save me!

"Interesting idea; New Age. But it's not new at all. In fact, it has been around for centuries." He wasn't backing off. "To be honest with you, this is what the devil has been trying to sell to humankind from the beginning, the idea of 'you can become a god.' I used to believe that, but not anymore. We all need to be saved from the eternal damnation we brought upon ourselves. If there's a God as a force standing for good, so the force that stands for evil should be as real as God. We call it the devil or Satan. For some reason, we are not able to see this picture clearly because the same evil force has blinded us spiritually. We cannot see the truth. We think we are gods or we can become gods. This pride has blinded us, and we can't understand what the devil is doing to us. We all think we are smarter than that, but we are not. We are just some children who have lost their father in the crowd, and we're so naive that we think everyone with a candy is our father."

His last statement was true. That was exactly what I felt—lost. But my pride didn't want to admit that. I didn't want to acknowledge I needed help, that I was lost, and that I needed to be found again. Most of my teenage and young adult years were spent nagging about whoever God was and about the hardships of life or why bad things were happening in the world, like I had nothing to do with them at all and it was all God's fault. I knew very well what he was talking about, but I wasn't brave enough to admit it. All I did was blame it all on God. My whole being was almost sure there was a God, but I was so self-centered that I didn't want to believe He was anything else except what I had been picturing all my life; God needed to be exactly the person who I had created in my mind.

Generally even though I always claimed to search for God I was mad at any kind of god who was part of this creation. Maybe the reason I was pretending to be searching for God was just an excuse to run away from Him. As a frustrated young man maybe I just wanted to find Him and slap Him on the face or shoot Him in the head!

Then I remembered the night before when I had asked God to kill me or save me when I wasn't even sure what being saved could mean! I knew Fernando was partially right, but I was filled with frustration, anger, and despair. However, I wanted to continue the discussion.

Fernando looked at his watch and then said, "It's time for dinner. I have to go now, but do you mind if we get together again and talk more?"

"Sure, I'd be delighted," I said.

He smiled and said, "Great, here's our address. We live in a trailer in the back yard of a cool church just two minutes walk from here," and he gave me a small piece of paper with a hand-written address on it. He had few more.

"That's great. I'll keep in touch," I assured him.

We shook hands and said good-bye. I went home that night with new thoughts blossoming in my mind. I was thinking about how cool these people were—my new friends, so simple, so in love with God, and probably so naive!

I was happy and calm. That night I had my best sleep in a very long time. After all, tomorrow could be a new day. Maybe it was God who had kept me alive until this moment for a reason. Maybe this old man, who some say is in control of the universe, had finally noticed I was looking for Him! And maybe Cheryl was right when she said, "He wasn't lost, you were, and He was after you!" Maybe He wasn't exactly who I had always pictured in my mind, and maybe, if I was able to shift my perspective, I would be able to see Him the way He truly was.

And maybe I was all the way wrong!

Close Encounter of the Second Kind

THE MAGIC OF LIFE IS that, regardless of the fact that there is nothing new under the blue sky, it still lures you to want to live it thoroughly again and again, even if you decide to end your life ten times a day.

I often wondered, *Isn't that a sickness?* I'm talking about myself back in those days—knowing what I had gone through, yet feeling the desire to live life again and again even though I knew deep inside that I would make the same choices! If it's not a sickness, then I don't know what to call it, maybe masochism! Having said that, I thought God must have been really something to let us live like that. My thinking went something like this: *What were we to Him? Lab hamsters? Even if we were, why such tests? Was there something He didn't know about His creatures? Why tests? Maybe what we call tests are nothing but the only way for us to know ourselves. Maybe what we call life (and the way it is) was the only (and the best) option God could come up with for us to become who we were destined or supposed to be. But if He was testing us, what were the tests for be? Why didn't He create us in a way that we wouldn't feel the pain so that He could easily continue His tests? And why had He given us the ability to reason all this? For this is even worse than physical pain. It is not all the sufferings of the world that drive you nuts; it is the reasoning behind it that can bring you to the point of madness and cause you to want to end it all. The ability to analyze such a meaningless test called life is even bitter and more painful than life itself. To me, pain was never an issue, but the awareness was! Was I right? Or I was just childish! Was I too philosophical to think about these facts, or I was just a no brainer?*

Even the idea of a God/Creator who planned a world like the one we live in and His decision to bring it to being and, after that, the idea of picking and sending some regular, messed up guys called prophets to tell people what is right and what is wrong sounded completely absurd and nonsensical—like a childish bedtime story or a myth. *So what?!* I thought. *You put people in jeopardy, suffering, and confusion, and then You send some messengers to tell them what to do to get out of that situation! What for? To prove Your sovereignty to them?* I wondered if I was blasphemous for thinking about these things! *Maybe.*

What about the whole universe? I wondered. *What about all the seen and unseen parts of the galaxies and star systems, not to mention the existence of the cosmic clustered dusts and black holes, light speed, dark matter/antimatter, the complexity of the atoms and DNA structure, and the comparison between the obvious age of universe as we know and the age of our species and the genesis of human beings (these numbers always drove me crazy).* I believed this comparison would make God and all His wise plans more incomprehensible and, therefore, very unacceptable.

Imagine building a giant spaceship like the Destiny (as in the Cancelled TV series Stargate Universe) and sending it into the vast space. Then imagine making some little semi-intelligent creatures that are, compared to space and the ship itself, unbelievably small and tiny. You somehow, through some communication device, tell them you created them and put them on the Destiny, but you don't tell them why and for what purpose. Then you give them a code of conduct and behavior and ask them, even though they don't know you and have no idea who you might be (maybe just a recorded voice), to listen to you and behave the way you tell them until you reveal your purposes to them (as far as they may understand). If they exactly do what you tell them to do, you will decide whether they deserve to know a little bit more about the ship and its destination. Then maybe you will decide whether you want to give them a second chance at another form of life, even though they don't have a clue about what their present life means! *What?! Second life? Why would I want to have another kind of life when I'm not yet clear about this one? Isn't being nothing and feeling nothing and, therefore, not being able to reason anything better than a chance to have another unknown kind of life with so many other uncertainties?! Man!* Even the idea troubled my mind.

I thought, *Isn't the idea of the next life something that the collective mind of humankind created as a satisfying reward for good works we might do in an incomprehensibly evil world, as well as a future haven from the bad things that others do to us that we have no power to stop or revenge? Isn't Heaven an imaginary place for the weak?* Here is a simple analogy for how what I was struggling with. What if a human father hid himself from his own baby son while expecting him to 1) believe he exists, 2) believe he is his father, 3) listen to him, 4) do exactly as he says, 5) trust him, and 6) believe in a completely different kind of life that is better than this world? To me it seemed like absolute lunacy.

What would this different world be like—a state of awareness in which you won't even remember who you used to be and what you went through? Somewhere that you will have no more idea of what sorrow meant, what evil meant, or what good and evil were? I knew that, according to some interpretations of religion, if after entering Heaven, you still remembered evil or the evil things you did, it meant that the evil still existed in your memory and was not completely destroyed, so it could come back to the surface and eventually happen again. According to this way of thinking, you would need to not remember anything of the past when you go to Heaven. Thus, to me it seemed that none of the tests and spiritual journeys of the past would make sense at all once you had entered Heaven.

Clearly, God's purpose in creating the universe was so incomprehensible that could only be accepted by faith. I'm not talking about questioning the existence of God at all. There is obviously enough evidence to cause some to totally reject Him and to cause others to totally accept Him, as we have seen many Christian philosophers during history deny their faith in God or, conversely, non-believing philosophers join the faithful after all.

In fact, the universe is so complicated in structure (but so simple in its nature) that not believing in a designer (just because it sounds old fashioned) is actually not so wise. There was a time when theism was a sign of intellectuality, but in current times it's the opposite that makes you feel intellectual. To embrace the idea of God as a possibility, we just need to be a little bit more humble. As a matter of fact, it's not just a possibility anymore, but a likely option. Those who claim to be cool by not believing in a mastermind designer try to cover up an obvious reality; deep inside they believe in Him because they know He's smarter than them, and they don't like that. The other reason for rejecting the idea of God is that they see injustice in the world, but rather than taking the responsibility for it, they blame it all on God. As a result of this frustration, they conclude there is no creator. Holding to this lame conclusion, they begin to feel pity for millions of so-called pathetic God-believing people around the world, and they try to awaken them by proving to them that they just believe in an illusion, or a delusion, called God!

My encounter with those two weird people made me think twice about what I had asked God the night after the party, but honestly, I thought, *What else could they or their God give me that I had not tried before? Seriously?!*

As Dave Gahan from Depeche Mode sings in "Enjoy the Silence," "All I ever wanted, all I ever needed, is here in my arms." All I wanted and needed was right there in my pocket; they were the only things motivating me to live another day—a little piece of opium, a bag of weed, and as much as alcohol I could ever want. If you had asked me, "But why live that kind of life?" I would have said it was because, as Metallica says, "Nothing else matters!" At the same time, there was another driving force working in me, and it was, as Bono says, "With or without you, I can't live," or "But I still haven't found what I'm looking for!" So I needed to keep looking; it wasn't an option for me, but was a code installed within me!

You may say, "There are other things in life worth living for," but that was not a reality for me. I had spent almost fifteen years trying everything you might (and might not) imagine in an effort to satisfy my soul and find a purpose for my life, but nothing had worked at all. I even tried to spend lots of time (as much as I could) with girls but that hadn't filled the vacuum either!

I began to think, *Maybe I'm gay! But if I am, why aren't I interested in men? Why do I still enjoy being with the opposite sex so much? So I am not gay.* The truth was, I was very attracted to Japanese girls even though I thought they were void of identity! All their knowledge about life was what the media and Hollywood told them to believe. It was very difficult to find a Japanese girl who was not possessed by American culture. At that time, I believed they were dolls living in a glass globe. I wasn't completely right about this, and later I met many Japanese girls who changed my idea about "dolls in a glass globe." However, few of them became and remained my best friends, even up until today.

For a while, I tried to stay cool and not check the address Fernando had given me, but that only lasted for two weeks. Another Sunday morning came, and I decided to go to Harajuku area, like I did every other Sunday while I lived in Tokyo. It was fun, interesting, and musical. In those days, every Sunday morning until evening, many amateur musicians and bands used to get together in Harajuku, closing the two ends of the boulevard and setting up their amps and musical instruments, which were brought there by trucks early in the morning. As far as I remember, they always started at 10 a.m. and played until sunset. Those Sundays were my best days in Tokyo, walking among hundreds of bands with different styles, including punk, rock, metal, pop, electronic, disco, and even classical. Every 50 feet, another band would take the stage with their own fans surrounding them. Many famous singers and bands got started with ten to fifteen fans in Harajuku, and they became so successful that later on they appeared on billboards and sold millions. If you were a musician, that was the best place to show off your talent. I had already made friends with some of them. They liked me, and sometimes they asked me to pick a guitar and play along with them even though I was terrible at the guitar. That made me popular among their fans, who were mostly girls. I didn't know how to play melodies, but could play along with some chords. The bands I used to play or hang out with mostly played songs from Scorpions, Dire Straits, Depeche Mode, The Cure, Eric Clapton, and the Beatles. It was fun, especially if I was drunk and high.

But that Sunday was different. Around 2 in the afternoon, during my tour in search of new talents in Harajuku Boulevard, I saw a simple group of girls and boys, mostly Caucasian, accompanied by two to three Japanese female backup vocalists and one good guitarist. They were playing a very beautiful song. It was so different, but so simple, that it drew my attention from a far. They wore blue jeans and white t-shirts. They were singing a heart-squeezing song to God, not to people or to the world, but a love song to God. That was one of the most unusual things I'd ever heard in my life. They didn't have much equipment, like the other bands did, but the sound was so captivating that, as soon as they started to play, people circled around them.

To my surprise, Cheryl was among them, singing with three other Japanese girls! And Fernando was playing an unbelievable melody on a guitar. Immediately behind them was a huge wooden cross with colorful writing on every side—phrases like "JC died for Rock & Rollers"; "Jesus Rocks"; "God loves Punks and Junkies"; and other sayings that put my heartbeat over one hundred. I was nailed to the floor right there in front of the band.

Many others gathered. Some tourists shouted out, "JC's number one" or "Jesus Rocks." I was drinking beer and smoking a cigarette. I wanted to applaud, but because of the beer and the cigarette in my hands, I just shouted and whistled, especially when I saw Cheryl and Fernando in the band. They both turned around to see who was whistling, and when they saw me, they waved at me and then looked at each other, nodded with a smile and a wink like there was something secret between them concerning me—something that they had talked about and had now come true!

I waited there for about half hour until they finished their little concert. It was very hard for me to be pleased by a song. To me, a song should have at least three elements to be considered a good song—original melody, meaningful lyrics, and a non-ordinary, out-of-the-box arrangement. For some people, a song is accompanied by memories—memories of the first time they listened to it, who they were with when they listened to it, and so on. But for me, music has always been a means of communicating a message or idea. The idea could be written in a memory of something or someone, but it is the way a musician communicates that memory or incident with others that gives life to a song and keeps the memory alive and ongoing.

What Cheryl, Fernando, and their friends played was a simple song. The words were even simpler. It was not a complicated chain of chords, just three or four. But there was something so powerful, so unusual, so touching, and so simple about it that I didn't want it to end. My future experience with that special kind of music later convinced me that these guys (who supposedly had changed the original song, *Our God Is An Awesome God* into something totally new) were probably part of the first generation of the creators of a revival in Christian music that took place almost a decade later and was picked up and followed by bands like Hillsong United, Gateway Worship, and (even later) Jesus Culture. This musical phenomenon took the world by surprise in the mid-1990s. However, I personally still prefer bands that communicate their personal experiences through a bright and hopeful approach to life, like Switchfoot, for example.

After Cheryl, Fernando, and their friends put aside their instruments, people began to shake hands with them and complement their music. Cheryl, however, cleared a path toward me and, with such a beautiful, life-giving smile, hugged and squeezed me hard. It was one of the warmest hugs someone had ever given me. We said hi, and she took me over to Fernando and then introduced me to the other band members. Fernando was awesome on guitar. I told him what I thought, and he thanked me with a humble smile and went on packing his guitar. Cheryl asked me to join them for a late lunch before the service started at 4 p.m.

I asked, "What service?"

She said, "You'll see if you'd like to come!"

I said, "Sure, why not?"

So we all went for my favorite food—sushi. I ordered some sake too. None of them drank with me except Fernando. He was cool.

After we finished eating, they took me to what they called The Harvest. It was just a big, simple room with chairs, a stage set up for music, and the capacity to hold about 200 people. I said to myself, "Wow, another good time with music! These guys are great." There were coffee and snacks on a table, and people from every ethnic group were standing around the table talking and laughing. What a place? I felt at home. It was a church.

To the Western mind, the rest of what happened is clear and predictable. For me, on the other hand, it was very strange and weird that they were singing to God. Some were even dancing in the front, and the rest lifted up their hands, waving to an imaginary presence. Some were jumping, while a few were crying quietly with joy. I couldn't help watching them. Everything seemed odd, but I had a good feeling.

After the music part was over, a huge Samoan guy (who was also leading the band) asked if anyone was there for the first time. I waved shyly. People began to clap for me! Those who were around me welcomed me by shaking hands with me; some even left their seats to hug me! I wasn't comfortable with that, but secretly enjoyed it. After that, the big guy introduced someone else, who was called by the title pastor—Pastor Kim, a Korean priest. I didn't know why they called him a pastor, but I thought he must be a very important fellow. Everybody began to clap and whistle for him! After he came up on the stage, he welcomed everyone again, and especially me. I thought, *Come on guys; it's embarrassing. If one more time anybody welcomes me, I will punch them,* even though deep in my heart I was so excited and happy.

Then Pastor Kim started his speech. He asked a question that blew my mind—a simple question, a question that was about the journey of life, a million dollar question! He asked, "How can we make sure we will enter the realm of eternal life after we close our eyes here in this mortal world?"

You can imagine how shocking this topic was to me. Many thoughts began to invade my mind at the moment. It couldn't be an accident that he had prepared a message about one of the most important questions I ever had. He could have picked any other topic to speak about. *Why that one?! Why that day?! Why?* But I told myself, *Instead of asking all these questions right now, you better listen carefully to what the man has to say. Whatever it is, you are here now, and he's going to tell you how you can make sure of entering the next life, so shut up and listen!*

Then he asked everybody to open up the Good Book to the place where Jesus was talking to a spiritually educated old man about how to enter the kingdom of God. He read the passage. For the next thirty minutes, something beyond explanation happened to me—something so simple, so powerful, so captivating, and so fascinating that it made me stay with that group of people for the next four months. All I heard that day was, "To enter Heaven, you need to be born again, not through books and philosophies of this world, but only through the Spirit of God." I found out that, only the things that are the same quality as God's can coexist with Him in His presence! No matter who I was or what I had accomplished, nothing could stand His consuming glory except what is made of His own Spirit.

The pastor said, "God is spirit, and only spirit-born beings can enter His realm and remain there!" It was a very interesting argument. I needed to know more about it.

I made up my mind to attend their gatherings twice a week; they called them "fellowship." After the second week, I noticed that two meetings were not enough to satisfy my thirsty soul, so I made it five visits a week. I stopped going out for drinks with my boss. I still liked drinking very much, but only at home after I was back from those fellowships. They were more like parties, only with coffee and live music. They began to call me the Wiseman, because of my subtle questions. I liked it. Among us, there were people from the U.S, Canada, the UK, Africa, New Zealand, Australia, India, Korea, China, and Japan. The church was supervised by Pastor Kim, who was from Korea. I was the only Iranian there. The church was called "Shibuya Harvest"—a base for young missionaries from YWAM (Youth With A Mission).

Every three months, a group of young missionaries was sent to Tokyo, as well as to some other cities in Japan, from the YWAM base in Honolulu, Hawaii. They slept in a trailer at night and evangelized in the streets during the day through mini concerts, dramas, and personal talks with young Japanese people. They called it witnessing! What they used to do was so similar to what I had done all my life, but they were very passionate and motivated, always joyful, and unbelievably friendly and kind.

For me, Jesus wasn't still who they claimed him to be, the incarnation of God Himself, savior of the world, Lord, and so on. For me, He was a man of love and wisdom. I had always believed that religion was not for the wise, and I considered myself a wise man. I had walked down the path of religion before, and it had taken me nowhere, nowhere at all. I thought religion was for the weak.

I liked all of the young missionaries, but there was something about Cheryl that I had never sensed or seen in anyone else before. She had some qualities that I, to be honest, envied. Even Fernando was different. I could have imagined myself talking to these two for hours without ridiculing them in my heart. Perhaps that sounds mean, but the reality is that too much philosophy had darkened my mind and heart and had given me a biting sarcasm that was closer to sickness than humor!

Frankly, there was something about Cheryl, Fernando, and the other kids that made me look down on myself. It was a good motivation though. What they had was something I knew I wasn't able to compete with. But I still found myself wondering, *What is it? Is it the fact that they talk about a God who unconditionally loves human beings? It can't be.* I had had conversations with many people during my pathetic life who had talked about a loving and merciful God, all of which ended in my glorious victory of opinion over their beliefs. *Why can't I challenge these people's simple belief in God?* I asked myself. It wasn't that I couldn't; I could, with my own standards, but I didn't feel good and victorious anymore, even when I was winning an argument. *Why, why, why?*

To be honest, there were things I was brainwashed with about Jesus while growing up in Iran, even though I wasn't a practicing Muslim. They were preached everywhere—in elementary schools, in classes at junior and senior high school, in Ramadan (the month of fasting), on TV, and in grandma and grandpa's stories of Muhammad, Ali, Hassan, and Hussein—even before the Islamic Revolution. After the Islamic Revolution took place, we heard thousands of other weird stories about the early leaders of Islam, which were all nothing but man-made stories to rule over the uneducated people in the name of God, just like what happened through some opportunistic Christians in the Dark Ages of Europe.

Today, after almost thirty-three years, nobody in Iran believes in those rubbish stories anymore. Today the most common form of religion that people follow in Iran is the religion of "good people go to Heaven," which is very much like what the New Age philosophy teaches. Another popular form of religion is something close to Sufism. It is called Darvishgari. In this belief system, there is a sense of spiritualism combined with a confessed love for an unseen God without the need to observe or practice the rituals and demands of any form of law. Younger generation believes in New Age Philosophy, but many Iranians still believe in the latter because deep in their hearts they don't want to be counted as Muslims, but at the same time, they also don't want to miss the chance to enter paradise, so they pretend to be Muslims, but modern ones! This combination of beliefs, during the decades, has turned into the most popular New Age mindset for Iranians all around the world. They believe in everything! From Abraham to Moses, from Plato to Emanuel Kant, from Jesus to Muhammad, and from Deepak Chopra to Paulo Coelho, they believe in it all. They believe in picking a moral flower from every garden of religion and philosophy in the whole world and combining it with the idea of good works, kindness in words, and the spice of democracy and human rights for all. It is essentially like what most other people in this world believe, regardless of being called a Muslim, Hindu, Buddhist, Zoroastrian, Christian, Jew, or even an Atheist. We all need to be respected and accepted! It has nothing to do with God or a so-called creator; it's all about us. After all, I am the one who make my destiny, right?

This "I" is still in progress, is still learning and experiencing new things. So, next year, I may not be who I am now because I'll learn new things. Beliefs can be changed, but the truth never changes. We are all in search of something that we sense is missing. Some of us are willing to pay any price to know the truth, and some of us just want to be around and have fun. But we will all come to a place at the end of this journey that could define our whole existence—the moment of death! Death defines who we have been in the process of life. All we do to achieve things in our lives is because we know we will die someday. And because of our uncertainty about the existence of a rewarding world after death, we try to cling to something that makes us feel secure, while we don't attach ourselves to any religion, considering ourselves to be "good." That was exactly what I felt. I didn't see the need to attach myself to a religion because I considered myself a good person, even though I did many bad things. And here is the problem with people who think like I used to think: We compare ourselves to individuals like Nero or Hitler, and we persuade ourselves that we are much better individuals than they were. This idea makes us feel good about our lifestyles and gives us a false sense of security. As a result, we begin to think that, even if there is a God, he would definitely notice that we are good people (according to our own standards) and would definitely let us into his Heaven. If this is not the case, then he is not just and doesn't even deserve our respect. Right?

But these missionaries were different, or at least, they looked different. They weren't pretending to be good people; they humbly claimed to be bad, but saved by God's loving grace. I personally witnessed them bringing old and stinky homeless beggars to the church, giving them baths, cutting their long, claw-like nails, giving them food and warm clothes, and taking care of them for several days so that they could have another chance at life. For this very reason, I made my mind to give it a try—not just to associate with them (which was very helpful in keeping me from the crazy habit of drinking every night and waking up at the door of my apartment the next morning), but to experience and see for myself how Jesus could possibly be able to turn those people into completely new individuals.

I personally didn't (and still don't) care much about the amount of good works people do. Everybody can do pretentious good works. Some believe they do them out of a pure heart as a virtue. I'm not sure about that. For me, being a better person was not that important or a big deal, but discovering the ultimate truth of life was what mattered to me.

When I got to know some of the church people, I found out that they all used to be bad people, very bad people. Some of them used to be drug dealers like I was. Some were convicts, others robbers, and some prostitutes. *How can it be possible?* I wondered. *It's not that these kinds of changes never occur in life. They do. But how can a man who lived two thousand years ago turn such bad people into loving and caring individuals today?* This change was so radical that they had left everything they had in the world by selling their possessions and spending their money to travel around the world and bring this news to others who had not yet heard it. I could imagine bad people doing good things, to some degree, in order to pay for the bad things they'd done, like a prisoner who tries to behave so that he can minimize his sentence. But becoming a totally good individual by no personal effort, regardless of education, IQ, age, social position, or spiritual awareness, didn't make sense to me.

They claimed they became good, not by their own will, but by Jesus giving them His Spirit! In fact, they told me that Jesus was alive and that He was living through them. I thought, *This stuff can only exist in words and can only be found in myths, bedtime stories, and ancient tales, but it can't be true for a twentieth century human being. There's supposed to be a practical way to reach that level of awareness, and that requires discipline, meditation, and access to some secret knowledge. It's another version of injustice if everyone can have access to it! What about all the challenges I went through, even the hundreds of hours of meditation, difficult practices of ancient sorcery techniques, and connections with other beings from other worlds?*

It was very difficult for me to see the whole creation, the problem of evil, the suffering and injustice, metaphysics, and everything else in the universe through the glasses of the Christian God. Either I was so preoccupied with my own mindset that I wasn't mentally able to accept a corporate way of salvation based on God's love, or they were all as childish as bedtime stories. I thought the first option was closer to the truth, but I didn't want to just give up on who I was. Otherwise, I would have gone through hell for nothing, which meant all my experiences and pains were as worthless as garbage.

So in order to get a firsthand knowledge about this new idea and to sound more professional in my conversations with these young missionaries (I still had my deceitful pride), I decided to read the Bible very carefully, and it became my major priority over the next couple months! In fact, the day before Cheryl flew back to the U.S., she gave me her own marked Bible. It was a tough day for me. I had gotten used to seeing her every day, and I took it for granted. In fact, the whole team was leaving. They were from different countries, but before they went to their homes, they had to first go back to the YWAM base in Hawaii. After giving a report on how they had witnessed to the Japanese, they would fly back to their own countries. Cheryl and I did not exchange any contact info. No email was used in those days, so the only option was telephone numbers, and I preferred not to ask for hers because, as I mentioned before, she was engaged. We just hugged and said goodbye. But before she left, she prayed a beautiful prayer over me, a prayer to her heavenly father, asking him to manifest his glory to me. She left a couple days before the others did. When they were all gone, for about a month there wasn't any other group designated for Tokyo. My time at church was shifted to home, reading the Bible Cheryl had gifted me. Meanwhile, my boss was angry with me because I wasn't rushing to the bars with him anymore.

I began with Genesis and went straight to the Book of Malachi in a month. As I had guessed, it was all like a bedtime story for kids. There was nothing much different in it from the Quran's stories, except the supernatural interventions of God. It contained almost the same stories that Muslims retell, with a little twist (of course, the twist came from Islam's side since Bible was written centuries before Islam showed up). At the time, I didn't care about the fact that all of those books could have been altered for the benefit of their believers or their leaders. For me, the important thing was to find a clue—a clue that could lead me to the ultimate truth I was looking for.

A couple of things interested me. In the Bible, God appeared to a few people during a specific time period—to Adam and Eve in the Garden of Eden, to Abraham, Isaac, Jacob, Moses, and some other leaders of Israel in different forms (in the form of an angel, for example), and to others who became prophets—all within the circle of the nation of Israel, with only one or two exceptions. I thought, *God taking human form to speak to people? How come?* My second challenge was His appearance. *How did He look like? Why did He come and show Himself to certain individuals who were not very much different or better than others?*

Another problem I had with Bible was the fact that God chose Isaac over Ishmael with no reason, promising Abraham to bless all nations through Isaac and not Ishmael! I didn't like His favoritism; it sounded like injustice to me. The same happened in the story of Jacob and his brother Esau.

And finally, the most challenging topic for me, as someone who had grown up in Iran, was the problem of the nation of Israel as a chosen people of God to carry out His name to the whole world! Why Israel? Were they better than other nations living on the earth? In Iran, we were taught that Israel began to occupy the Palestinian land after World War II. Many believed that. Many wondered, *Why would Israel do such a horrible thing?*

For some reason, from the time of Shah, even when I was a child, whenever I heard about Israel, something in me began to move. I had an unexplainable good feeling about them, and I didn't know why! Later, when I studied more and more on Bible topics, I understood many more realities. In fact, I found out that the land had already belonged to Israel thousands of years before. It was given to them as a gift by God (and if God is God, He always has a reason for anything He does, even if we are not able to understand why). And I also discovered that they used to be one of the greatest kingdoms of the past, especially during the reigns of David, Solomon, and a few other kings, even centuries before the Persian Empire was established by Cyrus the Great. The same Cyrus whose birth was predicted about 600 years before Christ (Isaiah 44:28-45:1); our own Cyrus who was mentioned in Bible by the Prophets as Messiah, The same Cyrus who freed the Israelites from the tyranny of the Babylonian Empire, the same Cyrus who blessed Israelites with gold and silver and helped them return to Jerusalem to rebuild their city and the house of God, the same Cyrus who kindly asked all Persians (Iranians) to freely and generously give towards this project and they all gave joyfully (The book of Ezra chapter one), for they also were familiar with and proud of noble Jewish men and women like Daniel who at the time of Cyrus (and Darius) was like Prime Minister to the king (Daniel 6 and 9:1), or Esther who later on became the Queen of Persia, and many other noble Jewish individuals who even decided to choose Persia as their second homeland, even until today. I'm not making up these stories. You can check them out in Bible.

After WWII, the Israelis tried to buy their old land back. The Palestinians seemed to be happy to sell their lands at a good price, but apparently later on they regretted it and wanted to take back what they had already sold for a price. This doesn't mean I believe Israelis are the most innocent nation in the world; no one and no nation is innocent in this world. Only a fool thinks he is innocent. The Israelites, as we see in the Bible, haven't been very faithful to their God, either. But that's the most distinguished virtue of God that I like; when He chooses you for His purposes, you are entitled to be called "chosen," and from that moment on, if you also choose Him, He will do anything to protect you, to bless you, and to make things work for your good so that you reach your highest potential, as He has destined for you. This revelation was awesome to me!

Predestination was another big question for me, even when I had no idea about the God of Israel. I used to think about this topic a lot. What if everything was destined to be the way it was? What if all we went through was mandatory and there was no other option? What if whatever we do we are supposed to do, and we have no control over our decisions? I thought, *Isn't this against the doctrine of the free will in all of the stories about God?* I had to figure this out.

After going through the Old Testament, I began to read the Gospels. It was around that time when the new team arrived from Hawaii—another young and passionate team of evangelists. The first day I met them was really interesting. Almost all the church members knew me by then, even though I had not yet embraced the Christian faith. But they were so kind to me, even the pastor. He had already let me attend the classes that were specifically for Christians. He told me once, "Bijan, your knowledge of the Bible has amazed me! I have never heard someone reading and studying the whole Bible in so much detail in less than two months! I just want you to know that I've been praying for you."

I didn't know why the concept of prayer was so important among Christians. In every so-called religion, you can see this act of praying, but as far as I had learned, this term had another meaning among the Christians. For example, in Buddhism and Hinduism, prayer means meditation, clearing your mind from the secular and mortal and finally detaching your awareness (spiritually) from self through mantras, becoming one with the universe. Or in Zoroastrian religion, prayer is a book that you just recite from. These prayers are dedicated to a god called Ahura Mazda and his angels, the creator of the universe and all that is good. They also equally believe in the existence of Ahriman, the evil one that created all evil in the universe.

In Zoroastrian religion, the idea of God does not have a very theological base and is not characterized as God in other Abramaic religions because Ahura Mazda only reveals himself through other angelic figures, so prayer as a means of communication with God loses its validity. The most obvious reason some Iranians like to relate themselves to this religion is because of the famous (New-Age-like) saying contributed to Zoroaster, "Good Thoughts, Good Words, Good Deeds." Even in Islam, most of the prayers are from books of Hadith and narrations of the lives of their spiritual/political leaders, or simply just reciting some verses from Quran. But the term is usually used as a reference to Namaz (Salat/Salah), an obligatory and prescribed practice that is repeated five times a day; it is addressed to Allah, but because of its soulless repetition, it loses its main purpose. Anything mandatory in a spiritual path will turn into a soulless practice, even if it began with a genuine purpose.

In my opinion, none of these prayers were more than some mantras or, at their best, some good thoughts toward a higher force that humans hold as a god, thoughts in which there is no power, no originality, and no active relationship between the object of prayer and the subject. They were just words that were commonly focused on praising a god or on maintaining a person's well being rather than on a relationship with our creator or a request for him to intervene in the lives of people or in the history of humankind in general.

By contrast, prayer had a much deeper value for these young missionaries. They truly, like kids, believed they could change the course of history through prayer. The funniest thing about them was that they even thought they could change God's decisions! *Silly kids!* I thought, *They didn't know that, if God would change His decisions, it actually and logically meant He was wrong about something and now, through the prayers of people, He was suddenly enlightened and aware of His mistake.* Any other explanation, in my opinion, was an effort to degrade God to a human level, thus taking away His divine absolute wisdom and power from Him. That was my understanding of God in those days.

When the new team arrived, I tried to get close to them and see if I could find someone like Cheryl or Fernando. I began to introduce myself to them, and to my surprise, they all responded with almost the same sentences like, "Oh, so you are Bijan, the Bijan?" or "We heard a lot about you" or "Oh yeah, the last team told us all about you!" But the weirdest sentence I heard was when they told me, "We've been praying and fasting for you even before we flew to Japan!" I couldn't believe my ears! *Why would they pray and fast for me when they don't even know me?*

I wanted to get closer to a particular guy named Steve because he was an awesome guitar player, even though he was only seventeen years old. I asked him if he knew Cheryl. He said he had heard of her, but never saw her, and he added, "Many YWAMers in Hawaii know you, man! You're famous!"

I was flattered.

Within the next month, Steve and Bonnie (who was also seventeen) became my best friends. Bonnie was a very sweet and funny girl. She always made everyone laugh. She was cute and very friendly. She used to make swords out of balloons and invite me to fight like the knights of old. I still have pictures of her with those sword-like balloons. Steve was tall and blond, with long hair. Japanese members of our church used to call him "Jesus"—as though Jesus was blond! Most Japanese thought Jesus was kind of American; I never figured out why. As I mentioned, Steve was also a professional guitar player. Years later, he sent me an instrumental piece on a cassette. He called it "Desert of Arabia." It was a masterpiece, like one of those Steve Vai's works.

Once the new group arrived, I began asking them the same tough questions I used to ask the other team. Yet no one (not even the pastor) was able to answer them. Finally I began to think about the possibility of taking my question to the source—the God of Christians. It seemed like a ridiculous thought. But if He was the writer and director of this huge play, who else could answer my questions, and who else could tell me who I was and what I was created for?

So as weird as it felt to me, I began to pray to Him.

Close Encounter of the Third Kind

As FAR AS I REMEMBERED, the only times I had talked to God were the times when I was so close to getting rid of myself, and I was filled with anger, frustration, disappointment, and hatred toward Him. I don't remember, at any other time, making an attempt to talk to Him. I guess that's the case with most of us. It seems useless and meaningless to try to speak with God when everything is alright—when we're in good health, have a good job, and have a full bank account. I usually heard people praying to God (in terms of talking to Him, not saying mantras or written prayers) only when something was wrong!

Isn't something wrong in the world already? So why not pray all the time? I didn't because, frankly, it seemed ridiculous! *Why would I even bother to speak to God when everything is alright? Doesn't He have more important things to care for? If He is God the Creator of the universe, He should be very busy, right? Why would He listen to me?* I used to reason, *Why would I bother myself and try to listen to an ant somewhere in a crowded city of Tokyo? Who cares for an ant? I don't. Neither would God.*

On the other hand, I also reasoned, *But if He had created me* (and if a creator creates something, He has a purpose for His creation), *then He must care for me; otherwise He is not God—a god maybe, but not God the Creator.* Therefore, I thought I must have value in His eyes and be worthy of attention, even if I was an ant. I realized that I didn't care about ants, whether in Tokyo or in the deserts of Egypt, because I hadn't brought them into the circle of life. I hadn't created them. If I had, I would care.

One day at church, I heard someone say something about Jacob wrestling with God. I thought, *Maybe I needed to wrestle with Him instead of complaining to Him.*

The fact that these people were secretly praying and fasting for me provoked me to think more seriously about prayer. I went deeper and deeper into Bible—early in the morning, before leaving for work, during my two fifteen-minutes breaks at work, during lunch time, and as soon as I got home! I couldn't help it. The excitement of reading the Bible in those days was like the excitement of watching the famous ABC TV series, *Lost*. I couldn't wait until the next episode, so I would watch the latest episodes over and over again to find a new clue, the hidden messages, and to read the symbols. The Bible was like the island to me, with lots of strange things in it. I knew there was something extraordinary about it, like a hidden treasure, and I knew I had been brought to Japan to be on this adventure. I had to discover this treasure.

Every night before I went to bed, I began to talk to God, asking Him questions about the injustice in the world, about poverty, about all the wars and famines, about sickness and disease, and about life. But my most important questions were: "Why did You decide to create the universe?" and "What am I supposed to do on earth?" However, He still seemed to be too busy to answer my questions.

I also told Him, "If Jesus is truly who He claimed to be, He must prove it to me!" Otherwise, how in the world could I know who was right or which philosophy or religion was telling the truth? Some people would say, "The truth is: Be good to all people (as if they always are), speak the truth (as if they've never ever told a lie), defend the weak (as if they've never passed by a wounded person in the streets), make your own belief system and live by it (which in fact means 'let me have my own belief system'), respect others (which means 'respect me'), respect people's beliefs (which means 'respect my beliefs'), stick to the law (as if they've never broken one), don't cheat (as if they've never cheated anyone), don't steal, don't kill, and defend human rights (for it is humane). If you do all these, then you will be a good person, and because you are a good person, God will definitely allow you to enter his Heaven. And this is your destiny, to be a good person, a good citizen of the world!"

To that I say, "OK, I got it. If I can do all these things that no one has ever been able to fully accomplish, then I'm a good guy!" We must ask ourselves, "Is that all? Is this the purpose of our existence? Is that why the whole creation came into existence? Is it just so that we can call ourselves good people? All of the science, astrology, physics, DNA structure, and other realities of the world exist just to tell us to be good people? Certainly there should be more to life than to be just a good person.

If we talk about a creator who had a purpose in creating all things, things that are unbelievably connected to each other, then the value of a conscious being should be much higher than just "being nice" to the people, animals, and plants around us, and it should have an effect, on a cosmic level, on a solar system that is 10 million light years away from us. I think we are worth more than that!

And I had this challenge with whoever this God was. My problem was that, if I accepted that there was a creator for the whole universe and whatever was beyond this universe, then in no way would I be able to believe in just "being good." The idea of being good, for me, was the most childish answer to the dilemma of the universe and God; it couldn't satisfy my soul or quench the thirst in me to know the truth. In that case, I would have to ignore and put aside the idea of the creator from any equation regarding life. I couldn't convince myself to accept the idea. If the whole world was connected through atoms and molecules, then the same law had to apply to the destiny of humankind in regard to the whole universe. By saying this, I don't mean that if a fly is eaten by a frog, it will have an effect on the destiny of humans; what I mean is that whatever we do and say and, most importantly, whatever we believe with all our beings can have an effect on the whole universe. I wanted to find my place in this puzzle and be part of that exciting discovery. I began to understand that I was much more important in this equation than I could have even imagined. And I believed that this would absolutely apply to everyone.

A friend of mine, a Canadian Y.W.A.Mer had introduced me to a Christian rock band called Petra. So I began to listen to Petra. It was interesting to hear a rock band singing songs about God, His forgiveness, His love, and the challenges of humankind in relation to the concept of God. They were forerunners in a new era in Christian messageful, non-worship music, which is still not accepted among a number of denominations, especially traditional streams of churches in the Middle East. Some of Petra's songs changed my perspective on the world and the person of Christ. I started having some feelings for Jesus! But I still needed more facts to completely surrender myself to Him; I needed a godly intervention.

Sometimes receiving an answer to just one of many questions can be enough to open up new horizons to understanding all of the other answers you're looking for. So I decided to focus on one question. If God was able to prove to me that Jesus was God Himself and who He claimed to be in the Bible, I would be able to accept all of the other childish stories of the

Bible as facts—if only Jesus was God! I had determined to pay any price if I only knew the response to that one question. I didn't know how it was possible for God to show me the truth, but if he was God, I knew He would find a way to communicate that truth to me.

So for the next few weeks, I kept reading my Bible and asking the same question over and over again before going to bed. But nothing happened. I saw no sign, and I was very good at seeing them and interpreting them. A couple of times I asked myself, *Is your heart really genuine in asking for such a huge revelation? Have you checked your intentions and motives? Do you really want to know the answer, or do you just want to add data to your knowledge so you can show off in debates?* But I already knew the answer to all these questions; I was willing and ready to die in exchange for the truth.

It was the beginning of December, 1990, when what I was waiting for finally happened—something absolutely mind-blowing.

I was at one of our Friday night meetings, and during the worship time, the big Samoan guy who was in charge of music asked everyone to pray out loud and say at least one thing they deeply wanted God to intervene in and fix. Several people prayed. Some people prayed for a sick friend or relative while others prayed for the salvation of their nations. A few of the Japanese prayed for Japan. Those who prayed stood up one by one and told God what they wanted. I was sitting on my seat, leaning my head over the chair in front of me. I had nothing to ask except the same question. So I asked Him in my heart, "God, You know how important it is for me to know the truth. You know what kind of life I'm living, and You know how I hate myself. If Jesus is who He claims to be, then I ask You in His name to show me a sign. Even if You don't care for me that much, at least answer me for Jesus' sake, for there is no strength left in me to continue this life. Please show me the truth!" I was saying this prayer in my heart, not even whispering.

The moment I finished my prayer, all of a sudden came the scary sign; the person who was sitting a few seats away from me stood up and opened his mouth, almost weeping and begging with tears: "Father, don't you hear him? Can't You see how desperate he is? Why don't You show Yourself to him? Why don't You tell him how You love him? Can't You hear how he hates himself? He's asking You for the sake of Your son, Jesus? Jesus, You say in Your word, 'You have not asked anything in My name yet; ask and you will receive, so that your joy may be complete,' and here he is asking in Your name! Father, show Your glory, in Jesus name!"

My body began to shake. No words could express my emotions at that moment. I was frightened to death. My heart was pounding so fast that I felt it was coming out of my chest; if not, it would explode. The guy who prayed that prayer was standing about ten feet away from me. He prayed as if he was begging for his own soul. I didn't dare to turn my head and look at him, for I was afraid I might see God Himself! I couldn't sit there anymore. There was a thick and heavy presence in the room, especially upon me. Everybody was quiet; there was no sound at all. I guess each and everyone had felt that heavy and holy presence. I had never felt such a persuading presence before in my life, even when that Darth Vader thing used to come and cripple me. This time it was different. I was experiencing the most incredible sense of belonging—a love that my being had never felt before. It was a combination of love, respect, awe, fear, joy, and excitement altogether. But at the same time, that presence was so pure, holy, and genuine that I couldn't bear it anymore.

I got up and ran out into the crowded streets in the Shibuya area. I just wanted to get lost in the sea of people. I wanted to get lost again. In fact, I was running away from that presence. All of the horrible things I had done up to that moment marched before my eyes. I kept telling myself, "I'm fine. I'm alright." But I wasn't. My body was still shaking. Now I hated myself more than ever. There was nothing in this world that could force me to go back to that room again. Thousands of thoughts invaded my mind. I began to analyze all the possibilities that could make that scene happen. Perhaps the forces of creation were just having fun with me. But what had happened back there in the church wasn't like anything I had ever experienced before. There was something truly divine in there. The scary part was not when the guy began to say that prayer, but when that presence came upon me and the whole church!

I was looking at people in the street, thinking, *What are we really looking for? What's this hurry in life?* We all looked like zombies, trying to survive without a clue about why we were there! Suddenly the difference between that moment at church and the scene I was looking at hit me so strongly that I began to lose my balance and direction. I lost my sense of direction for about a minute. When I came to myself, I noticed that I was walking against the streams of people like I was driving on a one-way street. Tokyo is so crowded that almost all of the sidewalks are as big as the streets, two-way sidewalks, I should say. People had to open a way for me to pass. They probably gave me some fingers and said some bad words, since I was breaking their rules of walking in a straight line. Those who have been to Tokyo know what I'm talking about, especially on a Friday night. After I noticed that I was walking in the wrong direction, I corrected my course and gave myself to the right stream of people.

In that area, there were some fortunetellers sitting by the sidewalk telling people about their future in exchange for money. I knew they had no special powers; they were doing what I used to do many years ago back in Iran—using some short wooden sticks to tell people about their future. It is called *I Ching*, an ancient Chinese method that is based on a book with predefined conditions of the sticks when you throw them on the floor or on a table. You just needed to remember the definition of each mark, and you can tell people some stuff and charge them for it! Most of the fortune tellers were young or middle age ladies.

Among all those ladies, there was an old man in his mid-eighties who, most of the time, didn't have a customer. Perhaps he was charging people too much or maybe just because there was something scary about him. I had wanted to talk to him many times before; he was different. The corner of the street where he had chosen to set up his simple short table was half a mile away from the other fortunetellers. It was right by the door of our church. I had been walking in the opposite direction for a while, but then changed my route and walked toward the church because it was on my way back to the subway station. I wanted to go back home and drink until I passed out. I was in my own thoughts and still shocked from what just happened at the church when I heard someone say, "Anata!" which means "You!" in Japanese. I turned around and saw the same old man looking at me. I ignored him and kept walking. Again I heard him say, "You, traveler!" but this time in English! I turned back and saw him pointing at me, "You! Come here, I have something to tell you." I took a look around me to make sure he was talking to me and not to someone else; he was talking to me!

You may guess how surprised I was when he told me he had something to tell me. I had never seen him ask anyone to come over. Other fortunetellers had the annoying habit of continually inviting people to their tables, just like when you pass in front of shops in Japan and the sellers keep saying "Irasshaimase," which is an expression like "Welcome" in English. But this man was not usually like that.

He did not even have a luxurious table, but was sitting on the floor with a very short and small wooden table in front of him. There was a small plastic baby chair there for the customers. He asked me to sit beside him. I told him that I didn't have money to pay him. He said, "I'm not

144

charging you!" He seemed more excited than I was, and this scared me. He asked me to hold the sticks in my hand, concentrate, and then throw them on the table. I did. He stared at the position of the sticks for a long time. I knew exactly what he was doing. I was an expert in reading *I Ching*, but I always needed the text to interpret the solid lines and broken lines. There was something a little bit different in his method. I used to throw the sticks once and then, according to position of the sticks, put them in order from top to bottom, six of them. But he had given me seven sticks. After a minute or two, he changed the position of the seventh one and put it on the top. And a little while later, he took it out and began to read the signs. I guess the seventh one was very important. It could probably change the whole perspective. He looked surprised. Finally after two or three more minutes, he spoke.

"You are a warrior looking for answers." Then he continued, "You have two periods of each ten years ahead of you. That's how far I can see! Everything depends on a decision you make about the two paths offered to you. One you know; one you will know soon."

His English was pretty good. I was surprised. "How soon?" I asked.

"Very soon. Based on your decision, you will have two completely different destinies. One will lead you to peace and balance; the other will bring you tough challenges and hardships!"

"Which one does a wise man choose?" I asked.

"I saw you. I had seen you before in this street. I had to wait for the right time," he paused for few seconds and then said, "And now is the right time."

He seemed very serious. I asked, "What do you mean by seeing me?" That was the expression only mystic teachers like Don Juan and some old prophets in the Bible used to use it; even Jesus used it when talking to one of his disciples.

"You know it. You are special, gifted! You have capacity. You are chosen. That capacity, if filled with the proper material, can bring capabilities, abilities." He replied.

"Aren't you supposed to tell me about my future? Tell me about that, please." I didn't feel comfortable when he talked about me being special, so I tried to change the subject.

"I already told you all you need to know. Everything depends on the seventh stick. I can't tell you more."

"But you made me more confused. So far I thought I only have one choice, but now you tell me I have two! What's the other one? You said I would know it soon, but how soon?" I asked him anxiously.

"You have learned a lot from many masters. All the paths you took and all you experienced in the last ten years have been leading you to this moment. You should have known by now which choice I am referring to."

I didn't know what choice he was talking about. He scared me when he said that I had learned from many masters. "Is he the incarnation of Don Juan?" I thought. "Or maybe the spirits are talking through him." I was frightened of the thought. For some reason, I felt I was mad at him. He was part the cycle, the cycle that had brought me to that moment. I was mad at all the masters he referred to. What was happening was too much for my brain to handle. I guess he sensed my anger and confusion.

He took a paper and pencil. He wrote down something like an address, folded the paper, and gave it to me.

"What is this?" I asked.

"Your second choice," he said. He smiled. I had never seen him smile before. He was always in a trance state whenever I saw him on that street. His smile made me hesitant to take the paper from him for a second.

I opened it. I was right; it was an address. Somewhere in Yokohama Port, about a forty-five minute ride, south of Tokyo.

"This is the address to a secret society for the gifted," he said, "a school for people with capacity to learn the ways of universe. Go there and tell them I sent you. They'll tell you what to do. Leave the rest to us. That place is where you belong. That's why I picked you tonight, for it was the time. This is your second choice." Then he looked at somewhere behind me and said, "And there is your other option."

I turned around and looked in the direction he was staring at; I saw Bonnie leaning against the wall ten feet away from us. She was watching us with concern in her eyes. I was filled with joy when I saw her. I waved at her and asked her to join us. I wanted to tell her about this old guru and his secret school for the gifted. She said she was fine and that she would wait. Seeing her there gave me goose bumps. I thought, *What is she doing here? Isn't she supposed to be at church now?*

There were thousands of other thoughts flying through my head. This old mystic teacher, probably a Buddhist Master, had told me it was the time. *What did he mean by that? How did he know I had been learning from other Masters?* I was excited and confused at the same time. I'd been looking for a true spiritual guru or a mystic school my whole life, and if he was right about what he said, it could be my only chance to achieve my ultimate goal in understanding the creation, the universe, and my very own existence—and now it was right in the palm of my hand. I was not yet able to digest his offer. It seemed too good to be true. I thought about that horrifying but convincing presence back in the church. *What about what I had been praying for? Was this the answer to my prayer when I prayed to the God of Christianity? Why did he refer to Bonnie as my other choice?* I was baffled!

I couldn't believe I was right there in the centre of a cosmic activity. *So it was true after all. There was a God, a higher power, a force beyond our understanding who cared for me and watched over me every step of my life.* I began to realize that He had hidden Himself from me so that I would begin to look for Him. He had been always there, even in those suicide attempts back in Shiraz. He was there when I was called for interrogations. They could have killed me without a trace, and they did not have to give an account to anyone, but He had saved me. Perhaps it had even been Him who had helped me out of that endless pit the last time I saw that disgusting, ugly creature. *And now He is offering me to join Him,* I thought.

The old man was right; the time had come. I looked again at the paper in my hand, knowing what I had to do. The old man was in a trance, meditating. But I thanked him joyfully anyway and said goodbye to him. He opened his eyes and looked at me, nodded, and went back to his trance. I got up and walked toward Bonnie while I gently squeezed the piece of paper in my hand. I threw it away after I had walked a distance from the old man. I had made my decision.

Now I knew what I had needed all of my life; I needed my Creator. I did not need to know if I was going to have a peaceful life or even a challenging life. I did not need to know the deep secrets of life, the mysteries, and the magic behind all things. All I needed was to personally know my Creator, the only one who knew why I was created, why I was still alive, and what my destiny was. I didn't need a school of mysticism to teach me about the mysteries of life. Who was better than God Himself, the almighty creator and sustainer of life? He held the key to all of the mysteries of the universe. But at that moment, no mystery could be compared to the love of God himself. I was about to sail on the ship of adventures, excitements, challenges, wisdom, knowledge, and wrestling with the forces of life—but this time I knew I was not alone. He had finally showed me that He cared. That was the true peace.

Bonnie looked disturbed and worried. As I got closer to her, I put my arm around her shoulder and said, "I want to know Jesus better." She smiled. I could see the joy in her eyes. She asked what it was I had thrown away the moment before. I said, "My ticket to another rabbit hole, but it doesn't matter anymore."

I took her to a coffee shop. She asked me why I had left the church in such a hurry. I told her the story. She and the others did not know about the life I had lived up to that moment. They just saw my enthusiasm to learn and grow in the knowledge of God. On numbered occasions, I had told them some stories from my past, but nothing about drugs, spirits, or demons. It wasn't easy for me to tell everyone who I was. Friendship with these missionaries from every walk of life and background had gradually helped me to see the world from a different angle, but not fully until that very night.

I told her about my recent prayers and what had happened at church that evening. I told her about that convincing presence hovering over my head. I said, "I couldn't bear it for another second. I had to run out."

"And the enemy was waiting for you outside, right at the corner of the building by the church!" she said.

"I don't know about that," I said. "But when I saw you there, I knew you were representing God; it was like a choice between you and the old man! I'm glad I chose you!" We both laughed.

Then I asked her what she was doing there! She said, "I was praying for you when you left the room, and I suddenly heard God telling me to go after you. I ran out to talk to you, but I lost you in the crowd. So I just walked around in hopes of finding you. When I was on my way back to the church after about ten to fifteen minutes, I saw you sitting there at that corner talking to the old man. I'd never had a good feeling about him. I was always wondering why he is sitting there right by the church. So when I saw him talking to you and telling you things based on those sticks, I knew why God had sent me out after you. But when I wanted to intervene, God told me not to! He told me that it was your decision and that I should not intervene. But I kept praying for you all the time you were talking to the old guy."

As I was listening to Bonnie, I began to see the whole picture. There was another side to this coin, and I had just begun to understand what was going on. It was still hard for me to believe there was a supernatural battle going on in the air in hidden places just because of me. Of course, later on, when I went through the details of what happened that night, I found out that it wasn't all planned for me. The Samoan guy who had asked the folks at church to pray for their friends and relatives, the guy who got up and scared the death out of me with that prayer, the fortuneteller who was waiting for me outside and called to me from among the crowd, and finally what Bonnie told me—those things weren't just for me. All the elements of this magical story were woven together to once again prove to all of us that there was a battle going on in the universe and to prove to us that God cared and that He was there working in His creation for His eternal purposes. It was not just about me, it was rather about His absolute power and His own glory!

"What are you going to do now?" Bonnie asked.

"I need to go home and think about what just happened." I replied.

"Are you kidding? After all that happened? You're so stubborn!" she laughed.

I humbly said, "No, it's not just that. I need to talk to Him."

"OK, I see. Sure, why not? Go ahead. I'm sure He has things to share with you, too," she said.

"I'll walk you to the church; then I'll go home. Maybe the old man's still there waiting for you for revenge; you stole me from him!" This time I laughed.

"No way! Angels are all around me, no weapon shall prosper against me!" she said and showed me the long red balloon she always carried as a sword. We both laughed again. She was a joy!

On the way back to the church, there was no sign of the old man!

I got home around 8 p.m., heated up a cup of sake, sat down, opened the Bible Cheryl had given me, and began to read. There were many marked lines in her Bible, mostly about how God had protected His people in times of trouble and despair. There were also parts about how He stood aside and let them do what they thought was right for them after they had already rejected His counsel. It was around 11 p.m. that I noticed something; the old man had been right about the times. It was the time. I grabbed my Bible and ran out!

It was 11:45 when I got to the church. I knocked on the door and rang the bell impatiently. Steve opened the door. As soon as he opened the door, I told him, "I want to give my heart to Jesus, right now!"

"Wow, Congratulations! Come on in, man." he said with a big smile on his face.

He ran ahead of me to let others know about my decision. "Hey guys, Bijan's here with good news!" he shouted.

They were all in the trailer getting ready for sleep. As soon as they heard I was there, they all gathered in the main sanctuary. They began to jump around me and hug me. They also told me how badly they had been waiting for this moment to come. It was three weeks until Christmas and four weeks until the end of 1990. It was almost four months since I had first met Cheryl and Fernando. How I wished they were there.

They took me to the backyard and circled around me. Bonnie was speechless, she told me later. Steve asked me to let him pray over me.

"Sure, by all means, man!" I said.

And he began to pray over me by laying his hand on my shoulder. All of a sudden, I felt the same presence I had run away from earlier that evening. I didn't know what was happening. I was afraid again, but being with those lovely people took away the fear.

Steve was thanking God for me. I didn't understand why someone should thank God for a person like me! But in a strange twist, he started to ask Him for forgiveness on my behalf for the things I had done. In my amazement, he started to name the most terrible things I had done. I began to feel uncomfortable.

He continued, "Lord, please forgive him for all the people he has hurt by teaching them wrongly about You. Forgive him for the poison he put into lives of others. Forgive him for all the satanic rituals he performed to gain power over people. And forgive him for disrespecting his parents by doing things he knew would hurt them. Father, forgive him for the souls he pulled away from You on his path. But You are a righteous God, a just God who gives a second chance to everyone who comes to You with an open heart and a humble spirit."

He continued the prayer and asked me repeat after him. As Steve led me in prayer, I accepted Christ into my life and asked Him to forgive me for all the wrongs I had done to people, to myself, and to Him. The moment I began to thank Him for His love and grace, I began to shake, weep, and cry out loud like a child. I lifted my eyes to the sky and yelled with all my strength, "Father, please forgive me!" And right in that moment, I actually saw something like a white laser coming out of the pitch dark sky right toward me. It hit me on the head and went out of my toes. It was so real and so unexpected that for a second I thought it was my death. I fell on the ground like a dead man.

I have no memories of what happened to me next except few blurry pictures. All I know is what the others told me later. They told me that they had never seen such a drastic conversion before. They were scared. They didn't know what to do. They said that I was on the floor moaning, weeping, yelling, rolling back and forth, shouting, and then laughing, jumping up and down, singing melodies in a very strange language, and again rolling on the floor repeating the same pattern. The cycle continued for almost three hours. All I remember from those three hours is the moment I came to myself and noticed I was covered in dust with a huge wet towel beside me. It was wet from my tears.

Steve and Bonnie were still standing by me, but the others were coming and going. Those who were yet up gave me hugs and welcomed me to the family. Steve told me, "Wow! It seems like God had a hard time cleaning you up, man!" Everybody laughed.

"How are you doing?" Bonnie asked me.

"I don't know! I still feel like I'm not here in this world, but I guess I'm going to be fine!" I replied. I could hardly speak.

They asked me to stay the night there, and I accepted. I asked them for a blanket. They gave me one, and I went to the sanctuary and lay down by the altar, right under the cross. I went to sleep like a little baby. I wasn't worry about anything anymore!

The Return

"It's a wonderful, wonderful life, no need to run and hide; it's a wonderful, wonderful life."

I'm sure some of you remember this beautiful song by Black. That's how I felt about life when I woke up the next day—it was a new day. It was Saturday, and I didn't need to go to work. After breakfast, we talked a little bit more about my experience the night before. Everybody believed they had never seen such a strong manifestation of God before at the moment of salvation. They admitted they had heard stories about people who were touched by God in the way I was, but never seen one like mine. I thanked them for all their prayers and fasts. I badly wanted Cheryl and Fernando to be there. I knew that the news would spread fast, and they would know about it soon, but I wanted them to be there.

As a beginning of a new era and as a gift, one of the girls I knew at church gave me a very thick and big silver ring with a golden cross carved on it. Her name was Kaoru. She was Japanese. For many years afterward, I wore that ring as a reminder of what had happened to me in Tokyo. The ring was one of a kind, and for many years it attracted people to me. It was a symbol of an era in my life. You will hear about it again in the last chapter of this book.

After breakfast, we sang some worship songs, and for the first time, I participated in singing the songs along with them. At 10 in the morning, I went to the backyard and grabbed the same 10-foot long wooden cross the teams were always carrying around, and I went out to Harajuku area, where thousands of Iranians used to get together to find jobs, trade currency, and even get drugs!

It was my first day of preaching Jesus, and I was almost killed by an angry Iranian Muslim when I began to claim Jesus as God. He attacked me with a knife, and other Iranians had to grab him and hold him so I could run away with my heavy cross. Not bad for the very first day!

I didn't know a thing about how to evangelize to Muslims. Imagine you are talking about Jesus in a free country and all of a sudden someone pulls a knife on you! So I decided to study the Bible more and get some advice from my Christian friends on how to share the Gospel with Muslims.

But before we go farther, I need to tell you a truth. Honesty is the glue that attaches a writer to his audience. This is a confession as well. As you will go on reading the rest of the story, you will notice that over two decades my understanding of God has been a process rather than a series of beliefs. Christianity as a religion has failed me many times, as you will read in further chapters. Christians have failed me, too. The concept of God has been changed in my understanding. And finally, I should add that I did not become who I am now in a single night, so I myself have failed me more than anything or anyone else! Although the principles I believed in have never changed (Biblical truths and the Apostles' Creed), it has seemed that the nature of the challenge has. Over time, God proved to me again and again that He is the only reliable source in the whole universe; I can trust in Him. Churches failed me, people failed me, believers failed me, and the ones I loved so dearly denied and rejected me as you will see, but He remained the same to me. Whether you believe in God or not, you always have the right to close this book at any point and never come back to it again. This book is not intended to advertise a religion over other religions. It's not even written to praise Christianity, for as you will read in the chapters that follow, I suffered a lot at the hands of my fellow Christians. My intention in writing this book is to present an account of a seeker of truth, an account based on facts of the life and common ground, regardless of where I was born and what culture I have lived in, so that I might encourage others like me who might be in the same situation, and to tell them that there is still hope for them because of a super-loving God who is worth all of their trust and who is willing to stand by them no matter what. What has happened to me might happen to any individual anywhere in this planet.

We all have a part in the search for the truth, and in this search, we become part of this truth. The important thing is not what we *expect* to find or become, but it is whether we *are found* in the truth. I even believe that the journey itself is not of first value. The most important element in life is how we influence each and every person we meet on our path by constantly encouraging them to keep searching for the ultimate truth and not just a truth. I believe that the truth is alive and desires to be unveiled by genuine seekers and warriors who are not just after fulfilling their own dreams, but long to be a part of the fulfillment of the dreams of others.

Revelation of the truth does not depend on your social status, your education, your wealth, or even where you were born or live; rather, it is based on a genuine heart desire to embrace the reality that "it's not about me; it's always about others." This revelation comes only to those who seek the truth. And despite what many activists claim these days, the amount of good works you do in your society and your conversations about human rights and democracy have nothing to do with your genuine search for the ultimate truth or your connection with the truth. It is the truth that defines and values all the good works you do in your society, and not vice versa. We all can talk. Words prove nothing. It's not about how many followers you have on twitter; it's about how many souls you touch and put back on the right track. The only thing that matters in the earthly realm is human souls! Satan is trying to destroy them; God is saving them. Some of us are just putting our own garbage in the spiritual containers of others. We have to be careful. Either we're helping the devil, or we are helping God. There is no gray area. So don't preach the truth if you don't have it. I was selling what I didn't have. That was a true crime—an act of mass murder!

During the next sixteen months of my stay in Tokyo, I brought many Iranians to the church. The invited were many, but those who chose to accept the faith were few. I met many old friends in Tokyo, and a number of them decided to give their hearts and lives to Christ. One was a friend of mine from the military whose face had been deformed by a renegade explosion right in front of my eyes.

One day, a national Japanese TV channel found out about an Iranian who had become a Christian in Tokyo and who was evangelizing to illegal Iranians living in Japan, most of whom gathered in Harajuku.

So this TV Channel News approached me to help them interview some Iranians on the quality of life for foreigners, housing, the job market, and so forth. They just wanted to know under what condition they had been living (everybody knew how poorly illegal foreigners were living in Japan). They asked me to interpret the interviews on site. I agreed.

As soon as we arrived in Harajuku, carrying the camera and other equipment, Iranians began to run in every direction! Many covered their faces with their jackets or shawls. Most of them had been staying in Japan with expired passports or visas; they were afraid of being caught by the police and deported back to Iran. A few of them, who had recently arrived in Japan, were kind enough to grant us an interview, but they didn't know much about the misery of others.

Most Iranians wanted to save some money and send it to their families. Rooms in Japan are very small, but the rent was so high that they had to live in groups of five to seven people in a 75-square foot room. Some landlords did not like that. To avoid conflicts, two or three people would sleep in parks twice a week so that the landlord would not throw them all out. Most of them had to work in underground facilities. Unlike many other Iranians, I had decided to keep it legal by travelling to South Korea every three months in order to renew my tourist visa, but I had to spend all of my savings for these trips. I had also applied for an immigrant visa to the Canadian Embassy in Tokyo. After a year, my application was still under evaluation. In going to South Korea, there was also the risk of being denied re-entry into Japan by the authorities at the time of arrival at the Narita Airport or sea borders, but I still wanted to be truthful, at least to myself, at any cost.

So many Iranians, because of loss of job and being thrown out by the landlords, began to steal things from each other such as money, gold, silver, passports, or anything with worth that would enable them to live on for a few more days. All of these facts had made them very agitated, edgy, and hateful toward the Japanese; for this reason, seeing another Iranian working for a TV channel could have pulled a trigger. When we finally set up for an interview, I sensed that something was going on around us. I told the guy who was in charge of the crew what I felt. He said that it was OK and that he was sure nothing would happen.

The reporter began asking his questions, and I translated. We were interviewing the newly arrived Iranians, and they were telling us that their living condition was not as bad as some claimed. Less than five minutes into the interview, I began to notice some murmuring around us in the crowd. I began to worry! When the reporter asked how many people sleep in a single room, I just heard someone yelled "sons of ...," and in a harmonized move, a mob of ten angry guys with huge wooden and metal sticks attacked me and the crew. They kept swearing at us in Farsi, English, and Japanese. Hundreds of other Iranians stood around us just watching. There seemed no way out. They began to push us, kick us, and beat us with the sticks. The cameraman was holding the camera over his head, and the camera was smashed into pieces! Two of the men caught me by my jacket, and one of them, who seemed to be their leader, began to punch me in the stomach, swearing.

Everything happened so fast; they caught us off guard. I wasn't worried much about myself, but about the TV crew and the reputation of Iranians in Japan. I was so embarrassed.

We were watched by the other Iranians for about two minutes, but it wasn't long until the observers came to rescue us. They proved that those frustrated, hopeless people who were beating us were not the true representatives of Iranians. In a sudden heroic move, all who had been watching the incident decided to come to rescue us. This time, it was the mob who was surprised! The crowd began to catch them one-by-one and pull them away from us, yelling at them, "What the hell are you guys doing? They just want to help us." We really wanted to. Some others came to help us by picking up whatever was left from the equipment and opening a gap for us to escape. We started running toward the van.

Two angry guys ran after us, spinning the sticks over their head, cursing and swearing at us. I noticed that their curses were different from the other ones! They were cursing me, "You filthy Christian, son of a ..., you infidel mother ...!" Yes, they remembered me from the other day, the first day I took the big cross and went to preach to them! So I ran faster until we all got into the van and drove away as fast as we could. Thank God they couldn't catch us. We drove until we reached a safe place. I asked if everyone was OK. Fortunately, no one had a major injury. I told them how sorry I was for what had just happened. They were quiet. I knew what was going on. They were developing a sense of hatred toward Iranians. They did not talk to me for the rest of the ride. They took me back to the church, where they talked to the girl who had introduced me to them in first place, and then they left.

That was the day I began to feel that maybe my destiny was not to minister to Iranians; maybe I needed to bring the good news to Japanese, Koreans, or even Africans, but definitely not Iranians!

———

Months passed, and I was growing in my Christian faith. I had learned how to pray, how to communicate with God through the Bible and bringing my thoughts to Him. The only things I was very interested in were, first, knowing Him better, second, understanding His plan for the world, and third and most important, understanding what I was supposed to do, what my destiny was, and how I was supposed to fulfill it. Other revelations were just complementary.

In my mind, Iran was off the table for me, especially after what had happened with the TV crew. I thought the Iranians I had brought to church so far were enough to be listed on my heavenly account. No more Iranians for me.

Then one day early in March, 1992, I received a letter from the Canadian Embassy that regretfully informed me about their final decision to reject my application. The following day, YMAM leaders in Japan decided to enroll me for the next training season in their regional district; finally some good news. However, I needed to renew my visa so that they could accept my application. I had to go the immigration office to discuss the possibilities of renewing my visa because, for the first time during my stay in Japan, my visa was expired, though only for a little over a week.

When I got to the immigration office, I saw many young people from different nationalities, including Iranians, with handcuffs sitting there waiting for the cops to take them to Narita Airport to deport them. It was a heartbreaking scene. After about two hours of waiting for in line, finally it was my turn to talk to an officer about my problem. He checked my passport and asked me if I knew my visa was expired. I smiled and said, "That's why I am here. I was wondering if there's a way you could renew it just for another week so that I can enroll in a Christian school."

"Did you see those with handcuffs waiting outside? They were caught because of the same reason," he said.

"But my visa was expired only a couple days ago," I replied. "I wasn't caught or arrested; I came here on my own to ask for a solution."

"It makes no difference," he said, holding on to my passport.

"You mean there's no difference between me and them?" I asked him. "They have handcuffs, but I have none!" I showed him my wrists.

"We received a letter from the Ministry not to renew any visas from specific nationalities. The only way for you is to go back to your country and apply for a student visa, and your school can follow up your application on your behalf." He said that it was the only suggestion he could give me.

There was no other way except to tell him that I had become a Christian and that, if I went back to Iran, they would probably kill me for that matter. I told him the story. He listened carefully. Then he picked up the phone, called his superior, and told him about the situation. In a few seconds, another Japanese man wearing a suit and holding a cup of coffee came to our desk, shook hands with me, and asked if I had become Christian in the last few days. I told him I had become a Christian about a year and a half prior and that I wanted to stay in Japan and enroll in a Christian school. I told him I could be a great help for Iranians in Tokyo, too. The second man turned to the first and told him about the stories he had heard about persecution of Muslims who become Christians in Muslim countries. Then I went farther and told him that I would even be able to work for the police as a translator or help in any other matters related to Iranians if they would help me with my visa. He thought for a while and then asked the other officer to have a private conversation.

After they talked for a while, they went to someone else's office, apparently a higher ranking officer. He looked at me from behind his office window and wrote something under my application and signed it.

Then the first officer came back to his desk and asked me to sign a paper he put in front of me. I asked him what it was. He said, "You have one day, only today, to decide. My boss told me to give your passport back. He will be in trouble if anybody finds out about this.

I said, "What am I supposed to do in one day?!"

He said, "If you have truly believed in your God, you should have asked Him what to do, not the immigration office." Then he continued, "It's your God who should tell you what to do!" His words were like a hammer on my head.

He handed me my passport back. I felt embarrassed. I was ashamed of my fears and all the effort I had put into staying in Japan. Hearing that sentence from someone who didn't even believe in God was like a slap on my face.

I began to think, *What they did was a miracle. They had the full authority to handcuff me and send me back to Iran. How many times should I be saved until I believe God is in control? How many times must God save me from simple daily incidents until I believe He is there watching over me?*

We all tend to call these interventions good luck and bad luck rather than taking them as actual interventions of a highly intelligent God. Sometimes that amazes me! In fact, counting all interventions as mere luck, odds, and chance is true superstition and ignorance.

I took my passport back, stepped out of the office, found a corner, and sat down on the floor; all of the seats were taken, and many were standing and waiting there for another chance. They were from many nationalities—Bengali, Pakistani, African, and even some Americans.

I began to think about the reasons Iranians decide to leave their country. I asked myself, *How could a person run from a prison to another one worse than the last one where he cannot even show his face in fear of being arrested?* For some Iranians, Japan was even worse than Iran.

The problem, in my opinion, was something spiritual—both a vacuum in our souls and a dark, heavy presence over the country. We all are familiar with the spiritual void. It's a common thing in all of us. But the dark force is not a common case. It is a force working behind most of the Middle East countries, a force that even Muslim leaders of a country like Iran were not and are not aware of, a force that had little to do with what regime was ruling over Iran or other Middle Eastern countries. I knew it was always there. You can feel it when you talk to Iranians, no matter where they've immigrated to. To me, it was more like a captivity from within—a sad, suspicious, desperate, and broken spirit.

I said to myself, "I have to do something about it." I just felt the urge.

I opened my bag, pulled out my Bible, and prayed for few minutes. I asked God to talk to me and tell me what He wanted me to do, for that was why I had put my trust in Him—He knew what He was doing, and He knew why He had created me.

I had heard many stories about Christians asking God to be their fortuneteller and about those who used the Bible out of context to get confirmations for what they wanted to do—like getting married, changing jobs, or even simple daily stuff—and that most of the time they got it wrong! It was difficult to resist the desire to ask Him to keep me in Japan. I told Him that if He kept me in Japan, I would be more useful to Him and that He could educate me in the word through working with YWAM. The Bible Cheryl had given me was filled with green and orange highlights. I opened my Bible, knowing that He already had something to tell me. I just wanted to hear it loud and clear. And there He spoke.

The page that I opened had only one highlighted passage. It read:

And when He got into the boat, he who had been demon-possessed begged Him that he might be with Him. However Jesus did not permit him, but said to him, "Go home to your friends, and tell them what great things the Lord has done for you, and how He has had compassion on you" (Mark 5:18-19 NKJV).

I was hit again, but this time it was so convincing and so obvious that resistance was futile. An ocean of peace came upon me, and I felt like a baby in his mother's arms. The passage was so powerful that no logic could argue with it. I knew it was from Him, and I accepted it like a soldier. I thanked Him, put my Bible in my bag, and went back to the office of the same person I had talked to a few minutes before. I told him, "My God showed me what I need to do. I'm going back to Iran for good, and I just wanted to let you know about my decision."

"But you know if you go back you might be killed for your faith," he said.

"Yes, I know. But that's what I need to do. He will protect me," I told him.

He asked me for my passport again, and I gave it to him. He went to his boss's office and came back two minutes later. He handed me the passport and said, "We extended your visa for another week. I hope you made the right decision."

I was surprised and asked him why they gave me a week. He said it was complicated, and I just needed to take advantage of the opportunity. I smiled, shook hands with him, and thanked him for his help.

On the way back home, I went to an Iranian Airline Agency and bought my ticket for the end of the week. I was so happy that I began to dance on my way to the train station. People looked at me like I was a lunatic! I was so surprised at how happy and peaceful I was regarding something that had scared me for the last three years—going back to Iran.

I had already left my own apartment and moved to a place called Joshua House a year before. It was one of the bases for the YWAM missionaries. My friends at Joshua House showed different reactions to my decision. Some were mad at me because I didn't share the idea with them and didn't ask for prayers on the topic. Some admired me for the decision. Yet, others told me that they would keep praying for me to receive clear wisdom on how to take the next steps.

I threw a goodbye party, and many showed up. That day, my Irish friend's fiancé gave her heart to Jesus after hearing my testimony. It was a perfect day. The next morning, I left the house I had lived in for more than a year, a house with so many wonderful memories. Before I left, I called my parents and told them I was on my way to Tehran. They were shocked.

During the few months before I went back, I had written many letters to my parents in which I explained about my new adventurous faith in God, without mentioning anything about Jesus. They knew something unusual had happened to me.

When I landed in Tehran's Mehrabad Airport after fourteen hours of flight, all of my family members and friends were there to welcome me back. My parents could not believe how different I looked. I had put on weight, and as they later said, I was glowing. I arrived in the airport around midnight, and we got home around 1 in the morning, but we were up talking until the dawn—me, my mother, and my youngest sister. My dad went to sleep right after we got home.

That night I told them what had happened to me. I told them that contrary to what we usually thought God wasn't lost, as we had so often heard people say; it was humankind who was lost. They patiently listened to all I had to share. It was an unforgettable night for me, especially when I gently took my mother's hands and, in tears, asked her to forgive me for all the bad things I had done to her and all the hurts I had caused her. I promised her I would never ever do anything that might harm our family or break her heart again. It was in that moment that I truly saw what I had done to her, to my dad, and to all my relatives and friends.

I could see the waves of tears in her eyes after I finished my story. She seemed to be hesitant about sharing something with me, but she finally spoke. She began to tell me about a dream she had had a couple of weeks before I told them I was coming back.

She said, "We were at Mehrabad Airport. The whole family and friends were there waiting for your flight to land. I was thinking about how different you should have been now. I was standing at a corner all alone by myself. For some reason, I was worried about you. We heard the announcement that your flight from Japan had just landed. Everybody got off the plane, but you were not among them. After a long time, all of a sudden your Aunt Mehri ran to me shouting, 'They brought Bijan; they brought Bijan!'"

She continued, "I said to myself, 'Why is she saying that they brought Bijan?' Everybody ran to the huge window toward the Airport runway to see what was going on. I opened my way toward the window and almost fainted at what I saw; the huge back door of the plane opened, and I saw four people carrying a casket. It was a very beautiful casket with a blazing golden cross on it. It was shining like a bright sun. Mehri said, 'Didn't I tell you? They brought Bijan.'"

And that was all she had seen in her dream! She told me that she had kept it to herself for weeks because she didn't know what it meant. I told her what she saw was truly a dream from God, showing her that the Bijan she used to know was completely dead on that glorious cross. I told her about what the Bible says about those who believe in Jesus and how they die to their old nature and are born anew from God's Spirit in a way that they become God's children.

She said, "Now I know for sure that you are changed, and whatever or whoever changed you is worthy of praise and admiration." Then she hugged me and said, "I forgive you!"

My youngest sister joined us by hugging us both, and to change the atmosphere she said, "I forgive you, too, big bro!" and we all laughed. It was almost dawn when we went to bed. I couldn't sleep for another thirty minutes. I was just staring at the ceiling, thanking God for all the love He had shown me. I pondered how easy it was to be free, happy, and at peace at last. I had been found by God in Japan, but now was back to Iran—where I discovered how I could operate in the same environment I had run away from, the environment in which I used to live in as a drug addict, drug dealer, and spiritual Guru!

I had no idea what I was supposed to do next. I just knew I couldn't keep quiet. And I knew that, sooner or later, I had to pay a price for my faith.

The Act-ivist

TEHRAN LOOKED COMPLETELY DIFFERENT FROM the picture I had in mind from before I travelled to Japan, or maybe it was just because I had changed. Everything looked new. Young people had begun to dress more fashionably again. There were new cars everywhere in the streets—from Japanese cars to Korean cars. Shops were selling more up-to-date merchandise. Some shops even had revealing lady's underwear behind their windows. What had happened? Apparently after the war was over, the government had decided to loosen the reins a little bit. Ayatollah Khomeini had passed away two years before I came back, and now Ayatollah Khamenei was the Supreme Leader of the Islamic Republic. Ayatollah Rafsanjani, who had been one the closest people to Ayatollah Khomeini, was the president. It is said that during mid-90s, his name was on the list of the top thirty richest people of the world. He was a smart person. Before he became the President he was the Chairman of the Iran's Parliament. In fact it was him who successfully convinced all other Ayatollahs to vote for Khamenei as the new Supreme Leader, but years later, in a clash of powers, he got into trouble because of that.

Since the success of the Revolution, there've been two main streams in the Government. One stream didn't have much of a problem with establishing diplomatic relations with the West, especially the United States. Rafsanjani seemed to be the head of this stream. They believed there were many benefits, for both nations, in opening diplomatic channels with America. On the other hand, the second stream believed that they could become a giant military and economic power—not only in the Middle East, but in the whole world—without America. Although people didn't like either of these two streams, sometimes you have to choose between the bad and the worse. So most people were in favor of the first stream. The reason was clear; the second stream was willing and ready to sacrifice anything to stay in power, even the country and its whole population.

During the Shah's reign, we had close bonds with the U.S. The definition of the word *freedom* was what we experienced in that era— freedom according to the Hollywood standards, music industry, and fashion. Media was and still is the greatest means of conveying ideas. Media has the power to twist the truth and sell us a colorful lie as a standard for life. Even during the Shah's reign, not many people were aware of the high number of political prisoners who were in prisons of the regime. But as a child of a military man, I used to hear many stories about how the political prisoners used to be tortured in prisons (of course, it was not comparable to what is going on now in prisons of Iran under the Islamic regime).

The Mullahs had already tasted a tiny flavor of power in politics a few decades before the success of the Revolution, but only for a short time, and they wanted to regain that power at any cost. Since they had also been insulted and mistreated by the Shah's father, the founder of Pahlavi Dynasty (Reza Shah), who knew what the Mullahs were capable of if they gained power, after Islamic Revolution they had the chance to get their revenge on Pahlavi's Royal Dynasty and fulfill their lust for ruling over millions of people whom they thought never appreciated their service to the community (and what that service might be, we have no idea).

For some clear social and, of course, psychological reasons, they not only hated the Royal family, but also all other manifestations of the western civilization, whether it was the dress code (like a suit and tie), or art, or music, or even dancing. On the top of this list, they hated America, which was considered to be the Great Satan who brought all these calamities on Iran (and by "Iran," they meant "the Mullahs"). Their hatred and the thirst for revenge and power had blinded them. They even hated the middle class of society for desiring the cultural appearances of the western civilization. Mullahs hated the "city people," which is the title they called them by (many Mullahs were from the smallest villages, as their last names usually show). They thought they were oppressed by all other classes of the society. They were mostly from the lowest layers of society, and their survival depended on preaching the death of others—whether it was the death of the leaders of early Islam in war against the evildoers of the time or the death of the ordinary people. Their job was always to say some words at a funeral, which was more like a lamentation about poverty and the humbleness of the founders of Islam and how unjustly they were killed by the rich, evil authorities.

The same story is still going on in what they preach, but now on a global scale. This time they have the military power to revenge all those infidels (evildoers) who have been oppressing Muslims (read Mullahs) during the centuries. These days in Iran, everyone who wants to exercise power over someone else, or everyone who hates a group of people for any given reason, becomes a Mullah. It's like a fashion now. Of course, the story is much more complicated in the higher ranking authorities, like in Government, but still the same motifs persist.

The first stream of power, headed up by Rafsanjani, knew this kind of behavior would never work in a global level, and they also found out that not everything in the Western Civilization is evil. Plus, they reached the conclusion, "Since we have the power, why not negotiate? We both will benefit and stay longer in power if we put our heads together with the Western Governments, because they have been there longer, and they should have known better!" But the second stream in Iran wanted all the power in the world for itself; it wanted everything and at any price (and it still does). Any conversation or negotiation was pointless and meaningless to them. Not surprisingly, this is the stream that supports terrorism and chaos just to remain in power. As far as it can be observed by any intelligent mind, the second stream of power (led by Ayatollah Khamenei) has no other drive, values, or standard except to remain in power and rob the nation of its wealth and riches until there's nothing left for anyone. All other national or even international political games are the means to maintain the first goal (you can even see this behavior in their claims about their peaceful nuclear activities; they are truly after military advantages over the West through making nuclear weapons). They just want to create global chaos everywhere so that they can remain in power longer. You can't find any correctional pattern in what they do in terms of the political actions they take. And we all know that if there are no recognizable behavioral patterns, there will be no certainty or chance of predictability. The Government of Iran, which is mostly run by the second stream, is like a virus or a bacteria with no brain to analyze the consequences of its behavior. Its only drive is to remain in power—in other words, survival.

Unfortunately, people of Iran are caught in this battle between the two streams of power, and they have no other option except to go with the first stream, which as you probably know, has been called the Green Wave since

June 2009, but in fact, they came to the surface during President Khatami administration.

Recently (and finally), it is becoming more clear to Iranians that the problem at hand is not a choice between a liberal or conservative Islamic regime, but the Islamic regime itself. Religion is not to become a ruling force or government, because its nature is very personal. We saw what Christianity did to Europe for about a thousand years; I'm glad the Iranian Islamic regime will not last that long!

The history of Europe has been carrying the marks of such horrible theocratic governments for about ten centuries in the name of Christianity and God. The inevitable outcome of this horrible theocracy was the Age of Reform, the Renaissance, the separation of government and religion, the Age of Enlightenment, the Industrial Revolution, and so on. But to be honest, it truly took Europe few centuries to finally overcome the side effects of such a tyranny. I understand that some believe these two examples are not really comparable (the rule of false Christian leaders and false Muslim leaders), but in so many aspects, they are.

However, in Iran's case, one specific factor could change all of the above equations sooner or later, and that is the educated, zealous, and modernized young generation. What took centuries for Europe to realize and, therefore, act upon may only take few years for Iran. We have not yet seen what the young generation of Iran is capable of. All we have seen since June 2009 is a sober, controlled behavior. It has only sparked on few occasions under a very weak leadership, a leadership that belongs to the first stream, but still has its own beliefs rooted in Islam's principals. The first stream yet believes in what Ayatollah Khomeini started—an Islamic regime. But so far, we haven't yet seen Islam bring a solution to the slightest world crises, and we all know why. Spirituality is a very personal element in life, and if it comes to rule as a solution-making system, it definitely fails because of the very reason of being a personal matter. What is good for me is not necessarily good for you. That's a fact. But the rule of a common law to protect everyone's right in all societies is a necessity as long as humankind exists, and the vehicle to carry out that common protective law is what we call a government. But this government, as history has proven, cannot and should not be of a religious kind.

Unfortunately, I'm observing the same process being initiated again among Christian movements, specifically in North America. How can they make the same mistake twice? I have no idea. Those who believe Christianity (or Islam, Judaism, or any other religion) should come to power and occupy governmental positions to improve the moral life of people and to expand Christendom (or any other religion) are as awfully wrong as the Islamic regime in Iran. To me, as one who has lived under this sort of religious government, this point is so obvious that it needs no further argument.

———

When I returned to Iran, the reason for such a visible change in Tehran's look was the fact that the war between Iran and Iraq had ended and the main focus of the Government had become (or at least it seemed to be) to rebuild the cities and strengthen the economy. For this very reason, they had already allowed some foreign countries and companies to help them in the process. They had signed many agreements with Russia, China, South and North Korea, and few other countries, but not with the U.S. or the UK in a direct way (except for some political agreements behind the curtains). The United States was still called the number one enemy of the regime. And since the capturing of the American Embassy in November 4, 1979 which had been referred to as a Spy Nest, no Western country felt safe in Iran anymore. This became especially true when the Iranian authorities began to use that term for every other embassy, consulate, foreign company, and any gathering of religious minorities that were still active in any way—like Jewish synagogues, Zoroastrian temples, Baha'i gatherings, and even Christian churches. So I had to be careful in my search for a church.

I had been home almost two months, and I had not found an active church. I wasn't even sure if there was one. I didn't know any Christians in Tehran to ask them about the churches, so I had to do my own search. I knew there were some Gregorian, Orthodox, and Catholic churches, which were more like historic places, but I was looking for a Spirit-filled church.

One day, when I was walking along a very quiet street in down town, I saw a sign in Korean with a very tiny subhead in English that read Korean Evangelical Church. I ran to the door, which was more like a gateway to a very big garden. I rang the bell few times until an old man showed up by the door. He opened the door just enough to see my face and said, "Yes?"

"I'm a Christian and just came back to Iran from Japan. I was wondering if I could talk to the Pastor!" I said.

He looked at me with suspicion and said, "The church is closed. And it's only for Koreans!"

"May I speak to the Pastor or someone who's in charge?" I insisted.

"No. Nobody's here, and as I said it's only for Koreans." He said that while pushing the door against me to lock it.

I was surprised at his reaction, but so far it was the only non-historical church I'd seen in the past two months, and I didn't want to miss my chances. So I asked him about when I could come back again to see the pastor.

"I already told you what you needed to know; you better leave now." This time I sensed a harsh tone in his voice.

"At least tell me if there's any other church I can visit. Would you?!" I didn't give up.

He took a look around at the street and told me that there was another church, an Assemblies of God church, near Tehran University on Takhte Jamshid Street, and then he shut the door!

I was kind of disappointed at his rude behavior at first, but I didn't care for too long; I had an address now. I had heard about this denomination in general when I was in Japan—Assemblies of God. There were many in my church back in Tokyo who believed in the manifestations of the Holy Spirit. I had considered myself a Bible-believing person—someone who believed in the Scriptures as the truth and as an application for real life. I didn't like it, though, when people gave it a name or title, like charismatic, Assemblies, Pentecostal, Baptist, or Methodist.

Anyway, the next day I went to the address and found the church. I rang the bell with some hesitation. This time a young lady came to the door. I told her I was a Christian who had just come back from Japan looking for a church. She smiled and politely asked me in. I was surprised! She asked me to wait, and she went upstairs. In less than a minute, a huge guy came down to greet me with a big smile.

"Hi, my name is Johnson. How can I help you?" he said, while he stretched out his hand toward me for a handshake.

"Hi, hello, my name is Bijan. I'm looking for a church to join. I was wondering if I could talk to someone in this church to learn more about your services," I said.

"Sure, why not? I'm the youth pastor here. We can talk in my office, if you'd like." He was still smiling.

"That would be great!" I sounded too excited.

He led me upstairs to his office.

He politely asked the young lady to bring us some tea. Her name was Narges. She and I became good friends later on. Johnson and I talked for three hours. I told him my whole story—my past life and how I met Jesus. He was amazed by my testimony. He then asked me to have lunch with him. I accepted, and we continued our conversation in a nearby restaurant. He was very open and asked me to attend the next service the next day, a Friday afternoon service. Then he explained to me that they had two public services during the week. The other one was on Sunday afternoons. He also told me that there were many youth groups and Bible studies during the week. Some were held in houses and other ones in different rooms at the church.

Before we said good-bye, he said, "I usually don't trust people so quickly, but the Holy Spirit spoke to my heart about you today as I was coming down the stairs to meet you."

"Are you serious? What did He tell you?" I asked him with excitement and curiosity.

"Well, He simply said, 'I have brought him here, take care of him!' and I just did. So please come back tomorrow and worship with us. Next week we are going to have a youth camp; come and share with us. Your testimony would be very uplifting for our youth."

I was filled with joy on the way back home. I couldn't wait to share about my new church with people I knew. I had already witnessed to hundreds in just two months. I wanted them to be part of a church, but first I had to find one! Now I was able to invite them to my new church.

Worship style was always an essential factor for me for experiencing God's presence in a church. I had written several worship songs by then, in Farsi and in English, and I had already begun evangelizing among my friends and relatives through those songs. There were even times when I was invited to house parties on weekends, and they always asked me in advance to prepare some of my own songs and play them with my guitar.

At one of these parties, when I was asked to sing a song, I began to tell them a little bit about the one I loved, the one who was the reason I wrote those songs. I took the chance to briefly explain to them who I was and what I used to do. They couldn't believe I used to be so bad. They started asking questions. They circled around me and listened carefully to what I shared with them for the rest of the night. I told them about a God who loved them and a God who was after their hearts instead of their good behavior. The funny thing is that these kinds of parties were usually like a club with loud dance music, alcohol, and drugs—just like what I used to do in my old days. This time I wasn't dragging them to hell with me; I was leading them to God's presence. It was very exciting to be there and talk about a God who was not exactly what they had pictured in their minds.

In Iran, when you talk to people about God, you notice that they have a very fixed concept about who He is. The title is normally associated with Allah, who is called Merciful and Forgiving, but he actually isn't. People, even those who claim to follow Allah, have a fearful image of him. All they do is to try to quench his anger and please him with so-called good deeds. But the God I was talking about was so different that it drew many young people, relatives, and friends to Him. They were surprised to see me singing love songs to Him. Usually, at the end of the parties, there were a number of them who would want to know more about the God I had introduced to them. So before I even began to attend that church, there were many who were ready to be harvested. When I found the Assemblies, I needed to make sure it was a suitable place for these young people, and thank God it was.

The first day I entered the church, I saw young boys and girls on the stage with musical instruments lifting up their voices and singing songs to Jesus. Some of the songs were familiar to me for they were the songs we used to sing in Shibuya Harvest in Tokyo but translated from English to Farsi. Not only that, but also all of the members of the church were worshiping God in the very same way that we used to worship in Japan. I was surprised that under the Islamic regime they had that kind of freedom. The only difference was the women's dress code! They had to observe the Islamic law of Hijab (shawls on their hair), even inside the church. It wasn't a strict order or bill. It was the church policy to keep the authorities and fanatic Muslims away. But that was OK as long as we were free to worship in a place altogether.

You can imagine how happy I was to join the Assemblies.

The next week, I attended the youth camp and made friends with more than 120 passionate young adults. I shared my testimony, and then Pastor Johnson introduced me to the lay leaders of the youth groups, and I was put into one of them.

Within a couple weeks, I had met with almost all of the main leaders of the congregation. Within a couple months, they let me sing my own songs in some worship youth services, and since my music taste was different, I became popular almost instantly. This was not a norm in the Assemblies churches. For security reasons and the test of faith, they wouldn't usually let anyone move up so quickly in the church, but they made an exception for me—it was God's favor.

In six months, they asked me to run a class for new believers. In less than a year, the leadership asked me to be one of the youth leaders. And in a year and half, I became the familiar face of every worship concert, not only in the Assemblies, but among other churches in the city as well. One of them was the same Korean church that I had first attempted to join.

In those days, Bishop Haik Hovsepian Mehr had already begun a campaign for Mehdi Dibaj, who was in prison for nine years for his unshakeable faith in Christ. The Government of Iran had already executed a pastor who had been arrested in Mashhad (the second most religious city in Iran). He used to be a Muslim, and he fell in love with Christ at a young age; his name was Hussein Soudmand.

Dibaj had been in prison for the sake of the same love for Jesus. He too was sentenced to death, but Bishop Haik's international humanitarian activities finally resulted in Dibaj's freedom. Dibaj himself told me later that he was very excited in prison, waiting for the sentence to be carried out, because he would be finally able to see his lover, face-to-face. He then added, "It seems that God has another plan for me, but I still prefer to be with Him."

He didn't need to wait too long to see his dream fulfilled.

After his release, Dibaj and I usually talked a lot when we were both at church. I always liked philosophical or theological conversations, but with him, none of it mattered; the only important thing to him was the love of Christ. Nothing else mattered. You could see it in his eyes, especially when he was talking to the youth at the church. I had never seen someone talk about God's love like that, especially considering that he had been in prison for nine long years, waiting everyday in his solitary confinement for his death sentence to be carried out. Now he was free to tell everyone about this love. That was dangerous!

Bishop Haik had already become an icon and was on the cover of European magazines because of his humanitarian activities. He was invited to conferences around the world to speak about persecution of the church in Iran and those in prison like Dibaj. And that was dangerous, too.

A few months after Dibaj was released, Haik was kidnapped and murdered. His body was found slaughtered somewhere outside of Tehran about a week after his disappearance.

Shortly after that, Dibaj was also found dead, along with other pastors and Christian scholars and some leaders of political parties or organizations.

The Regime blamed the murders on an anti-revolutionary terrorist group called Mujahidin. Later on, they claimed to arrest the killers. They were condemned to death in a fake court, and a few weeks later they confessed their crime on a fake TV program; we never heard of them again. The Government never took responsibility of any of these murders until years later, under the investigations of President Khatami administration. Many departments and units in the Ministry of Information were involved in the plot, even the Minister himself. Many high ranking officials' names from among the authorities came up after the investigation, even Khamenei, the Supreme Leader of the regime.

The investigation committee of the Khatami administration arrested some of the lay leaders of the operation. One of the high-ranking agents in the Ministry of Information took the most responsibility for murdering the leaders of opposition; his name was Saeed Emami. Later on, he was murdered in a mysterious way while under interrogation. They called it a suicide! All the secrets of the serial murders were buried with him. Dibaj was given the title Reverent after his death. The church declared all the murdered Christian leaders and pastors to be martyrs. The earth did not deserve their footsteps. I envied them.

A few months later, I was assigned as the Director of Discipleship and Training for new believers. In the spring of 1994 my second album was released. In those days, CDs were not yet used (at least not in Iran), so it was all on tapes. It was produced during the toughest period of persecution. My close friend, Jemis Rashidian, who was one of the most talented musicians in those days in the Assemblies, along with Rev. Vruir Avanesian, who was the pastor of worship and arts, believed in what I was doing and helped me produced the album. Unfortunately, we lost the original files, and I wasn't able to transfer them onto a CD or make a digital file out of them in later years. Maybe one day I'll be able to re-do them.

While I was in charge of new believers, many of them asked me to meet with their family members, and I did. As a result, many others dedicated their lives to Jesus. But we had to be very cautious, first for the sake of their own lives, and second, for the sake of the church.

I managed to oversee a number of new believers and lead the youth in a house church, as well. Among those who were coming to Christ were some who not everybody wanted to deal with—the demon possessed, people under spells, rock and rollers, drug addicts, and so on. Many times

I was called to hospitals or houses to pray over those who were, according to doctors, about to die in a few days, and not only did they recover (after a prayer), but also lived long lives in wholeness and total health. One of them was a 14-year-old boy diagnosed with a deadly tumor. He wasn't supposed to live more than three more days when his brother came to our church and asked me to go with him to the hospital and pray for him. He was a relative. When I went to the hospital, I noticed that many others had tried to heal him using all kinds of weird written prayers, prayers to so-called holy figures in Islam, but nothing had worked so far.

Jesus gave me an undeniable assurance that He was going to heal the kid. Before I said a short prayer for him, I told his parents that he was going to be immediately healed; they looked at me like I was crazy. I prayed over the kid, and then told him to get up and pull out all the tubes and go home! He smiled. I think he knew he was healed. A few hours later that night, his doctors were contacted by the hospital and were asked to come and comment on an unprecedented case. Yes, he was completely cured. None of the doctors could come up with an explanation. They kept him there for another day to do more tests, but finally had to release him in the next day. Recently he found me on Facebook. He's in his early 30s now and is still healthy and handsome!

There were many other similar cases, as well as horrible cases of demon possession. I had to prepare myself for days before any attempt to resolve such cases—fasting, prayers, and reading the Word. Sometimes leaders of the church would ask me to accompany them for such cases. Even the most difficult-to-deal-with believers and the toughest new believers were always assigned to me. Theological issues, whether it was a wrong teaching or something others believed to be a sin, were very important to the Assemblies. But I always tried to use those challenges as a common ground to bring people closer to loving God. Who was I to condemn people of sin? The only thing they needed was a little love, attention, and respect; the rest was just a natural response. Isn't that what Jesus did during His earthly life? Of course, new believers had challenges understanding the deity of Christ or the holy Trinity (like all other Christians), especially with their Islamic background, but not every challenge in understanding the difficult topics of the Bible is a blasphemy or heresy, a false teaching, or even a sin. Wrestling with your doubts are part of your growth.

Because of my involvement in cinema and the music industry, even some very well-known public figures and celebrities also came to Christ through me—from Iranian movie and TV stars to musicians, from cinematographers, directors, editors, and producers to authors. But I can't disclose their names unless they officially announce their faith.

I also used to be one of the worship leaders of the church, and we would take advantage of every occasion, like Norouz (Iranian New Year), Christmas, Easter, and Pentecost, as an outreach to invite Muslims to the church. My friend Jemis and I were also in charge of creating and planning other occasions for the youth and their non-Christian friends; music was always the strongest way of communicating our message with them in a country in which music was almost banned. Outside of the church, the Ministry of Culture and Guidance was in charge of approving or disapproving any song, poem, book, film, magazine, or play. As a result, there was not much good music on the market. I can boldly claim that, years before any underground band or musicians began to play rock/pop music in the Islamic Republic, we did it in the church.

The main sanctuary of the Assemblies church had the capacity of about 600 people. It was as big as some cultural centers that were used for live performances in the city. Sometimes we had to hold the concerts for three consecutive nights because of the popularity of our music style. We were usually asked by the pastor to finish our rehearsals early so that people wouldn't line up outside of the church; it was risky. I will share more about our music activities later.

In my early days of joining the Assemblies, I was introduced to some key leaders of our church, and one of them helped me find a job in a newly established company. The company's main project was to buy airplanes and helicopters from retired (or at work) military high-ranking officers in Russia at a very cheap price and then sell them for three to four times more to different Ministries in the Government of Iran, such as the Ministry of Defense, the Ministry of Transportation, the Ministry of Post, Iran Air, the Revolutionary Guard, and some fresh-out-of–the-oven airline companies (mostly run by the VIPs inside the Government).

You may ask how on earth we did that. Here's the short version. The founder of the company was an Iranian smart guy who was just back from the States after finishing his education (that's what he told his rich dad, but he actually hadn't.) He had married a nice Ukrainian girl back in the States, and by chance, the girl's father was a general in the Ukrainian Air Force! By a very simple mathematic calculation (rich and influential dads on both sides + a young ambitious couple + a country in need of technology + cheap prices + and some proper connections with greedy people in both governments), this company sold out many Russian airplanes and choppers to the Islamic Republic of Iran and benefited a lot. I was the second person who was hired in this company. The interesting part was that the guy who introduced me to my future boss, Kevin, had already told him that I was a Christian, but Kevin didn't seem to be bothered; he didn't have any problem with Christianity. His rich father and his younger brother, on the other hand, did.

At least six or seven other people were hired during the first month. Although I didn't have any academic education in any related areas of the company, in just three months, I became Kevin's most trusted employee. In the first six months of our operation, over one million U.S dollars were spent just on advertisement and bribes (I never had anything to do with the latter). Kevin didn't trust anyone with that money except me. All of his checks, all of his cash, and all of his bank accounts were under my supervision because he trusted me. That's what his younger brother didn't like at all.

His father wasn't happy about the fact that I was a Christian, an ex-Muslim. His father was a Hadji, which means someone who has visited Ka'aba at least once in his life time, and he had done that a dozen times. He was a very strict Muslim, but because of his son, he had to bear with me! Once he tried to prove to Kevin that I was not right for the job or even for the company, so he went to a Muslim fortuneteller and asked him to seek the spirits in order to get a confirmation for his opinion. The fortuneteller, after his communication with the so-called spirits, told him, "He's the most trustable person in the company!" But the father didn't believe the guy and went to another fortuneteller. In his surprise, he heard the same thing from the next guy, too! He did it for the third time to make sure. The answer was the same. He finally gave up and decided to get closer to me to see why the spirits said the same thing about me!

You may ask, "How come the Muslim fortunetellers told him such a thing about you?" to which I would say, "I have no idea!" Maybe a much more powerful force commanded them to say so, just like the story of Balaam in the Old Testament (see the book of Numbers chapters 22, 23 and 24 and the book of Joshua 24:9-10), or the story of Saul and Samuel's ghost (see 1 Samuel 28). Whoever intervened, it was a divine intervention to assure me of my job and the support I needed for my family. That's all I know. There may have been other reasons behind the whole picture, but I don't care to know.

Kevin's father was not the only one who decided to get closer to me. The nature of my job required me to be in constant contact with high-ranking authorities in the Ministries I named before. We travelled to Moscow many times, and we took these primitive people with us to Air Exhibitions held in Russia. And I was in charge of them. My mission was to protect them from getting lost, to order them pork-free foods, to help them exchange money, to make sure they were not robbed, and finally, to look after them so that they would not be tricked into bed by Russian girls! I wasn't always successful in my mission, though.

They usually challenged me for my beliefs (even though they didn't know my little secret). I used to talk to them about God from a biblical point of view, without directly referring to the Bible or mentioning Jesus. They liked to engage in conversations with me. Once, while we were on a flight to Moscow, the Deputy Minister of Post asked me to sit down beside him for a talk. He shared a lot with me about his different views on God. He was an open-minded person, but it was too risky to disclose my faith to him. I was just preparing these people's hearts for a future day when someone else would share the good news with them in a more direct way.

I had to be present at all of the meetings. After a while, Kevin asked me to oversee the company while he was on his long or short trips to Russia and the Ukraine, where his wife and her family actually used to live. Sometimes Kevin had to spend six months or more in Russia, the Ukraine, or Belarus to make new contracts with Russian authorities. So even though I didn't have the title of Vice President, still I was the Director of all things!

My friendship with Svetlana, Kevin's wife, was a very interesting one, and even Kevin used to tease us for our conversations about materialism, God, and Christianity. She was a materialist, as you may have guessed. She used to come to the company just to sit down with me and challenge my beliefs. That was another thing that Kevin's younger brother didn't like. And the younger brother would make a stop at the company almost every day to check on all the employees and report to his dad.

It didn't take long before I finally felt there was a serious danger in sharing my thoughts with everyone, especially since I was active in and out of church through evangelizing and music, particularly after the martyrdom of our pastors. So I talked to Kevin and asked him to let me go. He disagreed first but finally understood, and as a sign of his generosity, he gave me a good sum of money, which was enough for six months. But I preferred to gift the money to my parents. So that was my job as an airplane salesman!

After that, I decided to turn my translation hobby into a job. In fact, I had translated seven Christian books by then, along with some movie manuscripts and some university courses on theology. As a matter of fact, I was the only Christian who had gotten permission from the Ministry of Culture and Guidance to publish one of the Joy Dawson's books called *Intimate Friendship with God,* which not only sold one thousand copies within our Christian community, but also sold ten thousand copies in the book market (for half a dollar each). Iran had not then and still has not signed the international copyright agreement. This meant that none of the translators or musicians in Iran needed to ask for the permission of the owner of the work to translate or re-perform an art work. Plus, the age of the internet and email had not yet started those days, at least not in Iran. We lived in a closed society. There was almost no way to contact a writer for permission. And who knew whether, after contacting a foreign writer, we might be accused of spying for a foreign government!

Over the last thirty-two years, Iranians have been under the wildest persecutions you may or may not be able to imagine, both personally and corporately. The Mullahs turned Iran into an occupied land and did whatever their sick minds wanted to do in their lust for power. The same went on in publishing industries. Even the Church was affected by this attitude and began to censor the songs and books sold inside the church. Of course, they did this in the name of theological doctrines. I personally witnessed the removing of young, passionate guys and girls from the worship team or the choir just because the guys had long hair and the girls wore too much make-up. My last album in our church in Iran didn't receive permission (from the leaders) to be released just because we used some distortion guitar in some of the songs!

Regarding the book *Intimate friendship with God,* I would like to take the chance to ask Joy Dawson to forgive me for an unauthorized translation and publishing of her work. But I also proudly announce that the book was one of the all-time bestselling books of its kind as far as I remember, and it opened the way for other Christian books to receive permission from the Ministry of Guidance. I should also mention that the main benefit from the sales went to the publisher and not to me. Many were touched by this book. Bless you, Joy Dawson!

Between 1992 and 2000, I translated over twenty five books on different topics, such as the Fathers of the Church, ancient Christian poets and poetries, theology, and the power of faith, as well as books with topics such as Self-Help, Politics and Cinema. Soon after Mr. Khatami was elected as the President of Iran in 1997, I translated a book called *The Power of One,* written by Sharif M. Abdullah. He was an advisor to the White House, an international speaker, and a university professor. This book was the exact match for who Khatami was and what he had begun to do in Iran as a modern age leader. I dedicated the book to Khatami. A few weeks later, I received a letter of appreciation from his office for my attempt to translate such a valuable book!

Before the Khatami administration took power, of course, there was a different story. The church, media, news, music, and publishing industries were all under a severe censorship. By entering the publishing industry and performing music publicly, I was trying new things, new wineskins for the new wine; Christ's message of God's love and freedom. Everything seemed to move in the right direction, at least from my point of view and a Christian point of view, especially since I met a girl who I thought to be an angel sent by God, someone who could become my suitable helper, as God willed for Adam in the Book of Genesis—my Eve!

Kathy

SHE WAS A BEAM OF light! A friend of mine brought her to our church. We had another concert, and almost a thousand people showed up. The church's building didn't have that capacity, so many were standing outside. The show was sold out. We actually had to send at least 300 people back home. We told them to come back the following Thursday night. We had to use this opportunity to reach out to as many as we could. Fortunately, my friend had already bought her a ticket.

She was introduced to me minutes before the concert started, so we didn't have much time to chat. The only info I got was that she was a student in English Literature at Tehran University. Let's call her Kathy.

When you expand your network, others within your network do the rest for you by bringing more people into the circle. That's how I used to work, or even evangelize. As I mentioned before, I would go to house parties, sing songs, and share with the rebellious young generation. As a result, most of the new comers to our church were the fruit of those social activities. Even those who were atheists liked to bring their friends to our church at least for the sake of the music, and as a result, I made friends with all of them.

That night the concert went very well. A huge number of new comers came to the front and asked the leaders for prayers while we were still playing a soft tune. That was our norm. After the concert, I was invited to my friend's house party, the same friend who had brought Kathy to the church. I accepted.

I had just quit my job at MKR (the airplane selling company) and was living my life by doing some translation jobs here and there. It wasn't bad, but I still had to think about finding a way to keep helping the family.

My father's retirement salary was not enough to manage the expenses. My sister, Sherrie, had already managed to go to Switzerland, and after a year, she had moved to Canada and married an Iranian businessman. She was concerned about the family too, so she decided to help our parents immigrate to Canada. The file was going through its regular process, but nobody knew how long it would take them to finally fly to Canada. Thank God for all the efforts and support my sister and her husband put into this, for my parents were really desperate. My youngest sister was still working at a movie-related magazine, but what she got was hardly enough to handle her own expenses. So, in my concern for them, I had practically stopped thinking about myself, my future, my dreams and my marriage. My pastor, on the other hand, was concerned about my marriage. But I didn't want to think about it until I was sure about my parents' situation and my financial condition.

After the concert my sister and I, along with some other friends, went to the party. It wasn't like other parties I usually attended; there was no craziness! I thanked God. I had the chance to talk with Kathy a little bit more that night, and we had good times. My friend gave me winks the whole night while I was talking to Kathy. I guess he was thinking about hooking us up. *Silly him,* I thought.

During the conversation, I learned that she was from Gorgan, the capital of a province in northern Iran. Her father was a doctor and a member of the city council. Her older brother had also graduated recently as a family physician. Her younger brother was in his last year of high school. I noticed that she didn't want to speak about her mom. She was living in a huge penthouse, which was like a dormitory for girl students.

There was something about her that made me want to talk to her more. So I asked her if she had had a good time that evening at the concert.

"Oh yeah, that was one of the best times I'd ever had in a long time!" she replied.

"Which part did you like?" I wanted to know more about her likes.

"Your voice! And the lyrics! They were different! Did you write them all?" she asked.

"Thanks for the complement! Well, most of them were mine. There were some songs that I translated from English. Glad you liked them."

"Do you have them on tapes or cassettes? I mean, I'd love to listen to them again." she said.

"Sure, I mean yes. I have them on tape. I will get you one later. But how about the message the pastor spoke after the concert?" I wanted to know what she got out of the message.

"Well, I would prefer the songs to speak for themselves. They had a strong message about love, hope, faith, and life. I wouldn't add a speech to that. Plus, the short talks you had in between the songs were much more touching than what the pastor...is that what you call them, pastor?" she asked with hesitance. I nodded.

She continued, "Yeah, they were much more touching. I guess these days this is the best way someone can approach young people regarding God."

"Me too. That's why I started adding non-worship songs to the format of worship concerts. What am I talking about?! You probably have no idea what's the difference between Christian music or worship music!" I wasn't sure she knew the difference; many Iranian Christians, even the leaders, didn't know the difference.

"I have a clue, especially after tonight. I'd never been to a Christian concert, but I have been to a Catholic church a few times for prayers, when I was feeling down. But the way you and your friends played music tonight was so different. It was even better than many other Persian bands I know inside and outside of Iran! I believe a big number of young people tonight felt the way I felt."

"Wow, thanks! It means a lot to me. So you're saying you will stop by the church again, maybe next week?" I asked her with anticipation in my voice.

"Sure, I liked it very much. Plus, I need to get your album, so I guess you will see me again." She smiled. In fact, her heart-melting smile was the first thing I noticed about her, and it was the first thing I liked about her. However, later on I found out that having a beautiful smile is not enough!

Our friendship was very simple. From my point of view, first she needed to know more about the true God. I didn't want her to come to church for any other reason, except to know Jesus. In my youth group, I had often heard questions like, "Brother Bijan, is it OK to date or even marry a non-Christian?" and I always had to come up with what the Bible says and what our interpretation of those verses could be, according to the situation.

My answer was always something like this, "I really want you to understand that there are things we need to choose or decide for ourselves as God calls us to freedom, but He also wants us to have a personal relationship with Him. And personal means there are things that are truly personal, between you and God. Something that is not good for me might be the right choice for someone else. So you need to get your own conviction in your spirit. But if you want my personal opinion, I would say that I'm not in favor of marrying a non-Christian!"

It was not easy to advise those young guys and girls, especially considering the mindset that was formed in them by the media. All they knew about Christianity was what they had seen in the movies of Hollywood. They used to think all Americans are Christians. Many of them did not believe in Mohammad and Islam anymore when they accepted Christ, but they didn't have a clear understanding of Christianity, either. Unfortunately, for some of them, there was no difference between the western culture and Christianity as a religion!

Despite public opinion in the West, I can assure you that Islam has lost its meaning for the new generation of Iranians. They are not Muslims. In fact, more than fifty percent of the young people in Iran do not even believe in God anymore. New Age philosophy and Universalism is the new fashion in Iran. It is the new religion. Do not judge the situation based on the fact that young Iranians had to choose between bad and worse during the Presidential Election in 2009. It was not for the sake of Mir Hussein Musavi (the other candidate who was running against Ahmadinejad) that they came to the streets in millions, but it was for the sake of freedom and democracy. We all know that. What I mean is that they may have grown up in an Islamic environment, with teaching of the Sharia law in schools and through the media, but they don't believe in Islam anymore. So when you approach Iranians, do not consider them all as Muslims; in fact, sometimes they are offended by this idea that "all Iranians are Muslims." Rather, approach them as human beings and don't bring up Islam!

Since Kathy had been coming to the Assemblies for quite a while, I decided to talk to Rosa, one of my friends at church who was in charge of the new believer girls and ask her to approach Kathy to see how she was doing. I had already given her a Bible to read, and I needed someone to follow up with her. Rosa had a 20-year-old girl and was a very good communicator; she was the perfect person to work with Kathy as a mentor.

So they began a weekly meeting. I was right; Kathy needed someone to speak to. She seemed to have some burdens from her past, mostly regarding her mom. That was why she never talked about her. Soon they became best friends. Rosa and I used to share a little about what was good for her or what was the best way to help her, as far as the confidentiality principle was not violated.

She was attending the church regularly. That was a good sign. But still there was something about her that kept me concerned.

Kathy, just like many other Iranian women I knew, was interested in one specific story in the New Testament, the story of the woman caught in adultery. What interested her was the fact that everyone wanted to stone her, but Jesus did not hold any accusation against her. I wasn't very surprised at her choice. Because of Islam's pressure on women, this is one of the most beautiful pictures you can use to present God and the Gospel to Iranian women. This is true, first because of the social condition they were living under in the Islamic regime, and second because most of the women I knew, at some point in their lives, had had a relationship that ended in a sexual affair, whether by their own choice or under pressure. As a result, unconsciously they've been carrying a heavy burden of guilt within. In that story, Jesus saw that genuine guilt in that woman, contrary to the pretentious people who caught her in adultery. They felt guilt too, but for different reasons. Some of them might have been among those who had already slept with that woman and wanted to stone her to get rid of their own shame or guilt. Others might have pictured sleeping with her and wanted to destroy the source of that so-called evil temptation. But Jesus saw the brokenness in her. That was enough for Him to forgive her.

Kathy was dating a guy. They met within her first few months of living in Tehran. Later on, before she began to come to our church on a regular basis, they broke up but they were still in touch. She told me that they had never had an easy day. They always fought. But she never told me the cause of those fights. I didn't want to know, either. It wasn't my business. I was just helping her find her purpose in life. A few weeks after they broke up, her boyfriend told a mutual friend of ours that it was almost impossible to get to an agreement with Kathy on anything at all. When I heard that I thought, *He is only mad at her and wants to blame Kathy for their break-up.*

Kathy gradually made friend with my sister, and as a result, she spent more time with us in our house. I was happy for her. She was away from her own family, and I hoped she could somehow forget about what was bothering her concerning her past. My mother liked her very much, and she seemed to like my mom, too. It was difficult not to like Kathy. She was beautiful and charming. She sounded wise and reasoning. Once the widow of Rev. Haik Hovsepian, Sister Takoosh, referred to Kathy's face as the most innocent face she had ever seen. She even said if she wanted to make a movie about Mary, the mother of Jesus, she would definitely use Kathy to picture her innocence.

When she was at our place, she would hang around the kitchen and help my mother with cooking and the chores, even though once she told me she hated kitchen work. She made many visits to our home and spent lots of time with my mom. While I was at church doing my music rehearsal or having my meetings or working on my translation material, they got closer and closer until one day my mother told me she wished Kathy was my bride! I told her I wasn't ready for marriage yet and that, even if I was, it needed to be the one God had for me. I really didn't want to be influenced by any outside source in making my decision for marriage, even if it was my mom. The only important thing for me was to see her become more intimate with God on a personal level.

One day, Kathy told me she felt that English Literature was not her real passion, and to my surprise, she told me she had already quit it. I was shocked. I told her it would have been better if she had received counsel from a few people before she quit, like her family members and maybe some instructors at her university. She said, "I did what I did because I felt it was the right thing to do." She didn't want to talk about it anymore.

To be honest, it was the first time she talked to me like that. I felt a strange stubbornness in her. I did not continue the conversation, but I wasn't very happy with her sudden decision.

Six months passed, and one day I received a call from Rosa. She told me that Kathy had finally given her heart to Christ. I've been waiting for that moment for many months. I thanked God and then asked Rosa if Kathy had talked to her about her mom. I really wanted her to be free from her past and whatever was bothering her. Rosa said, "Not yet; I still feel she needs more time."

I was sure she would come to our place that night to let us know about her decision. On the way back home, I bought some flowers (she loved Narcissus). I was right; she was at our place. As soon as I stepped in, my mom said, "Someone has some good news to share!" but when she saw me with flowers, she said, "And someone seems to know it already!" We all laughed. Kathy came to me, hugged me, and said, "Thank you, Bijan. It was all for your prayers and kindness. You, your family, and Rosa helped me a lot. I'm so happy; it's like I'm a new person. Thank you!"

"I'm so happy for you, too." I said, "You made the right decision. Welcome to the family. Now you're a child of God!"

She smiled and hugged me again.

Around that time, Rev. Edward, who is one of the best preachers I've ever heard in my life, was ordained as the Bishop of the Assemblies. He was always one of my few examples to follow. He was tall and large in figure. His presence always carried the anointing of the Holy Spirit. Some of the youth were afraid of him, but in fact, it wasn't him they were afraid of; it was the presence of God who was with him all the time. It was the same presence that on many occasions scared the agents of the Ministry of Information, too. He had been called to the Ministry many times for investigation on Rev. Haik, Rev. Dibaj, and Rev. Mikailian's deaths. The Government wanted him to admit that they were killed by the Mujahedin terrorist group. He never admitted that. He stood firm against them and openly told them he believed they, the Government of Iran, had killed them. He was right, we all knew that. The plot involved many other intellectual reformists or leaders of opposition groups. At least 100 people were on the list (the list leaked out later on).

Edward was a true man of God, though of course with his own flaws. To me, he was always the closest example to my biblical hero, Paul. He was very successful in his marriage, too. He had three daughters and a son. His wife, Sister Anahid, was the pastor of women. Her solid, strong, and loving character and manner made her a peaceful refuge for all the girls and women in our church. She was able to see through people. On one occasion, I asked Kathy to get an appointment to see her at least once, but she said, "I feel more comfortable with Rosa." She truly deserved to be the first official female Reverent in the Assemblies of God in Iran. Unfortunately, she didn't live long to see that happen. As far as I remember it was in the year 2001 that cancer took her to Heaven into the arms of her Creator! May she rest in peace.

After Rev. Edward was ordained as Bishop of the Assemblies, we needed another pastor to take his place as the senior pastor. There were two or three candidates, but we essentially knew who would be the next senior pastor. His name was Vartan Avanesian, and at the time, he was the pastor of one of our two Armenian branches in the east of Tehran. During his recent visits to preach in our church, we had had the chance to build a good friendship.

Meanwhile, Kathy was gradually growing and had begun to open up to me and to Rosa more and more. The things she said about her mom didn't sound that bad. When she was sharing her stories with us, she just wanted us to listen and not to comment. I noticed that her conflicts with her mom were really a big deal to her, to the point that, whenever I tried to say anything to soften the problem, she got angry at me and did not talk to me for days. I tried different ways to help her overcome her unpleasant feelings about her mom, but it didn't work. I noticed that she had a serious issue in this regard, and it worried me.

She had already joined the youth in our church. She wanted to be under my supervision, but I asked Rosa to introduce her to one of our female youth leaders. I was praying and waiting for the right time to talk to Rev. Edward about Kathy. Talking to the senior pastor about someone you were interested in was like a tradition in our church. Those who liked another person would first start to pray for that person for a while, if necessary fast, and after at least two or three months, if they still felt that the leading was from God, they needed to share it with the senior pastor. He would pray with them, too, for a while, and if he felt the same vibe (at least in some important areas), he would then talk to the other person, whether the initiator was a guy or a girl.

To be honest, I wasn't yet 100 percent sure if the feelings I had for her were prompted by God. Since I was in the publishing industry, I began to search for some good books on dating, relationships, and marriage. According to Rev. Edward, after the salvation, marriage was the most important decision a Christian could make. And as far as I remember, he also said that after the Bible, books on relationships and communication were the most important books for Christians to read. So I began to expand my horizons.

One day, before I reached a solid conclusion about my feelings, she called me and said she had to go back to Gorgan because her Grandma had passed away. She wanted to see me before she left. It wasn't safe to meet outside, so I asked her to come to our place. She did. My mother was at the kitchen when she sat down and began to talk.

"I needed to see you before I leave." She seemed a little anxious.

"Sorry about your grandma. I know you loved her so much. But I'm glad you'll get the chance to see your family soon." I said.

"That's why I wanted to see you, Bijan! This might be the last time we see each other!" she said.

"What do you mean by 'last time'? What's happened?! Why do you say so?" I wasn't expecting that.

"My dad called me yesterday. Since I quit the university and my expenses in Tehran are too much for him, he said it was better for me to go back to Gorgan and stay with the family." She sounded very disturbed.

"Well, I understand why your dad has asked you to go back. From his point of view, it is the best option for you and for them. But I don't think it's a serious thing. If God wants you to live here in Tehran, He will make a way." I said that with confidence, but she didn't agree.

"You don't understand! When my dad says I need to go back and stay with them, it means going back and staying for good!"

"Kathy, I do understand, but you need to respect your parents. Again, I'm sure if it's God's will for you to be back in Tehran, you will be back again in no time. You're just going back for your Grandma's funeral. Plus we can pray about this. I'll ask Rosa to join us in prayer." I knew she wanted to hear something else from me, but I couldn't tell her anything before I was really sure. Plus, I thought that by going back to Gorgan she would be able to solve some of her issues with her mom. I was thinking about her family and the opportunity she would have to share about her faith.

She picked up her purse and put it on her lap; then turned to me and said, "I think I made a mistake in coming here. Obviously you don't care much about what happens to me if I go back to Gorgan! I better go now." She seemed mad at me. I never understood why women got angry in such situations. I did later, though.

"Kathy, please! I do care...I mean, it's important to me, too, but you need to learn to see things in a different light now. Sometimes what we consider as the worst turns out to be the best. I just need you to know that God is aware of your situation and of your heart. He won't let you down. Perhaps there's a good in this." I tried to encourage her.

"I don't understand why God wants me to do something so stressful. I just do not want it. Honestly, if I go back to Gorgan, I will kill myself. I really will!" This time it was her who made me mad!

"Now you speak illogically. You will never kill yourself." I thought it was good to remind her of how well she was doing in her life after she came to know Jesus, so I said, "You just came out of a very stressful situation. You came out of an abusive relationship. You found God. You have peace and joy. And it's just the beginning of a new life for you. You think I liked it when I first began to think about coming back to Iran from Japan? No, I hated it. But when I asked Him about what the best was for me, He told me, 'Iran!' And look at me now; I'm an instrument in His hands to help people know their true Creator and reconcile with Him. I got the chance to be who I was created to be. I'm doing all the things I always dreamed of—making music, writing and translating, being useful to my society. I thank Him for making me come back. I'm glad to have so many good friends, including you. So take this chance and turn it into something wonderful."

"It's impossible. I know my family. They will laugh at me and make fun of me if I tell them about Jesus. I even hate to think about it. Anyway, I need to go now. I haven't packed yet. Thanks for everything." She got up and went to the door without even saying goodbye to me or my mom.

"Are you mad at me?" I asked her gently.

"No, I just need to go now. Maybe I expected something else!" she said, and then she left.

I knew what she was expecting, but I couldn't tell her about my feelings yet. That was why I was planning to meet with Rev. Edward. She was so defensive that I didn't even feel comfortable to pray with her. I learned that day how stubborn she could be in such situations. Her emotional behavior was the main reason I had not yet made up my mind about her.

She left for Gorgan the day after. The same day, I asked Rev. Edward if I could meet him. He was always kind to me. Sometimes I felt like he thought of me as a rebel in our church, but I guess deep inside he knew I was trying to create a new wineskin for the new wine. I was judged by many for my clothing style, music style, approaching style, and evangelizing style. I was even considered a danger for the church through publishing Christian literature outside of the church. Few years later others follow my footstep and began to publish Christian books outside the church. Rev. Edward never let me down. As soon as I asked him for an appointment, he agreed to see me without even asking for the reason.

Considering the amount of work I was doing in and out of church, I needed some advice for my own calling, too. I was involved in many services just because I didn't have the boldness to say "No" to anyone. Whenever people asked me to help them in their ministry, I would say "Yes." So besides my interest in Kathy, there were also other things regarding my ministry that I needed to talk to Rev. Edward about.

He invited me to his place. We spent a very good quality time. He helped me understand what Jesus meant by saying that our yes should be yes and our no should be no. One aspect he shared with me was to learn how to say "No" to different ministries inside the church. I was doing whatever I could for all different parts of our church, from kid's ministry to youth and young adults, from healing ministry to training new believers, from music and worship to dubbing movies, and from translating Christian literature to cleaning the church. But I needed to stop saying "Yes" to everyone; I was burned out. Rev. Edward helped me draw a line and pick only the services I felt were closer to my call.

The next subject we talked about was Kathy. When I told him about this certain girl in the church, he jumped in and said, "I think I know who you're talking about."

I was surprised, "Really? How come?"

He said, "I guess you are talking about the girl who always sits right in front of the pulpit in the third or fourth row from the back! Am I right?"

"Yes," I said, "That's her!"

"But I don't remember her name," he continued, "I guess Sister Rosa introduced her to me few weeks ago!"

"Oh, I see. Her name is Kathy, and she's from Gorgan."

"Yes, Kathy. Is she from Gorgan? That's the city brother Haik was sent to for the first time as a pastor!" He said.

"Really? Interesting! I didn't know that," I said, while thinking whether it was a sign of confirmation or otherwise. I was still looking for signs in everything. Since then, I have learned that too much sign reading can turn into a spiritual sickness because it can take away your logic and your will power and put you in a very uncomfortable situation during the process of decision making. Fortunately, I'm not into the signs anymore, except in rare cases. Now I directly talk to God and make my decisions not based on just signs but based on His direct guidance.

Rev. Edward then told me that I was one of those he was always concerned about regarding marriage, but since I was a little bit different in character, behavior, and style it was difficult for him to find a match for me. We both laughed. He then asked me to tell him what I was thinking about her. I did. He asked me to give him a week or so to pray about us. I agreed.

Three days later, she called me. She sounded anxious, stressful, and sad. She told me that she was so depressed that she really wanted to kill herself because she couldn't take it anymore. I asked her if anything bad had happened. She said that everything was bad. I asked her to be patient, but she just cried.

After we finished talking on the phone, I called Rev. Edward and told him about Kathy's decision to harm herself and how desperate she sounded. He asked me to keep praying for her and said he was doing the same. I asked him, "Do you think it could help if I tell her about my feelings?"

He wasn't in favor of the idea and told me it was not the right time, yet. He believed she had to deal with this problem according to her faith. He said, "She needs to pass this test by herself."

I agreed, but my heart was telling me to call her and tell her how I felt. The Bible says, *"The heart is deceitful above all things ... who can know it?"* (Jeremiah 17:9). I ignored my pastor's advice and listened to my heart.

Perhaps Happily Ever After

IT WAS A WARM, MID-SUMMER day of 1996; we both were excited and nervous at the same time. It was almost a year and a half after we had first met. It was our wedding day!

Wedding days are always the most stressful days for the couples. You can't sleep the night before and have to get up early in the morning and run all day long. The car, the flowers, the church decoration, the wedding dresses, the after wedding party, the food, and the photographer are the easiest parts. It's the small problems that drive you crazy, especially when there is no wedding planner and you have to do all the things by yourself.

After I called her that day and told her how I felt, she managed to be back in Tehran after a week. She later told me that she couldn't hide her joy during the mourning days for her Grandma and that everybody had noticed her unusual, indescribable happiness. Her friends were the first to know about us. She somehow managed to convince her parents to let her go back to Tehran, provided she made a decision to go back to university. It was the most important thing for them, boasting about the fact that she was a university student. Entering university was the toughest challenge of the youth in Iran, and at the same time, it was the most prestigious success you could achieve in your young age! I never knew why! Maybe it was because the number of applicants in those days was ten times more than the capacity of all universities and because, in order to be accepted, you had to pass a very difficult exam.

When she was back in Tehran, we went to Rev. Edward, and we prayed together. Rev. Edward seemed to be a little bit upset, but didn't say anything. We'd been dating for about six months when she was baptized and officially joined the Assemblies. We had our difficult times, like any other couple. She seemed to be content and happy with our relationship, and we began to plan our wedding. She was a little bit worried about our finances since I wasn't officially working, even though I was paid very well for my translation job. I didn't have much savings. My youngest sister was also engaged, and they were planning their wedding for mid-spring. Ours was planned to be in mid-summer.

Canada had finally accepted my parents as immigrants, and they were supposed to fly to Toronto right after our wedding day. My father, who had sold whatever was left from our small amount of possessions, gave me and my sister an equal portion of what he had. It helped us a lot. It was enough for the rent of a decent apartment for at least a year. With my income from my books, we were able to live a good life.

We started our life as a married couple in the summer of 1996.

My income from the translation job was enough for a relatively good life, so I asked Kathy to continue her studies in whatever course she liked. I did not care if she worked or not; I was confident that I would be able to manage our lives. I wasn't concerned about other things that the older generation of men were concerned about regarding their wives. Many of them wanted their wives to stay at home, clean the house, cook for them, sleep with them, and give birth to a boy. The new generation of men, on the other hand, thought it was necessary for women to be socially active.

After I went to Gorgan to ask her dad for her hand in marriage, I learned a lot about her family. Her mom was one of the nicest women I had ever met. She was reasonable, kind, a professional cook, a book reader, and a well-educated woman who had sacrificed her own career for the sake of the family. She had studied nursing, but since her husband was a doctor, she decided to stay home and take care of her step-son. Kathy's dad had been married once before and had a son from his previous marriage. This son had just graduated as a family physician, and he was the pride of his father. Kathy was their first and only daughter, and Mazi was their last and youngest son from the second marriage.

Kathy was daddy's girl. She always got whatever she wanted. Her mom didn't like her husband's attitude; Kathy wasn't supposed to get whatever she wanted. If she didn't get what she wanted from her mom, she would go to her dad, and by making up a false story about bad behavior from her mom, she took revenge. That was her style, as her mom told me months later when we got closer. It sounds cute if you picture a little girl doing that, but when you actually see that behavior in an adult, it doesn't look cute anymore; it is rather scary.

At the beginning, her dad didn't like me much; I was the one who had taken away his little girl from him! Kathy was showing more attention to me than to him when we were together. Plus, his wife, Kathy's mom, had become one of my fanatic fans! She liked me very much and was very proud to have me as their future son-in-law. During the time we spent in their town, I managed to find common ground with her dad, too. He liked to talk about politics and watch action movies. I didn't like the first, but I was a fan of the second. So to make him happy, I got him action-packed movies as gifts, starring Arnold Schwarzenegger, Jean Claude Van Damme, and Sylvester Stallone. He was a very emotional person too, easy to cry, easy to laugh, but also easy to anger.

That was the main problem in the family. Everyone except Kathy's mom was always angry about something at least once or twice a day—and over the silliest things you could imagine. I'm not exaggerating. In my successive trips to their town, while spending time with them, I never passed a day without hearing them yell at each other or use inappropriate language. There was always something to fight over. Kathy's mom was the only one who was calm and had to put up with everyone else, especially her husband. He had diabetes, and he had to inject insulin at least twice a day. Unfortunately, he had learned how to have his own way and get things he wanted by using his illness. It was no wonder Kathy behaved the same way. Sometimes I felt a deep empathy with Kathy's mom. To me, she was an admirable woman, and she was nothing like what Kathy had pictured for me, but I wasn't allowed to say anything in her defense in front of Kathy. I just prayed for their relationship to be healed.

As far as I could tell, the problem was in Kathy's view of her mom, not in something her mom had done to her. It was more like she looked at her as a rival in her relationship with her dad. So, whatever her mom did, every word she said, and every thought she had were considered by Kathy as a plot against her relationship with her father. And since she strongly felt she had to fight with this evil (figuratively speaking), she had to be prepared by constantly planning against her mom's behavior. Being suspicious can turn into a horrible psychological illness.

Every vacation, every holiday, and even some weekends, we were asked to be with them. They had a summer beach house that was only a two-hour drive from Tehran, and we usually spent most of the holidays there. I began to get closer to the family. A few months passed, and I noticed that they truly loved and respected me as their own son. Her dad's only concern was his social reputation and the possible troubles my beliefs could cause for him.

One year passed. During this period of time, I witnessed an odd behavioral pattern in Kathy that began to confuse and scare me. I remember once, after a beautiful worship service, everybody came to me and shared how God had touched their hearts through the music. She didn't like when people circled around me and gave me complements. But I wasn't aware of it in those early days of our marriage. When I learned about it, I began to keep her close to me right after the concerts so that she could feel that the success was ours both. I had to constantly remind her that all I was achieving was because of God's grace and her support. That night when we were on our way back home, I took a short cut to avoid the traffic. The road was under construction. There were no houses or shops around the area for miles. I noticed that she was holding to the handle of the door. She looked nervous. When I asked her if she was OK, she hysterically said, "Where are you taking me?" She sounded both angry and frightened.

I laughed and teased her, "I'm not taking you to any bad place, and you know that!"

This time she screamed, "'Where are you taking me?' I said!" she was shaking.

"Honey, it's just a shortcut. We will be home in few minutes!" I was shocked at her tone.

She moved closer to the door. That was the first time I was really frightened being with her. I thought, *What if she opens the door and jumps out?* I gently asked her to be calm and then slowly reduced the speed. All of a sudden she began to scream again, "Are you going to kill me? Are you?"

She wasn't joking.

We were not far from our home, but I decided to slowly turn around and go back to the main street. I told her what I was about to do, and she said, "Please, take me home, I beg you."

We got home about an hour later. It was late, and she went to bed immediately. I stayed up and aimlessly tried to figure out what had just happened. The next morning, when I asked her if she was alright, she hugged me and kissed me and then said, "Why not honey? Whoever has a wonderful husband like you is the luckiest girl in the whole world."

Whenever we were in Gorgan to visit her family, things like that happened, some as scary as the one I just mentioned, some milder. A number of other odd behaviors happened whenever she saw her dad or mom talking with me. I guess she always thought we were talking behind her back. The funny thing was that she kept insisting that I needed to have a better relationship with her family because, in her opinion, they didn't like me as much as she wanted.

My responsibilities at church were getting heavier, especially after I decided to be more focused on what I was best at—music, literature, teaching, and training. My name was added to the list of candidates for the upcoming deacon election. I was proud that I could get there in four years. Most people who were listed as candidates for such a promotion at the Assemblies had been serving at church for at least a decade. Pastor Vartan asked me to take more official responsibilities at church.

As a youth pastor and the Director of Discipleship Training, I had to be in touch with many young people. I had to meet with them, encourage them, pray with them, and give them counseling—whether it was a theological problem, love story or a family issue. Kathy asked me to decrease my hours of service at church and find a second job with a higher salary even though my translation job and book publishing was making more than enough for us to live on.

One day my former boss (at the airplane selling company) called me and asked me to help him with the new company he was starting. It was a great opportunity to rebuild my career. I talked to Kathy about it, and she loved the idea; we considered it a gift from God. But I knew accepting that job would mean I had to spend more time out of the home. I shared it with Kathy, and she admitted that, if we wanted a better life (financially), we both needed to make some sacrifices.

Since our financial situation was getting better, I encouraged her to go back to university, as she had promised her parents, and she agreed to do her best to pass the big exam. At the same time, she suggested that, since we were trying to make a better life, she could try to find an office job somewhere. She said she didn't feel good about seeing me work until late at night to manage our lives. I assured her that it was OK for me, and I asked her not to be worry about anything, but to focus on preparing herself for the big university exam.

A couple months later, she was accepted into the Spanish Literature program, and we celebrated it together with a romantic dinner and after-dinner fun. I gave her the perfume she loved. We had a great night. We were up until 3 a.m. fooling around playfully. I told her how much I loved her before we went to bed. While playing with her long brown hair, I thought to myself, *"What else can I do to make her happy?!"* She turned her back to me and put my arms around her chest. We both felt lucky and happy.

A week later, while she was gone for her university registration, I finished my meetings early and ran home to prepare another memorable night by cleaning up the house and cooking before she was back. She got back home an hour earlier than I expected, before I had finished cleaning. She was very picky about dirt, like Monica in the TV series, *Friends.*

She took a look around, and without saying hi or being surprised that I was at home so early, she went to the bathroom. After two to three minutes, she came out. She walked toward me, and without any warning, she began to angrily beat me like crazy! I could feel her hatred through her nails under my arm's skin and chest. She kept smacking me on my head and scratching my arm with her fiery fists and claws, screaming at me, "I hate you! You disgust me! I hate you! I wish you dead! Die, die!"

I was so caught off guard that I couldn't make any move in the first few seconds. My arm was all bloody, and my head was spinning around under her fists. After about ten seconds, I came to my senses, got up, and ran to the kitchen like a scared poppy who didn't know why his owner was beating him. She stood there, shaking and swearing at me. I couldn't believe my eyes and ears.

Finally I opened my mouth and said, "Honey, it's OK; it's alright. I'm sorry. I'm sorry. Please just tell me what happened. What did I do wrong? I just wanted to clean up the house and cook for us tonight. I wasn't expecting you this early. I'll clean up everything, I promise."

She looked at me with eyes wide open for few seconds and stared at my bloody arm. Then she ran to the bedroom and slammed the door behind her. I kept staring at the door for quite a while. When I finally sat down again, with my head in my hands, wondering what had just happened, she came out, walked toward me gently, knelt by my side, held on to my bloody arm, and wept softly. I cried too, holding her head upon my chest.

"Let's start all over again, a new beginning," she said.

I wasn't able to say a word. I was just so frightened.

The next morning, after taking a shower, I went back to the bedroom to get dressed. She looked at me with surprise and said, "Oh my God, what's happened to your arm? What did you do to yourself?"

"Oh, you mean the scratches?" I replied. "They're just scratches. A kitty catty did it to me last night!" I thought I was teasing her. But she didn't look teased. She looked at me with unbelief. As she began to walk toward the bathroom to take a shower, she said, "What kitty catty? You can't fool me. Were you playing with yourself?" and then she laughed sarcastically.

She really did not remember what had happened the night before.

Rejection

BECOMING FAMOUS AND POPULAR WAS a good thing, but as a Christian it was also risky.

I was getting prepared for another concert, and I needed to be careful about my identity. I had been using a nickname for almost five years, but I had a feeling that a confrontation was almost inevitable. Using a pen name on my books did not cause any problems, but to get further permission for releasing a CD or for having concerts, I had to personally go to the Ministry and sign some papers with my real name. To the Western mind, getting permission from a government office to release a song or have a concert, or even publish a book, may sound ridiculous. In Iran, every song, poem, or book has to be examined by the Ministry, and only those found "harmless" by the Islamic standards will get permission to be publically published or distributed. Believe me.

Many talented people had to escape Iran in order to continue their career. Many writers, singers, and movie stars left Iran. I personally know many talented musicians who went underground. They recorded and distributed their work on their own. A few of them are very popular right now, but unfortunately, they cannot sell their music publically, and it's obvious why.

In my case, most of the books I got permission to publish were categorized by the Ministry as a positive thinking series. Even the first book I wrote, *Dew of Faith,* was categorized as Islamic Ethics, while it dealt with Christianity and was filled with quotes from the Psalms and the New Testament. I was very surprised when I got the permission for it. Maybe it touched the heart of the person who was in charge of reading and rating it. Or maybe God closed the person's eyes to the Christian elements in the book.

A newer generation of musicians had immigrated to North America or Europe because of the censorship, people such as Kaveh Yaghmaei, Shahkar Bineshpajoh, Shadmehr Aghili, Mohsen Namjoo, and many others who used to publicly hold concerts in Iran.

I had previously thought I would be able to make it, but as a Christian, it became obvious that I would not be able to continue using a nick name for a long time. Even non-Christians had difficulty getting the permission for their works. In fact, around that time, the Ministry rejected me when I applied for further concerts. I had to find someone else to sing my songs; I could play and sing backup vocals, but not as the front man. There was a young man in our church who had been rejected by the leaders at the Assemblies to sing in some of our concerts because of his long hair as I mentioned before. He was a bit disappointed by the decision, and since we were friends and familiar with each other's music styles, I said to myself, *Why not giving him a chance in the band?* At church, he was known as Yuna. In my opinion, he was a rising star with a great look and a very warm and smooth voice, much better than mine. So the decision was made, and he agreed to be the lead singer. We went to the Ministry, and based on his looks and his voice and the fact that he was not yet known as a Christian, we got the permission for live performances. So we began to practice.

At the same time, some of the church leaders were not happy about my evangelistic activities outside the church, such as concerts, publishing, writing in newspapers, and so forth. I tried my best to help them understand that what I was doing was the new wineskin Jesus was referring to in His Word, but as He said in Luke 5:39 "And no one, having drunk old wine, immediately desires new; for he says, 'The old is better'" (NKJV).

Kathy was already going to university, and her uncle had offered her a job to help her build better social communication skills. He had talked to one of his friends, who had recently started a company, and he agreed to hire Kathy as his secretary.

One of the reasons she didn't want me to be involved in church ministry was that she was afraid something would happen to her dad because of my evangelistic activities (it was ironic that her dad's name was Bijan, too), but I wasn't sure if that was her main concern. Things were quickly becoming more complicated since Kathy had begun to go to university and work at the same time. She didn't respect me or my opinions anymore. Whenever we had to make a financial decision, she quoted her boss or her instructor at university as people with better understanding than me. What I thought wasn't important to her anymore.

A few months later, I found out that she had been hiding her money from me, even though I had never asked her about her salary. She had changed her bank and separated our mutual account. It was then that I remembered what she had said in one of our pre-marriage hot arguments. That day, after a discussion about how to save money by investing some of our future savings in the shaky business market in Iran, she very aggressively said, "If I had enough money, I would never get married." I didn't take her words seriously; whenever she was upset, she would say things that she later referred to as mere jokes.

In those days, I had already begun to work with my old boss again, but this time we weren't selling airplanes. The authorities had forced him to sell the company to them or at least give them 51 percent of the shares, but he refused. So the Government found another way to bring him down; they approached the lay retired authorities or even smugglers in the former Soviet Union in order to directly buy whatever they wanted. They were successful; they took the business into their own hands. Right now in Iran, almost 60 percent of small cargo or passenger airlines are using Russian airplanes like the Topolov and Antonov.

As a result, my boss shut down the company and came up with another mind-blowing idea. The new company's plan was to sell materials made out of plastic or glass, materials with a high density that were being produced in secret labs in Russia. This technology wasn't yet out publically. And he was the first one who had the guts to make such a risk. These condense plastic or glass materials could be used in many different industries, from building airplane bodies to bulletproof vests! He was even discussing buying a camouflage material that could make you almost invisible out in nature (it could be used in the military). This wasn't a new thing in the West, but it was new for the Iranian Military. Of course, these materials were not the only things they'd been in negotiation for. I didn't get into this business much, because he put me back in charge of some other responsibilities that were still in connection with what I used to do in MKR. However, this time my job was to get work permission for Russian pilots and crews. It wasn't as exciting as my old responsibilities, but the salary was very good, and I didn't have to work as much as before.

I used to come home early at least twice a week to surprise Kathy with cooking and flowers. I guess, based on my schedules, she knew what days of the week I would do that. She began to come home late. One night, she didn't show up at all, and I waited for her until 9 p.m. The food went cold. She didn't answer my calls at work, and finally when she showed up, she pretended to be tired and went straight to bed.

After few minutes of wrestling with my thoughts, I went to bed and laid down beside her, but she moved away from me and harshly said, "I told you I'm tired. Don't you understand?!"

"I understand, honey. I just want to lie down beside you." I continued, "In the last couple of weeks, we haven't even had a simple conversation with each other. I'm just concerned. You seem to be tired all the time."

She said, "I'm not in the mood for a talk. Do you mind going back to the living room? I just want to sleep, alone!"

That wasn't the Kathy I knew. Our sex life was very exciting and we both enjoyed the gift of intimacy very much but only the first few months after our wedding; things changed as her behavior changed. My man-brain wasn't able to analyze her behavior. I didn't want to even think about what might have been going on in her work place, but her constant quotations from her boss (who was also the founder of the company) made me uneasy. I went back to the living room to avoid an unnecessary fight.

I poured a glass of wine and drank it all up. The next morning, I woke up on the couch. She was gone, and I was late for work.

This pattern continued for a month or two. I had a big concert ahead at church and another one in Shafagh Cultural Centre in Tehran in a couple of weeks afterward. She didn't seem to care. All she was doing was complaining about our need for a luxurious car and a bigger place. In fact she had already been complaining about church stuff, about the leaders (she called them pretentious) and about Christianity in general. I could understand her dreams as a woman, especially being the only daughter of a rich family. She had already begun to despise my parents as irresponsible parents who had never thought about the future of their children, even though she knew we had lost everything we had to some greedy people in the government. The money they had lost was between $300,000 and $400,000. She knew it was taken by the government.

Her arguments and accusations were absurd. I was unable to understand why she was behaving that way. I had recently learned through a mutual friend that most of the nights when she came home very late it was because she was actually with some of her unmarried friends watching movies. However, she was always against me staying out late with my old friends; she considered that a kind of cheating! I also knew some of her female relatives (unmannered middle-aged women) had been recently talking to her on the phone. I never liked their lousy behaviors.

The company she was working for was an import-export company. I never figured out what they imported or exported. When I eventually asked her about the nature of her job, she replied with anger that it wasn't my business to ask her about that. I was surprised at her response, but as always, I didn't want to get into fight with her. But as our relationship got tenser in every area, fights became inevitable.

Once, out of curiosity, I went to her work place in the middle of the day. She also used to make unexpected visits to my work place to check on me. But she got angry at me for doing that. She thought it was right for women to check on their husbands at work, but that if a man did that it meant he already pictured his wife with another man. What a logic! That night when she got home, she accused me of disgracing her in front of her boss. She believed I had destroyed her reputation and that I had proved what mindset I had toward her! I was sure they were not her own thoughts; somebody had injected those ideas into her brain.

Apparently, something (or someone) was pulling her away from me. I do know that in our second year of marriage I was too busy, both in ministry and my career. But there wasn't even one night that I missed a dinner. We used to talk on the phone up to five times a day. But since she had expanded her network, she gradually walked away from me. She began to feel she didn't need me anymore and that she was a modern woman now. Maybe she began to think she was too good for me. She used to be proud of me, but now she was avoiding me. She was even reluctant to introduce me to her new friends and co-workers. Among her relatives, there were other men who had the same problem with their wives. I guess it was epidemic in her family! As far as I remember, none of them were old fashion men. We all belonged to the new generation of young, responsible, and understanding men—growing to be more flexible and sensitive to women and their needs. We all studied many books on relationships. But none of our wives liked to do that, just because they thought it was the men who had to change! It was sad. We were all taking care of our families with at least two jobs.

We all believed in women as equals, despite what many North Americans or Europeans think of Iranian men. In the new generation of Iranian couples, men are much more attentive to their wives and encourage them to expand their social networks. What you usually hear on media in the West is not exactly what is happening among the new generation of married couples. What the media wants you to hear is only one side of the story, and it's just about women suffering under the tyranny of the fanatic, uneducated, traditional Muslim men who have an unsatisfied lust for sex. This is not the truth. Like everywhere else in the world, like North America, Europe, Russia, Africa or South East Asia, and like almost every other town, city or country in the world, there are cases in Iran too in which women are abused by men. But at the same time, there are many stories in the West where fathers or brothers rape their daughters or sisters and chain them in their basements for years. In some cases, they have even had children with their own daughters or sisters!

To think that all men in Iran are the same is as nonsensical as if Iranians thought all men in North America or Europe are like those fathers who rape their own daughters. These kind of news stories are like food for the media. Of course, I'm not here talking about the political freedom or the democracy that we don't have in Iran or the unfair arrests and the tortures in prisons, which are crimes against all Iranians and not just women. I'm just trying to correct a misled public opinion in the West regarding how miserable all women in Iran are. If you look at some of the pictures and articles on the internet about Iranian girls (or Persian girls), you will see how well-dressed, fashionable, competitive, and feminist they are. In fact, I believe that, by saying these words, despite any accusations of some short-minded critics, I'm not degrading women's position in Iran, but I'm upgrading their role in my so-called third world country. And I hereby declare that the role of the women in recent scores against the Islamic regime, through demonstrations and the sacrifices they made, is far greater than what we know now. This is not something I just came to understand during the recent demonstrations against the Islamic regime. This is what I have always believed about Iranian women.

In days of Khatami administration, I translated and published a book about the most successful women in the world. After finishing the work, I asked a publisher to help me publish it. He did. The book was called *Our Power As Women; The Wisdom and Strategies of Highly Successful Women* by Helene Lerner (Berkeley: Conari Press, 1996). This book was a selection of advices from successful women, such as Beverley Sills, Gloria Steinem, Patricia Ireland, and Paula Zhan. The book was published and sold out immediately. I have always been proud of Iranian women and wanted to contribute to their remarkable role in elevating the Iranian culture in Iran and around the world.

But during my own marriage, I carried a frustration within. None of the books that I had written or translated and none of the articles that I'd written in any magazine or newspaper had been read by Kathy. Her reasoning was, "I already know you, and I know what kind of opinions you have. Why would I bother to read them in a book?"

She used the same reasoning for not coming to my concerts, too. On one occasion, she even told me that she was embarrassed to admit that I was her husband because there were only 500 people in the Cultural Centre at the time of concert. To her, it was a disgrace that only 500 people came to our performance. She was especially embarrassed because I had personally invited her colleagues and boss. After that night, she stopped coming to my concerts. She had already stopped coming to church long before that night.

While I had magazine interviews and recognition in society, my own wife hated me more and more until she almost stopped talking to me. It was a very uncomfortable situation. I had to leave her notes on the dining table or refrigerator in hopes that she would read them.

I had been praying for us and was thinking of taking our problems to our pastors. She always hated the idea. I didn't know what to do, especially after the night when she beat me hard and forgot about the whole thing the next morning. To be honest with you, I was afraid of her. Before she had stopped talking to me, she would have fights over the slightest things with me. It was unbearable. And everything was getting worse.

One day, we were having a Bible study in our place. There were about 20 of us. I used to encourage the youth to read more books on different subjects like poetry, literature, and postmodern arts. I used our Bible studies to talk about modern philosophies, music, cinema, dating, and many other relative topics that other leaders at our church were reluctant to talk about. I even asked them to read books and articles by atheists so that they wouldn't become religious fanatics. That day we were talking about relationships and the differences between men and women in order to have a better understanding of each other's behavioral patterns. To my surprise, Kathy showed up. She took a chair and sat down with us. She was pale and anxious. She was cold to everyone. I smelled danger, but there was nothing I could do. When it was her turn to comment on the subject (which was about the masks we wear in our daily life, especially regarding dating), she began an attack on everyone, accusing them all of wasting their lives with nonsense. One of the girls asked her what she meant by that.

"What I mean, sweetheart, is to stop making a fool of yourself. You think you are better than everyone else. You all pretend to be loving and kind. It's just a game. Like everything else you do. Even your leaders justify their deeds through white lies! Now you know what I'm talking about."

There was a long silence. But as the group leader, I felt I had to say something before everything got out of hand, so I said, "Well, Kathy, I'm glad you finally joined our exciting conversations. You are partially right. There are many Christians who behave like that, i.e., wearing masks. But isn't that what we all do, whether Christians or not? Wearing masks is a defensive or protective mechanism in all of us. We don't want people to see our weaknesses for we are ashamed of them. But if we begin to communicate and trust each other, little by little we will be able to put our masks aside." I thought that was an opportunity by which I could at least show her that we needed to talk and communicate.

She gave me an angry look and said, "blab blab blab, you're one of them, too! You haven't talked to me for weeks. You don't even come to bed with me anymore! All you care about is church church church. Get out of there, you all!" and she threw the chair aside and went to the bedroom and slammed the door.

Everybody had their heads down, staring at the floor. I didn't know what to do or say. That was exactly what I was afraid of when she showed up. She had lied to my face. It was her who had stopped talking to me long ago. It was her who shut the bedroom door on me. I was so confused! I couldn't understand why she was behaving that way.

I told everybody that she was probably tired from work. And I added that she didn't really mean all that. As I finished saying that, one of the guys said, "To be honest with you, brother Bijan, Kathy called me today and asked if we were going to have a Bible study, and I said, 'Yes, we are, at your home,' and she asked me not to tell you!"

I thought, *So, that was a plan?* I was embarrassed before everyone, and didn't know what to say.

I went to the kitchen and came back with coffee, tea, and some cookies. I announced the session was over and then grabbed my guitar and invited everyone to sing a song with me. That was the only thought that came to my mind to change the atmosphere.

After they left, I knew that they would spread the news. I'm not a person who gets angry easily. So I went to the bedroom door and knocked. I asked her to let me in. She yelled from inside, "Do you want to kill me?" thinking they were still there. I told her to drop the act and come out because they were already gone. She didn't say anything. The door was locked from inside.

I went back to the kitchen to prepare something for dinner, thinking about what she was possibly planning to do!

Three days later, when we had a huge concert in the church, Pastor Vartan, who had been ordained as the new Senior Pastor of the Assemblies, came to me just five minutes before the opening and told me that he needed to talk to me later that week.

I said, "Sure, what about?"

"I didn't want to tell you this now," he said, "but I guess you have some explanation to give about why you haven't been nice to Kathy over the last seven to eight months. She's been coming to our house once or twice a week for the past six months with so many complaints about you. But don't worry; I'll fix you," he laughed, as if it was a joke, and then he ran upstairs to his office to get his notes for the message he was about to share right after the concert.

It was as if I was nailed to the floor for what seemed to be an eternity. I felt like throwing up. There was a storm in my stomach. Something told me that Kathy had been working on a huge plan against me. But why? Six months was a long time. I had been an idiot to think that hiding our problems from the pastors was a good idea. I was still in shock about what the pastor told me when the doors were opened and people began to take their seats. I was still standing there by the stage. I couldn't move.

I finally stepped up onto the stage, grabbed my guitar, smiled to the band, and briefly welcomed the audience. My deep sadness affected the whole program that night. It was the first time after many months that Kathy showed up, sitting in the third row from the stage, right in front of me. That night's performance was the most emotional Christian concert I had ever led. Even the upbeat songs seemed so sad. The ironic thing was that many first-time visitors to our church (Muslims) gave their hearts to Jesus that night. Most of the time during the concert, my eyes were closed to avoid any eye contact with Kathy. But God was using all of that pressure to lead the whole program into a revival. I still have the video of that night. People wept so deeply that the cameraman could not help getting close ups. Every song, for me, was a prayer and a pouring out of my heart to God.

Sometimes when I look back to that night, I ask myself, *Was that night a destined night? Was Vartan destined to say those words right before I went up on stage? Were those who came to the front to dedicate their lives to Jesus already chosen and handpicked for that special night? Were the whole incidents woven together according to what God had planned to happen that night?* Predestination? Perhaps! Or maybe God simply used the whole situation to glorify Himself!

That night, Kathy and I didn't say a word until we went to bed, in separate rooms. It'd been a long time since the last time we had had any sexual intimacy. The last time I had insisted on having sex, she kicked me (literally) out of bed and threw me out of our bedroom!

I couldn't stop wondering why she had been visiting the pastor and his wife for the last six months, while she had always been telling me not to do that. She would tell me that when a third party comes into the picture, it would bring suspicion and, in some cases, favoritism, and they both could damage the marriage. I agreed with her to a degree, but after our problems got out of hand, many times I asked her to let me talk to Pastor Vartan, but she aggressively disagreed. I never complained to anyone or shared what was going on between us. I didn't want her to think I was doing something behind her back.

But apparently she was plotting against me. I couldn't believe she had done that. Within the next few days, I found out that she had been visiting my sister (who she hated), my uncles and other relatives, and many of our mutual friends, as well, telling them unbelievable stories about how badly I was treating her. Most of the nights that she came back home late, she had been sowing seeds of doubt and hatred in peoples' hearts and minds against me, even in the hearts of our pastors and some other leaders of the church. I was just entering a game I had already lost.

People changed. Even my sister and her husband began to complain about how badly I was treating Kathy. They were all brainwashed. One morning I went to my uncle's place in order to give him a device my father had sent for him from Canada as a gift. My uncle was surprised when he saw me and asked if I had seen Kathy on the way. Then he said, "She left just minutes before you got here!" No wonder my uncle began to gently rebuke me for the way I was treating her. My goodness, I couldn't believe my ears. She had told him stories that had never happened or stories that had happened, but in which I was the victim, not her.

I was completely confused and of course angry. I could not find a single reason for what she was doing. God knows how many times I tried to have a conversation with her, but either she went to our bedroom and locked the door, or she threw things at me, hit me with something, or bombarded me with words I'm ashamed to mention here.

The only thing hindering me from taking any other action, except waiting and praying, was that most of the time she did not remember what she had said or done to me (or she pretended not to remember). This pattern had been regularly repeated until I found out that she was talking behind my back all this time. Now I needed to take action.

One day, when I finally showed some boldness, faced her, and told her I knew what she was doing, she couldn't hide her smile and said, "You can't do anything about it now. It's too late. You've already lost the game. You should admit I'm smarter than you. The only one left on your side is your dear brother Edward. He is the only one still defending you, and I promise he will be on my side before you can do anything about it!"

Why was she doing this to us? What had I done to deserve this? Was she really serious about what she just said? Was she revenging me for something I didn't know about? Was she going through some psychological breakdown? Was she hallucinating or delusional? Was the whole thing just a game to her, a game of *who is smarter*? Or perhaps she was planning something I wasn't able to understand at all. She was planning to win, but win what?

Pastor Vartan asked us to have a meeting with him, together with Bishop Edward, who knew me better than Vartan or even better than Kathy. We went to his office at the Assemblies. Kathy came separately. We sat down, and we prayed a while with Vartan and Edward. Kathy did not pray with us. She was defensive from the first moment. Vartan then began to address me, "Bijan, we are here to see what kind of assistance we can give you both, individually and as a couple. Kathy has been visiting me and my wife for the past six months and has shared with us stories that we couldn't believe at first, but as they continued to happen over and over again, we felt we need to do something about it. The reason I didn't intervene for a while was that I trusted you as a leader and a teacher who lives what he teaches, but we have heard stories from Kathy that left us no doubt that now it's time for us to step in and talk to you! And, we are here," he continued, "to know what exactly is going on. I say this in front of Kathy; I don't think your problems are too difficult for God to solve. In fact, there is nothing impossible for God."

Bishop Edward came in, "Amen, and I too believe that if you two put more time and energy and love into this, in no time you'll be back to your good days, even better days."

Vartan addressed Kathy, "Don't you agree, Kathy?"

"Only if he changes his behavior and loves me again," she said, "instead of hating me!"

"Why are you saying this, Kathy," I turned to her and asked in shock! But she didn't even look at me. Something in me wanted to shout out loud and tell everyone that she was playing us all, but still, there was another stronger force within me which prevented me from doing that. I truly wanted to know her motives for going through all these troubles.

We sat there for about two hours. All she told the pastors was either a lie or a mixture of different occasions in different timeframes. I was sitting there looking down, eating myself from within until I couldn't bear it anymore and burst into a soundless weeping.

"Come on," Kathy said, "stop playing games, Bijan. These are old tricks; I've already warned Brother Vartan about this; crocodile tears!

I wanted to smash everything around me, break the windows, and throw myself out when she said that. I was mad at God for wanting me to stay humble and offer her my other cheek. The only reason I didn't take any harsh action earlier was because I still loved her, and in all my prayers, God had told me to bear with her as Christ suffered for us even when we had turned our back to Him.

But it was like she had been working on her plan for a long time. She had prepared herself for every possible scenario. What would you do if you were in my place? I didn't know whether she was mentally sick or she was cheating on me. I didn't know whether her forgetfulness was a serious illness or a pre-planned plot. Maybe she was planning on a divorce?

Kathy kept saying things that had never happened. When she finished, she turned to me and said, "You can now stop your crocodile tears!"

Bishop Edward turned to her and said, "Dear Kathy, I've been in the ministry for almost forty years now; these tears I see are not crocodile tears. I just need to hear more from Bijan, because we've already heard your side of the story, but Bijan has been silent all the way." Then he turned to me said, "Bijan, would you tell us a little bit about what Kathy is accusing you of? I just feel in my spirit that for some reasons you are not telling us what we need to hear to discern the truth. And if you keep silent, then we have to agree that she's right about everything she has told us!"

I was voiceless. After a long silence I said, "I know I haven't been exactly who I should be for her. I swear that I did all I could to make her happy and keep her happy, but regardless of all my efforts it seems that I'm still short. I have no idea why Kathy is telling you all these stories. I just don't understand what is happening. I'm so confused. Many other couples in our church have gone through the same challenges we've faced. I know this because they have come to me and shared with me. I have given them counseling that has been working in their relationships. And I'm doing the same things I suggested to them to do, but it seems like none of them are working in my own relationship with Kathy! Everything is messed up in my mind. It's like a horrifying nightmare. I have no power or reason to defend myself!"

"Alright, Bijan, I guess we need to make another appointment and dig deeper." Bishop Edward said. "And meanwhile, I like to meet you both individually."

I said, "OK, sure."

Kathy replied, "May I keep seeing Brother Vartan and Sister Anahid?"

"Well, I don't see any reason for you not to see them," Edward replied. "They are your pastors, but still I need to see you individually."

When we were leaving the room, Bishop Edward whispered to me "Bijan, please give me a call tomorrow morning to set an appointment ASAP." I nodded.

I didn't know how to open up to Brother Edward. It's hard to explain something to someone when you personally don't understand it. It's like when Christians try to explain the Trinity to non-Christians, for even the best Christian theologians can't even understand it with the standards of human logic, but they believe in it and know it as a fact.

Anyway, we met again the next day. I told him all that I knew and all my concerns. He told me that he still didn't feel convinced by Kathy's stories and that was why he wanted to see me ASAP. After two hours of conversation in his old office at church, we went out for lunch. During the lunch, he finally overcame his hesitance and asked me if I thought she was cheating on me and looking for a way out by forcing me to divorce her.

I didn't want to think about that option. I said, "No, I don't think so."

Then he asked if I had met her boss. I said I had and that he looked like a nice guy to me. I added, "By the way, he's not her type, I know." I continued, "But I remember last year in one of the meetings at church, there was a discussion going on about marriage, and one of the leaders said something about divorce. That was when Kathy began to behave differently. When we were back at home that night, she asked me about it. It was about the legitimacy of divorce from a biblical point of view, and I told her that divorce was allowed by Jesus under some circumstances.

Then all of a sudden, in my amazement, she said to me, 'Bijan, I just want you to remember that I wasn't the one who said divorce was eligible in Christianity; it was you who said it.' I laughed and said, 'I didn't bring it up; you did. I just answered your question!' Then she just left the room and went to the kitchen to prepare something for dinner. I always remember that night. She seemed happy when she was saying that."

"It's interesting because she has told the same story to Pastor Vartan but with a little twist that it was you who had brought up the divorce argument," Edward said, "and I think there should be a reason she's been insisting on this to Pastor Vartan, even though, to be honest with you, she seems so innocent and sincere in what she's sharing, and it has confused both of us. She even told us you've been drinking and smoking for a long time and that you are almost an alcoholic!"

He looked me in the eyes for a while to read my thoughts.

I scratched my head and said, "I drink sometimes, in family gatherings, but I'm not an alcoholic! I don't know why she said that. She even told me once that she thought it was cool to drink. But regarding smoking, I'm being honest with you. I began to smoke since last month. I was under a heavy pressure. And it's not like what you think; it's only one or two a day. I'm not hiding anything from you, Brother Edward. I'm telling you the truth; I wasn't smoking then. She is just using these things because she knows that the church is sensitive to these things! I know I'm in trouble for smoking, but believe me, she has driven me crazy by her odd behavior and accusations. A few weeks ago my car needed a service. The service man left his cigarette pack in the car. I was frustrated and stressed out. That was the first time I got tempted and smoked again after years of quitting."

"Do you know that it can affect your reputation and the outcome of this case?" he asked.

"Yes. But I'm willing to give up any reputation and all my services at church to fix our relationship," I replied.

"I'm glad to hear that, for then it will be easier for us to deal with the problem." He continued, "We can at least tell other leaders that you are willing to cooperate, even at the cost of your services at church."

"So, by that you mean that other leaders already know about this?" I asked.

"Yes, I'm afraid they do," he replied.

After talking to Bishop Edward, I was more persuaded that she had planned her every step from a long time before, but none of us knew why!

That day was the first day of a series of meetings and appointments on apparently the first unsolvable marriage problem in the history of the Assemblies of God in Iran. The most repeated sentence I heard from all of the leaders during that time was, "If this case would end up in a divorce, the Government will use this against all of us, and the reputation of the church will be questioned by many!" They seemed not to be worried about Kathy and me, but the reputation of the church, and I knew by "church" they meant themselves.

Since then, I had many meetings with the leaders who felt they were able (or anointed) to fix our problem, but all they told me was that smoking and drinking were the cause of all the problems we had. All of a sudden, everybody was against me. I tried to explain to them that it was not about smoking or drinking at all, but they had already made up their minds.

She was smarter than I thought. But I still couldn't figure out why she had gone through all these troubles to present me to them as a monster. She actually told them I was sexually impotent, incapable of performing any sexual intimacy, while it was her who kept kicking me out of bed. So they all, including Bishop Edward, suggested I needed to see a doctor. *Unbelievable!* How could I, as a Christian minister, defend myself against such an accusation in Iran? I finally gave in and saw a doctor; I was totally OK.

In some counseling sessions, they wanted us both to get into some agreements and follow them for at least a week or more and then report to them about the results. In all cases, after we were back at home, she told me she was not going to abide by any of those stupid agreements and if I told them what she had just said, she would simply deny it. I couldn't believe my ears. On one occasion, I told her I wished there was a microphone to record her words. That was the last time she ever spoke to me at home!

Soon after that night, Bishop Edward called me up for a meeting and told me that Kathy was afraid of living with me in the same place and that we needed to live separately for a while. He believed that living separately for a while might fire up the flames of our love again.

I knew what she was thinking; she was afraid of me recording her voice. I told Brother Edward what had happened the other night. But he insisted on his suggestion—living separately for a while.

It took me a while to convince myself about the benefits of the idea. So finally few days before my birthday, I packed my backpack, along with my acoustic guitar and some of my books, and left the apartment. I moved to a friend's basement. He was a young man I had met a while before through one of my recent street evangelizing efforts. His name was Pouyan, and he had just given his heart to Christ. A week or two after I moved in to his place, I invited him (and five other friends whom I had shared the Gospel with) to our church for a Sunday evening service. That night, at the direct command of Pastor Vartan, I was not allowed to enter the church by the ushers. I was told I was excluded, right in front of the friends I had brought to the service.

Pouyan was shocked when he saw that they didn't let me in. He turned to me and said with anger, "I will never go to a church that has excluded you! It was you who led me to Jesus. What kind of church is this?"

Others said the same thing and didn't want to go in.

I smiled and said, "Come on guys, I already told you that there are some issues between me and the pastor which we are working on. I will talk to the pastor later, but meanwhile, you guys go in and enjoy the service; it's an order." Then I laughed, while crying inside.

I asked the usher (Brother Reuben, who is with the Lord now) to let them in. Those days not everybody could bring strangers to the Assemblies because of the Government watch over the church, but he was kind enough to let them in. They all enjoyed the music, but as they told me later, they couldn't believe the message of love Pastor Vartan was preaching, knowing how he had cut me out of the church. It took me a long time to clear their minds of what had happened that night—especially when they went to the front to speak to him about the gift of the Holy Spirit that they had just received the day before when I prayed over them. As they shared their experience, Pastor Vartan confronted them saying, "Who on earth is Bijan to baptize you in the Spirit? He is excluded from the church!"

That was when they got into an argument with him about me, and they never wanted to attend the church again. But thank God for their love and submission to Jesus and to me; they went back to the church.

Many years later, in a conference in Armenia, I met Pastor Vartan and his lovely wife, Sister Anahid (who had been the strongest defender of Kathy). They both embraced me and cried in my arms. Maybe they felt guilty or responsible for the sufferings I went through in those days. I didn't have anything against them in my heart. I just cried with them. Sister Anahid said, "I know what you've been through...I'm sorry!"

Apparently, years after our last contact, they went through a similar rejection by the leaders and elders of the church (for reasons I won't discuss here), which caused them to resign and leave Iran. They too went through lots of hardship. We've been in touch through Facebook ever since we met in Armenia in 2007. May they be under an ever-increasing shower of blessing everywhere they go.

That night, I was rejected from entering my Father's house. I didn't realize, at the moment, that being cut off from your church could push you to the verge of spiritual death if you are not strong enough in your relationship with God, especially if you have nowhere else to go because of the accusations and because of living in an Islamic country. I was forced to go through things that, if I had not been in my right place with God, could have taken me back to the days of committing suicide. But I needed to learn not to put my trust in people—not even in church leaders, for that matter.

Was everything working for my good, as the Bible teaches? Was God a just God? Were the leaders of the church really being led by the Holy Spirit in every decision they made? I began to doubt everything except Jesus Himself. My old friends at church didn't want to see me or be around me, not because they thought I was a bad influence, but because they were afraid of the leaders of the church. In the eyes of the leaders, I was not a sheep anymore; I was a rebellious goat, a disgrace to them, a leper!

It took many painful years for me to deal with those feelings of frustration and rejection. The only friends I had were Pouyan, who I was living with, and the one I will introduce to you soon; I call her Brida.

American Spies

THREE MONTHS AFTER OUR WEDDING, Kathy and I were called to the Ministry of Information (the Iranian Intelligence Service). They never asked Kathy to be present in further interrogations. But they summoned me many more times. It happened around the last days of fall in 1996. In fact it was during the last months of the Rafsanjani administration that the serial murdering of the pastors and many other active politicians and journalists was disclosed publically through newspapers and few brave journalists. When Khatami won the Election in 1997 he started a vast investigation on the topic. It was during the investigations that many active and well-known journalists were also called for an interrogation. I remember that a number of other active Christians (not the main leaders of the church) were also called to the Ministry of Information. We were told by the agents not to tell anyone about the interrogations; otherwise, we would be in trouble.

Kathy's father was also stressed out by fear, both for himself, as an elected representative in the City Council, and for his family. Our home phone was tapped, and through our phone, they also tapped many other numbers_friends, relatives, and the church members. The Ministry of Culture and Guidance had already banned me from singing in my Band. We started the band in 1995 and called it "Green Rise" or, as we say in Farsi, "Tolou e Sabz" and we successfully continued until 1999. In 1995 there wasn't even any talk regarding a Green Wave in politics; it started fourteen years later.

The interrogations differed according to their purpose. In some, there was only one interrogator; in others there were two. Couples were interrogated separately and then again together. Mostly there were two interrogators with names such as Hassani and Husseini (like Smith and Jones here in North America). During the last months of Rafsanjani administration (for some reasons) they tried to treat you more humanely by calling you at home or at your work place, asking you to give them a visit. But if you ignored their calls and decided not to go where they asked you to go, next time they would arrest you, and you would definitely pay some price for ignoring them. In general, in those days, whether they arrested you or called you to be somewhere they asked you to be, they would usually keep you in a cold, dark room for at least two hours to play some mental games on you, to scare you, and to make you picture the worst that could ever happen to you. Then they would send you to another room, usually a very large and empty one where you could even hear the echo of your own heart beat. I've been there many times, and each time the scenario was different.

The first time they summoned us Kathy acted cool and very mature. She was there only once, but was interrogated twice during the four or five hours we were there—once with me present and then separately. She never discussed what they questioned her about in private. During the whole year, they called me at work or at home many more times and asked me again to go to the Ministry and explain more about my activities.

They would always keep me in that dark, cold room again for almost the whole day, and then they'd take me to the huge, empty room. In all cases, whenever I stretched my hand toward them for a handshake, they didn't respond, probably because they thought I was an infidel, an unclean person, according to the Sharia Law, but I kept doing it every time! The first person was always aggressive and kept yelling at me, while the other one tried to calm him down. I knew they were acting, but I didn't tell them I knew that! Once they threw a file on the desk as big as a huge dictionary. They didn't let me take a look at it, but they told me that it was enough to put a rope around my neck. I knew they were bluffing, but I wasn't sure. You could never predict what they would do to you, just like their Government.

From time to time, they would take out a picture of me somewhere in the streets or a paper with numbers on it and showed them to me as evidence. Some of the papers were official documents with a red stamp on them, and others were like hand written reports. They tried to confuse me by asking repeated questions or asking questions at the same time, tossing the papers to each other, yelling, and pounding on the desk. The angry guy even threatened to torture me, "Do you know we can take you down there (pointing to the floor) and get what we want out of you like this (he snapped)?

I smiled gently and nodded, "But believe me, I have nothing to tell you." He got up and leaned over the desk and stared right into my eyes and said, "You have no idea...."

The other one jumped in and gently said, "Brother Hassani, let me talk to him, please."

The same story continued for almost a three years. The last time they asked me to be there was a couple of weeks after I began to live with Pouyan. Three hours into the interrogation, they put a two-page document in front of me, asking me to sign it. I read the whole two pages and crossed out some paragraphs that accused me of endangering the national security. They wanted me to name all of the leaders of the church, leaders of the house churches and the youth groups, as well as the church's foreign connections! They were two different sheets. One was the accusations and the penalties of endangering the national security, and the other one looked like a confession letter. At the end, they wanted me to sign the confession letter right under a paragraph which said something like this, "Hereby, I [my name], willingly and in perfect health denounce my Christian faith. I repent from my sin and embrace Islam and cooperate with the authorities unconditionally in order to reduce my crime of apostasy." It was something like that.

I put the pen down and said, "I'm sorry brothers, but I won't sign this paper under any circumstances for I cannot and will not deny what I have seen and experienced in Christ. He has given me a new life, eternal life, and I'm not exchanging Him for anything in this world." Then I wrote down, "I believe in Jesus Christ" and signed the paper.

The angry guy pounded on the desk again and yelled at me, "Do you know we can keep you here as long as we want?" He repeated again, "We have the tools to make you cooperate, right here, under this room. Did you know that?"

I was about to say, "You would have no power over me if it wasn't given to you by God," but I changed my mind, because it could have been misinterpreted by them. They did believe in God (as Allah). It could have proven to them that they had authority over me since they still (up to this date) believe they are the vessels of God's Judgment on Earth. So I decided to keep silent.

The other guy shook his head in disappointment and told the other one to send me out. He took me to the first room again and left me there. I thought to myself, *"Here I am, Lord. Do as You wish. I'm OK with whatever decision You make. But please don't let me give them what they want. I love You."* Then I began to quietly sing a song.

An hour later, a guard opened the door and said that I could leave. It was a relief for the moment, but then I thought, *Maybe they just don't want to kill me here in the Ministry. Maybe they think I have already told some people where I was going today. Probably they think it is wiser to let me go now and kill me later in an accident.* It was a disturbing thought. For a long time afterward even until I was compelled to leave the country, I sensed and felt the presence of the agents all around me. It was disturbing.

I called Kathy and told her what had happened, just to give her a heads up. She wasn't very excited about it. "Don't worry, nothing will happen to you," she said sarcastically. "God's with you. Don't you believe that?"

———

After few more interrogations by the Ministry of Information, half through the year 1997, when my relationship with Kathy was getting worse, I received another call from Intelligence, but this time it wasn't from the Ministry of Information, but the intelligence department of the Ministry of Foreign Affairs. I was surprised. As usual, I asked the person on the phone to send me a formal letter. He said, "You will be at this address tomorrow morning at 11:00; no other option!" He gave me the address; then he hung up.

It is painful not to have anyone to talk to in times of trouble, but it is more heartbreaking when you are going into a lion's den and you can't even tell anyone about it. Surely Kathy didn't care. I didn't want to worry my sister. She and her husband had their own problems, like any other Iranians. They were both involved in media. If you know a little bit about Iran from the news, you know that even the movie industry is under a huge censorship, and even right now, some of the very well-known film makers and movie stars are in prison for believing in democracy and human rights. I didn't want to add to my sister's worries by telling her I was summoned to an interrogation. Those days things were much better than they are now under Ahmadinejad's. However, the media was always a big target for government attacks.

I knew I couldn't tell Bishop Edward, either. His phone was under control, too. And his house was watched 24/7. I had no one else to talk to, so I just wrote a small note about where I was going that day and left it on my pillow just in case.

The building was located on Villa Street, a central residential area with a population of mostly Armenian Christians (Gregorian). A military guard asked me to sign in at the entrance. The waiting room was cozy and decorated with all the modern furniture and paintings. A man dressed in a military uniform came out to greet me. In rank, he was a major.

He welcomed me with a hand shake and then led me to his office. I was surprised when he did that. I thought, *Doesn't he know I'm a Christian? What's going on in here? Or maybe it's not about my Christian activities! So what else could it be?* He offered me a seat. To me it seemed like it must be a very important situation if it needed to be handled by a major from the Intelligence Department of Ministry of Foreign Affairs. There was a nice, old European coffee table between us.

He introduced himself, just the last name and the rank. Then he asked me to tell him a little bit about myself. The comfortable and friendly atmosphere gave me enough boldness to ask him why I was there. He respectfully asked me to first tell him a little bit about myself. "We will get to that part later," he said, "and if everything goes well, you will be allowed to leave, and if not...we'll see."

His statement scared me. Thousands of thoughts came to my mind. But I had to show no weaknesses; I'd been in that situation before. So I decided to go with the flow until I'd figure out why I was there.

I took my time and, deliberately choosing my words, told him some general things about myself. I told him I was married, where I was working, and what my position was. I mentioned about my music activities and concerts. And I also told him about the books I had translated since I had come back from Japan. He took some notes while I was speaking.

After I spoke for about ten minutes, he asked if there was anything else I thought he would need to know. It would have been naive to imagine he didn't know about my Christian faith. So I said, "And of course, you know I love Christ, and I attend a church. I also like helping young people by giving them advice on life issues."

"I appreciate that," he said. "Now please tell me more about what you do at church. Do you lead a house church? Are you involved in leadership in general?"

I considered myself an intelligent and smart person. One aspect of being smart is not considering an Intelligence officer an idiot!

"I would tell you everything I can, as long as it won't be interfering with someone else's privacy or against my moral standards," I said.

"I'm afraid you have to answer my questions regardless of any privacy matter," he replied, "for it's not only a matter of national security, but your own life as well."

I was shocked when he said that. "Would you please be more specific?" I asked. "If I know what you are looking for, I might be able to help you in a better way."

He looked at his papers and played with them for a while. Then said, "I need you to be very clear and specific on what I'm going to ask you now." His tone of voice worried me more. He continued, "I have a ready to sign paper in my hand which has your name on it. This letter has given me the full authority to issue the final decision on your case and on behalf of two other men, especially considering the other records we have on you. So I need you to be completely honest with me. My superiors have reached an agreement on your case based on the evidence in your file that you are a danger to the Islamic Republic. It's up to me now to sign this paper. This is your sentence, and it only needs my confirmation in order to be carried out. I guarantee you I can go to both extremes, as you Christians say, 'to bless you or to...'"

He didn't finish his sentence. But he sounded very serious. All of a sudden, despite his outward gentleness, I felt he was ready to carry out any punishment for the sake of his national duty.

"If any inspector or interrogator approaches me the way you do, I will do my best to cooperate," I complemented him. I needed more time to pick up my thoughts and think about my answers because I had not yet understood why I was being interrogated by a major from the Ministry of Foreign Affairs. So I asked him about the other two he had mentioned.

He told me that they were American tourists who were arrested about two months earlier. He said they were arrested because of their suspicious activities. After more investigation, they found out that their passports were fake. He continued the story and said, "They entered Iran with fake passports, claiming to be Swiss citizens, which alone is a crime. But they were also accused of spying for CIA. They had been traveling city to city and had some meetings with a number of people. To be honest with you, their lives depend on my conversation with you as I'm the one in charge right now by the power given to me by the court. The only Iranian name associated with a phone number in their phonebook was yours. Since they were foreigners, it was the Ministry of Foreign Affairs' duty to follow up the matter." He continued, "As we investigated the case, we noticed that your name was associated with a file in Ministry of Information for evangelistic Christian activities within and outside the Assemblies of God churches."

In those days, our church was considered the second Spy Nest after the former American Embassy in Tehran.

He then explained to me that he had the full authority to send me right to be hung without further investigation, if only he was convinced of my crime. They probably had the advantage of keeping those Americans as long as they wanted and using the opportunity for political bargaining with America. That was my understanding from the case. But I, on the other hand, had no value for them, no matter how serious the case was. They just wanted to make sure whether they were spies. If they were, so was I. And based on my thick file, there was no need to spend a minute more on me; I would be hung from a rope.

My life (and apparently theirs too) depended on how I was able to use my mouth; the power of life and death was in my words in that moment; I believed that. It was not an ordinary case of arrest or trial of a Christian. To be honest with you, I was under so much pressure because of Kathy and what church had done to me that for a second the thought came to my mind, *"I could have used that opportunity as revenge!"* Assigning that smart and trained major with full authority over the case was a very smart move. I am still sure that they all knew what a vulnerable situation I was in— abandoned by my friends, dealing with the frustration in my marriage, facing unfair judgments from the church leaders and my own relatives, being accused of things I had not done, dealing with the very possibility of losing my career as a musician and a published author and translator, and finally coping with the anxiety of being hung soon if I would not cooperate with this smart man sitting in front of me.

Frankly, all I wanted to do in that moment was to smoke a cigarette! You may laugh now, but I really needed one. So I asked him if I could have one. He offered me a pack of Marlboro light, which was on the coffee table. I accepted. He took one, too. Believe it or not, it helped me relax.

For some reason this passage came to my mind in that moment. In Galatians 2:6, Paul says, *"But from those who seemed to be something- whatever they were, it makes no difference to me; God shows personal favoritism to no man—for those who seemed to be something added nothing to me".*

I would be lying if I said that I didn't think of revenging everyone, even myself (for not being able to be someone people expected me to be). I would be lying if I told you I was a perfectly moral man in that moment. I tried not to show the major what I was thinking of. I was so fragile. Think of it; no one even knew I was there. And I had no value to those I valued so dearly. I was all alone. It seemed like, apart from what I was doing at the church, I had no identity; I was nothing. I had almost stopped praying regularly. The only time I prayed was before the food or sometimes when I was playing a tune with my guitar. Some of my church friends thought (and some of them may still think) I had turned into a junkie, a heroin addict, and perhaps that was why Kathy had problem with me. Even after a decade, some of them still think I'm a homeless junkie living on the streets of downtown Tehran, even years after I left Iran! So to those who have nothing else to do except make judgments about others, I say, "Move on and a get a life." And as Paul says again in Galatians 6:17, *"From now on let no one trouble me, for I bear in my body the marks of the Lord Jesus".*

The major kept staring at me, trying to read my mind. From an earthly point of view, I was so close to giving up on the church and taking revenge on everyone who had put this unbearable guilt on me. What I was thinking about had nothing to do with Jesus Himself, but those who claimed to be something while they were not even able to discern a simple lie from the truth.

Then I began to think about my other option—being executed! That could be much better; I would go to Heaven, everybody would consider me a martyr, and they would all shed tears for me. I mean it could be a better way to revenge everyone while I would be in Heaven singing and dancing. I laughed at my thoughts.

This guy was nice and I couldn't keep him waiting. He was also very clever. I couldn't mess with him. He seemed very confident. He really thought he was doing his duty, job, or whatever, to his best. I had to be very careful. I finally talked.

"Well, I'm still on my word. I'll tell you all I remember. And I remember those two young guys. I spoke to them the first day they came to our church. I guess it was about four months ago. In fact, one of the brothers in the Assemblies introduced them to me. As far as I remember they introduced themselves as Dan and Tim. They needed an interpreter for the sermon. I was reluctant at first, but I accepted anyway."

I didn't tell the major that I didn't want to get involved in church stuff. But apparently he knew that, because he said, "I know why you were reluctant!"

I was surprised, but didn't admit I understood what he meant. I said, "Well, recently I was very busy with my books and music. So I thought these two guys might ask me to go places with them and translate, and I didn't really have that time," I said.

"What were their names?" He asked.

I told him the truth, "I already said I guess Dan and Tim." He smiled and nodded. "And then?" he asked.

"Then, as I predicted, they called me the next day and asked me to have a meeting with them. I told them I was busy, but they said that it would only take few minutes. I agreed and we met, at the church."

"Were the leaders of the church involved in that meeting? Or did they ask you to cooperate with these two men?" he asked.

"No to both questions. I guess they didn't want to have anything to do with them," I replied. "They were already in trouble being accused of having contacts with foreign sources. You know that!"

"And is that true?" He was shooting in the dark.

"Believe me when I tell you that our church is in less connection with foreigners than a simple and small export-import company. As you know, these days ordinary businessmen have more connections with the West than any journalist or any religious minority here in Iran. I know what I'm talking about. Our church is a very independent church. The only case I remember that involved the foreigners was the case with Rev. Dibaj and some other martyrs like Rev. Haik. Except that, they don't really want to have anything to do with foreigners." I said what I needed to say. After all, I still loved them so dearly, and the revenge thing I felt was only for a few seconds—just a carnal thought.

He played with his papers again. "That is something *we* will decide about later," he said and continued, "So what exactly did they discuss with you in that meeting?"

"Well, as far as I remember, they just wanted to know about the condition of Christians in Iran, and what they knew was pretty much the reality. We are not doing very well (I pointed to the whole room and our current conversation, sarcastically)."

He defended, "This is not about Christians or Christianity; this is about the national security. My job is to defend and protect the country. I have no interest in your Christian faith, and if I'm persuaded that they are nothing but some young idiot missionaries, I'll let you go. If not, you will stay here, and I'm afraid to tell you that my associates will take you directly to Evin Prison. But it will be a pity, for you are a smart man!" He sounded convincing. Something in his argument was telling me he spoke the truth. He was honest, but serious about his duty.

I told him all I knew and what had happened. I told him that these two young men, in my opinion, made a big mistake by coming to Iran as missionaries with fake passports. I told him they were not spies, but real Christians who were trying to understand the condition of Iranian Christians. I added that I warned them not to travel around the country and talk to people in every city. In fact, I had already warned them about being mistaken as spies if they did that. But they were young and not experienced in their approach as evangelists. I told the major all the details of our conversations in that meeting and their next few phone calls. I assured him they were not spies. And I begged him to free them and let them go.

"I believe they learned their lesson! Just think of their parents and their family members, please. Their parents should have been so worried about them by now. They probably think they are already dead. You know me; you know where I live or where I go for lunch or a coffee. You know my publishers. You've let me publish Christian books for years and have a band in the last couple years. I mean, you know how to find me; you can even keep me here, but please let these guys go home. They are probably scared to death. I hope they were not hurt or harmed! I beg you, please."

Suddenly I came to my senses after I heard my own last sentences! I wasn't talking to the major! In fact, without even knowing, I was interceding for them to God. I was praying. God was there in the room. I could sense His glorious presence, the same thick and cloudy presence I felt years ago in Tokyo and I was asking God to set His children free!

In a blink of an eye, the major's behavior changed. He put down the papers, stood up, and asked me to leave. He went back to his desk and, without even looking at me said, "Have a good day! You are free to go." He looked pale.

I didn't know what had happened in that moment. I was free to go; it meant he believed me, and it meant he was convinced they were not spies! The glorious presence of God was still in the room. I'm sure the major felt it too. He tried to avoid looking at me. I thanked him and went on my way toward the door. But I wanted to make sure he would free them. I felt I was bolder and braver then, so I said, "So, you are going to let them go, aren't you?" and looked at him with a funny smile on my face.

"Didn't I say you can go?" he said again, without looking at me, and then he continued, "Yes, I suppose so!"

"Thank you so much, Major. You're a very good person with a good heart. Thank you, and God bless you. Have a good day!" I said and then left the room. I felt like Daniel; the lion's mouth was closed, and I was safe. I thought about these young men's parents when I was walking back home. God was good. I was happy!

———

Two months later in the summer, I was a dinner guest at a friend's place, and he had an American magazine under his coffee table that drew my attention. I looked at the cover, and I immediately recognized the faces of those two young American missionaries. The cover said they were freed from an Iranian prison after two months (or so) with the accusation of spying for America. I thanked God with joy in my heart. And I thought, *Thank you, Major, and be blessed wherever you are.*

Brida

MIRACLES ARE NOT NECESSARILY A single or a series of supernatural events. You and I can be a miracle in someone else's life. And this is exactly what she was for me.

—

During the second year of President Khatami administration, in one of the annual Iranian International Book Exhibitions in the spring of 1999, a few weeks before Kathy and I began to live separately, I was promoting my last translated book, *The Power of One* by Sharif M. Abdullah. The book was about the chaotic condition of the world we live in and the eminent need for reformist leaders to emerge and lead the nations toward a new era. I thought this book would precisely define the character of Mohammad Khatami, the former President of Iran (based on the situation of Iran in those days).

One sunny and beautiful spring afternoon during the Exhibition, two girls stopped by my booth. They were, like most of the visitors, university students looking for the latest phenomena in the international literature world. Along with my already published books, I was also promoting *The Power of One*. As an evangelist, I also took the opportunity to share my faith with whoever made a stop at my booth. I had lots of Christian literature, New Testaments, and Bibles right under my table and in my bag.

One of those two girls, named Solmaz, asked me if I knew a certain writer (I don't recall his name now), but instead, I presented my new book to her, and she, after taking a look at the back cover and some of the pages, liked the book and began to talk about the world issues. I listened to her, and after she finished, I said, "Well, you are right, there are billions of problems with our world, and it's not just Africa, Afghanistan, Iran, or the condition we are living in right now; it's worldwide, and they are not going to be solved by a writer or a politician, even if it's Mr. Khatami."

"I'm aware of that," she said, "but no one has ever come up with a realistic solution; everybody just talks. They all think they have the right answer or solution to the world crises!"

"I see that you have been searching," I replied, "but haven't found what you're looking for! I have something that you might be interested in."

As I bent down to get her a New Testament, I noticed that the other one, who was standing three feet away from us, stepped forward in curiosity to see what I would come up with. She had not said a word yet. She took her shades off as she got closer to the desk. That was when I really noticed her. She was beautiful and elegant, but looked so unreachable. There was a quiet, shy, and smiley "hi" in her shiny eyes. She noticed that I noticed her. She asked, "Is that an Injil (the Farsi word for Gospel)?"

"Yes," I replied.

I gave the New Testament to her friend. She didn't seem to be surprised when I gave her the book. She said, "So you think the answer to all the world problems is this, a religion?" I wasn't able to focus on what she was saying. That was not me. I had never felt such a distraction seeing a girl—even when I met Cheryl in Tokyo. I had no idea what was happening to me. It was like I'd known her even before the creation of the universe! She was staring back at me right into my eyes, like she was feeling the same thing. I had to take control of myself. I had to scatter the clouds of her presence before I could continue to talk to the first girl. I took away my eyes from her and looked down to my desk and the titles of the books for a while to distract my mind until I was back to normal again.

The other girl kept asking me questions, and I explained to her as far as it was possible, for it wasn't wise to hold a long conversation about Christianity where we were standing, especially in a Book Exhibition with thousands of people passing by. But I asked her to read the book and think about what Jesus was offering. She took it. I grabbed another New Testament, and without saying a word, offered it to the other one. She took it too. Then to my surprise, she asked me if I could give her my phone number! Her friend quickly turned to her and gave her one of those angry looks that meant, *What the heck are you doing? We don't know this guy!*

I was nailed to the floor. It was like I was born without a tongue. After a long pause, I came up with the best I could, "No." I had no other words. My vocabulary as a writer had turned totally blank.

"But I need to talk to you about something." she didn't seem to be offended by my sharp "No". She continued, "I'm not sure if I can come to the Exhibit again. I really need to talk to you."

"We'll meet again, if we're supposed to." I finally said what I needed to say. Then I continued, "What I gave you is worthy of being taken seriously."

She stared at me with one of those "please trust me" looks in her eyes. I felt she had something to share, but wasn't comfortable bringing it up at that moment. It wasn't wise to give her my number. I didn't want to worsen my situation with Kathy even though we didn't live together at that time. But I was sure her intention was pure when she asked me for my phone number.

She was still looking at me, waiting for me to change my mind. I said, "Please accept my apologies; I can't give you my number. I'm married, and it's not right to give my number to girls. I hope you understand."

"I understand, and I highly respect that," she said, "but what I need to talk to you about has nothing to do with the fact that you are married. What if we won't ever see each other again? I need to talk to you about something very important!"

I lost my chemical balance; what did she mean by that? I had butterflies in my stomach. What was happening? Her friend was watching both of us alternatively with anger and surprise.

I said, "If we won't meet again then we were not supposed to."

"But I need to talk to you!" She sounded very serious.

I was confused. She was very honest and sincere. She didn't seem to have any wrong motives. I had already been accused by Kathy, at our recent counseling sessions, of having secret lovers, and I didn't want to give her any excuse to hammer me down again.

She seemed to be looking for another way of keeping us in touch, "I'm sure you won't mistake me with those girls who walk around and give away their phone numbers, but I need you to have this." Then she wrote down her home phone number on a piece of paper and gave it to me. "Please promise me not to lose it. Please say that you won't lose it, OK?"

"OK. I promise not to lose it. But I also need you to know that I don't promise to call you, either," I replied.

"It's alright. Just don't lose the number," she smiled.

Her friend was very mad at her for what she had just done. She took her by the arm, and they walked away from the booth.

—

When I began to write my story, my greatest challenge was not the artistic writing styles or characterizing the personas, but rather, whether I would allow myself to write about some of the individuals I met on my path and the kind of relationship we had—people who changed me for good or for bad. It's not because I was afraid to be stoned by some people for I know there are always more than a few who will stone you anyway. I just didn't want to harm those I love dearly or damage their current lives under any circumstances. But these people and the consequent changes they brought to my life are so important and valuable to who I am now that I cannot leave them out of the story just because what some people may think. To agree with Marina Nemat, I add that our life experiences, which in many areas are common to almost all humankind, should be a naked bearer of who we were and how we became who we are. I constantly remind myself that this memoir is not going to be just a book, but it is being written as a living testimony to the life of a simple human being and to the beauty of life, the necessity of love, the value of forgiveness, the importance of hope, and the power of faith—in ourselves, in others and in our Creator.

This is my purpose, regardless of whether some people react negatively to these events. We tend to deny the things we do not understand. But I have learned this; you can't deny or stand against destiny. Destiny is not a wild black horse we can tame and ride on. It has its own way of doing things. I know some people who do not believe in God, but they claim to believe in destiny. You may or may not believe in God, but in order to believe that there's a pattern in life called *destiny,* you should first admit there is a Creator, and this Creator works in mysterious ways! And if you don't believe in God, well I should say, in that case, you take the whole fun out of life!

—

The two girls never came back to my booth for the remaining days of the exhibit. I didn't want to think about the subject at all. I decided to forget what had happened. I didn't need any more trouble.

I mostly thought about Kathy and wondered what she really wanted out of life or even out of our relationship. I was ready to accept the fact that I didn't sacrifice as much as I was supposed to, in term of what Bible says to men; Love your wives as Christ loved the church and gave his life for her (see Eph. 5:25).

Sometimes I wished there was a Dr. Phil there to help us see what was going wrong. Something that drove me crazy was that, despite her occasional loss of memories, she acted very calculated and very deliberate in any other thing she did, whether at work or university or in the presence of our pastors. So far, no one had ever seen her bad mouthing (as she did when we were alone). Nobody had ever seen her furious anger. So everybody was still accusing me of treating her badly (except her mom). We were told by many to go through some psychological evaluation. I agreed. She didn't. She had closed all doors to any conversation and negotiation. Maybe she was afraid of not being able to fool the psychologist. Seeing a psychologist was her greatest fear.

I was still hoping to somehow get to a solution, but the more time passed, the more frustrated I became, especially after I found out that all her late-night comebacks were nothing but partying with her friends, watching movies, eating popcorn, and talking behind my back. A mutual friend of mine once told me that he saw Kathy with her ex-boyfriend. I didn't believe him and still don't want to. He thought I was so naïve not to consider this possibility.

One afternoon, about two weeks after the exhibition was over, I accidentally came across the phone number she had given to me. I'd promised her not to lose it, and for that purpose, I'd put it inside my Bible. I looked at the number for a while, but put it back inside my Bible. The only thing I was a little afraid of was my own vulnerable situation. I had no doubt about her motives; they were as pure as snow. She really wanted to talk to me that day. A few minutes later, I finally decided to call her.

I dialed the number. She answered the phone after the first ring, "Hello!"

I recognized her voice. "Hi, this is Bijan, from the exhibition," I said.

"Hi Bijan! How are you?!" she replied with excitement and without giving me a chance to say how I was doing she asked, "Do you remember my friend, Solmaz?"

"Yes of course I do. Why are you asking? Anything happened to her?" I asked.

"No, she's OK. She's here with me, sitting right beside me," she said. "And guess what? She just asked me if you ever called. And I told her that you would, at the right time. And then the phone rang, and I told Solmaz, 'Here he is,' before even answering the phone! And she laughed at me. And guess what? It was you!"

"Wow! So it really was the right time," I said with doubt about whether she was telling me the truth.

"Hold on a second," she said, "Solmaz wants to make sure it's really you!"

"Hello! Mr. Bijan?! Is that you?!" Solmaz asked.

"Yes, it's me. How are you?" I asked her.

"Oh my God, I can't believe it's you. We were just talking about you!" she sounded excited and scared at the same time!

Then she put her back on the phone, and we talked for about five minutes. She asked if we could meet. I wasn't sure if seeing her was a good idea. But when I asked her about what she wanted to share with me, she said that she needed to see me and tell me about it in person!

The curiosity was killing me. The day after was a Thursday, and Thursdays in Iran are like Saturdays in the West. And since young people do not have anything fun to do, they usually get together and go to the mountainside north of Tehran (we call it Darband). There in Darband, there is a narrow road that takes you to some beautiful rocky places. A river flows from the mountaintop north of Tehran right by the road which makes it much more beautiful. On Thursdays and Fridays, you can see the line-ups of people from afar, boys and girls in groups of five, ten, or even twenty. There are stations on the way up with small traditional restaurants and tea houses under the old trees by the river. I asked her if we could meet there. She agreed, and we made arrangements to meet at a bus stop at Tajrish Square.

"Did I do the right thing?" I asked myself. I wasn't sure at the moment. I prepared myself for evangelizing. *This is the only reason I agreed to see her,* I told myself.

I did not feel guilty, for I believed in my intention.

—

I got to the Tajrish bus terminal five minutes early. The butterflies in my stomach were killing me. I truly wanted to know what she wanted to share with me. A couple of times, I told myself to leave the bus stop and go home, but I couldn't. For some reason, the situation reminded me of the day when I met Cheryl in Shibuya Station in Tokyo.

There were hundreds of young people at the station waiting for their friends and gangs (good ones) to get together and rush into buses to get to Darband before it was too crowded.

I saw her from afar. I recognized her among hundreds of other girls dressed in almost the same fashion. She was wearing the same shades. Thank God for that; I didn't have to look into her big shiny eyes. She saw me too and waved at me. We said hi and immediately got into a shuttle. I didn't know what to expect or even what to say. Her presence was very strong, even though she was small in figure. She was smiling all the way to the last stop.

She began to talk first to break the ice; just simple words. She addressed me with respect. Her respectful tone made it easier for me to talk back to her. She asked how I was doing, and I still have no idea why I said what I said, "I'm just too nervous! I have butterflies in my belly. And I don't know why I'm telling you this!"

She laughed out loud and then said, "If you would have said this to another girl but me, I'm sure she would have been running away from you by now! But I understand. So don't be nervous, be excited instead. I have something very important to tell you."

The way she said that was like water on fire for me. I felt my confidence was back again, and I told her that she was a very wise and mature girl. She laughed and said, "You haven't seen half of it yet!"

When we reached some heights on the mountain, we decided to stop at a tea house. The rest of the day we talked. I gave her a glimpse of who I used to be and how God had saved me, not only from being lost, but also from where I was going to—hell. I told her about my spiritual transformation and about the unconditional love of God. I told her about my music activity, too. I felt I needed to be very honest with her, so I added that I wasn't feeling well recently because there was something wrong going on in my life.

"With your wife?" she asked me, while pointing to my ring. Apparently she was much smarter than I guessed.

"Um, yes. But enough about me. I'm not here to talk about me; I'm here to hear your story," I said.

She had listened to my story attentively. I didn't notice that while I was talking to her, I also walked away from her and from where she was sitting. Unintentionally, I had put a distance between us. She was sitting there on a bench-like piece of wood, and I was walking around and talking (teachers cannot sit when they're truly teaching, or maybe it's just me!). There was about ten feet of distance between us. When I finished, she asked, "Why are you so far away? You don't need to be afraid of me. You know that, don't you? Come closer."

I sat down closer to her, but still kept a proper distance. I wasn't afraid of her at all. I had the feeling I had known this girl before even we were born. She said, "Now I know for sure why I had to talk to you; you are the one." Then she continued, "Now listen to my story." Then she leaned back against the tree behind her and said, "Please let me finish before you say anything, OK?" Then without giving me a chance to say anything, she continued, "I was seeing someone for a while, and I still am, on and off. He is nice and caring. But there was something in our relationship that kept bothering me all the time. I'm as simple as you can see. I am a simple girl. I don't like conflicts or fights. I liked him and still think I like him, but I was in pain since the first day we began to date. Even though everything seemed to be perfect, but I didn't have peace."

I thought, *Why is she telling me about her relationships? I don't want to listen to that.*

She continued, "You know when something is wrong, even if it looks like perfect, right? We had good times. We've been together now for about two years."

"What do all these things have to do with me?" I said. I felt a little bit uncomfortable, with no reason! I was there for something spiritual rather than listening to a break-up story.

She said, "Come on, Bijan, I listened to your story, didn't I? Plus we are here because I wanted to share something with you." I felt embarrassed for what I had just said. Then she added, "I will get to the part that will have to do with you! Be patient." And then she smiled. She was like a five-year-old girl who wanted to share an exciting story, and I was treating her like an idiot!

"OK, as I said, I didn't have peace about the relationship. I wanted a way out, but at the same time, I still liked him. One night, a few weeks before I met you at the book fair, I had a strange dream. In my dream, I was lost in a dark labyrinth. It was like an endless cave with millions of crossroads at every corner. I was running through all the turns and corridors in search of a way out. I was desperate and terrified. I was scared of not being able to finally find my way."

I could see the small teardrops rolling down on her eyes. I used to have those kinds of dreams many years ago. They are so frightening and make you feel helpless. I'm sure some of you, my readers, have had those experiences, too.

I said, "I know what you are talking about. They are horrible dreams. I used to have them, too!"

"Yeah, but it's going to be more horrifying, or I better say, exciting," she replied. Then she went on, "While I was running from one corridor to another in search of a way out, suddenly, on a crossroad, a glowing figure appeared to me out of nowhere. He was all light. His presence was so friendly, peaceful, and loving that all my fears disappeared when I saw him. I knew in my dream that he was a holy man. I knew I could trust him. So I asked him "Sir, I'm lost in this labyrinth, and I'm so scared. Could you please help me find my way or show me the way out?"

He pointed to one of the corridors and said, "Take this one. Walk until you see a …

She paused and smiled.

I asked, "See what? What happened next?"

She said, "Time out, break time!"

I laughed and said, "What? Are you kidding? No breaks. Tell me the rest of the story. Come on! I want to know what happened next."

She laughed with me and said, "It costs you!" I asked her what. She said, "A cup of tea and some dates, fresh black dates, right from that old tea house over there!" she pointed to the tea house. I jumped up and ran to the tea house and came back with two hot cups of tea and a small plate of fresh black dates. I sat down and asked her to continue. She smiled, thanked me, and went on, "Alright, the shining holy man said, 'Walk in this direction until you see a man, with a table in front of him. He will show you the way out.' Then before I get the chance to thank him he disappeared. I took his advice and walked toward the direction he gave me. At the end of the corridor, I saw a man (I wasn't able to clearly see his face) standing behind a table filled with different kinds of books, like history, politics, religion, and so forth. I told him what had happened, and I told him that the holy shiny man had sent me to him to show me the way." He didn't say a word. He just simply bent down and took something from beneath the table. Then he showed me a small ark, a chest, which he brought out from under the table. He put it in front of me and asked me to open it and read what was inside. But I was so desperate to get out of that cave that I just asked him to show me the way. I didn't understand why he was asking me to read something." She paused.

I thought the dream was over, but out of curiosity asked her if it was over. She smiled and said, "Don't you want to know what was in the ark?"

"Of course I do, but I thought...I'm sorry, go on please." I replied to her. while telling myself, *What's wrong with you, man? You are smarter than that!*

She continued, "He put the ark in front of me and again asked me to open it. And I did." She stared at me for few seconds and then went on, "There was a book, an old book inside the ark. He told me to read it! I asked him again just to show me the way out, and I told him that I didn't have time to read a book. He insisted. Finally I accepted. I grabbed the book, and as soon as I opened it, a light began to shine from behind me. I turned around and saw an entrance or an exit opened toward a green field outside. I was so happy to see the doorway that I forgot about the man and began to run toward the light without even thanking him for his help. I didn't even say goodbye to him. I ran out into the green field; I was free at last. Then I was awake! Now I'm done." And she laughed again playfully.

"Wow, what a dream! I guess it doesn't need any interpretation" I said. "It was very clear and very exciting. It was like a scene from a magical movie." I continued, "The message is as clear as this blue sky. The cave is your life, and the corridors are the paths humankind is lost on. The man in light is Jesus, and the other one with the books is me! I gave you the Bible and asked you to read it, remember? If you do, the doors of Heaven will be opened to you." I smiled and continued by teasing her, "And you didn't even thank me or say goodbye to me!"

We both laughed. She looked thoughtful. I knew what she was thinking about. I was thinking about the same thing. I knew she knew it. My job was to only show her the way. Within only three hours, we had established a friendship that for others might have taken many years to build. We both knew that. But there was also a painful truth that we both understood in that moment; even as friends, our paths would separate as soon as she found the Way!

After a long silence, I asked if she had read the book *Brida* by Paulo Coelho. She had not. I asked her to read it. Then I asked her if she was yet willing to continue seeing her boyfriend after she saw that dream. She wasn't sure. She still had some feelings for him. She needed time. She was very wise, and it came clear to me as a truth when she turned to me and said, "I will pray for you and your wife!"

I smiled.

In the next few months, we became very good friends. Pouyan, my roommate fell in love with her immediately, like a sister he never had. I became her instructor. All we talked about was the Bible, books, poems, Paulo, Shel Silverstein, and fulfilling our destinies. Pouyan, she, and I used to go to the same mountainside and spent a whole day talking, laughing, and praying. Yes, she gave her heart to Christ in less than a month and began to go to church with Pouyan. She broke up with her boyfriend. She got freed from her past pains and sorrows. She became a new creation.

I used to call Kathy almost every day to see how she was doing. Her attitude was always the same, "Why do you call me? I thought being separated meant no contact. You can ask my friends about me. Do not call me at home or at my work place. You embarrass me." She didn't want to talk to me. Yet I kept calling her a few times a week to hear the same thing! She was my wife, and I was hoping to somehow deal with our problem while I knew there was nothing else I could do. I began to think, *"Maybe the whole thing was a big mistake from the beginning when I ignored my pastor's advice and rushed into the relationship by calling her at her grandma's funeral!"*

Some of my faithful friends at church told me that she had stopped attending the services because she believed she had more important things to do. Pastor Vartan was avoiding me. Bishop Edward ignored me. I began to think that there was something wrong; maybe after all, they were convinced they were wrong, but their pride prevented them from accepting me in church again. I casted the thought out of my mind like casting out a demon. I still loved them so dearly. But I had no one else to talk to except Pouyan and my new friend.

One day she told that she had finished reading Brida by Paulo Coelho. She was very excited about the similarities between her own character and Brida's. I told her that that was why I had asked her to read the book in the first place. Since that day, I began to call her Brida, and she liked it!

She was a poet. She wrote short poems, like Haikus. They were simple and beautiful, but striking and right to the point. They blew my mind away. The first one I read was the one she wrote on the back of my Bible in Darband, while I went to grab a bottle of water for her. A lame translation could be:

You have tossed me up in the air,
Like an apple I spin,

In all magic, in all mystery.
Why have you lifted up your hands so high?
To catch me?

This was the craziest poem I'd read in years. She was totally aware of my concern for her. I was worried about her. We were in the beginning of our friendship, and I was worry that our friendship would lead to somewhere else instead of what she saw in her dream. And by that poem, she just wanted to assure me that I shouldn't be anxious to catch her, but should trust God, and that despite all the spins, she would be capable of finding her way in the midst of all the other magical moments and mysteries she was going through.

She, Pouyan, and I were into literature. Since all three of us had a child within, one of the writers we discovered and fell in love with was Shel Silverstien. He was a genius. We began to pick up parts of his poems and use them as conversational pieces. Many people around us never understood what we were talking about.

My confidence, my hope, and my strength were coming back to me. All I needed to survive the pain I was going through was a couple friends I could share my heart with without being judged. I just needed to make sure there were at least one or two people in the whole world who were not judging me for what I was accused of, or even further, for what I had done wrong.

As a Christian and as a mentor to many others in pain, I always knew God was there with me. He was the only one who did not leave me or forsake me. He was the only hope I had to keep me breathing, living, and dreaming. But just like any other human being, I needed to see that reflection of unconditional love in a tangible way, a manifestation of His love through another human being. And God knew that! Sometimes He lets us go without it for a while, and sometimes, according to how much we can take, He will send an angel to watch over us, like He did for Jesus at Gethsemane.

Brida was that angel!

In Paulo's book, Brida is an apprentice of a middle-aged sorcerer while she is still in an uncertain relationship with her boyfriend. The sorcerer and Brida felt a strong bond between them, something that was not love, per se, but much stronger and more powerful than that. They were each other's other half, as the writer describes it. Of course in almost all other Coelho's book there is a mystical Christian element behind the conversations and symbols. It was that element that in those days attracted me to his works first. The sorcerer knew the truth from the beginning, and it made it so difficult for him to continue the mentorship. They were part of each other beyond time and space, but not in a sense of the human kind of love, which leads to a marriage and a life happily after. Deep inside they knew they were not meant for that kind of relationship, but still they were meant to be a very essential part of each other's life in a specific time period.

Life is not about completeness or perfection, but about doing what you are here to do. During your life, you meet with some people whom you feel you have a strange bond with. You wish you could remain in their lives and them in yours, but mostly they are not meant for that purpose; they are there to make your transition smoother and more comfortable, while meeting them on your path has its own complications, even pain.

She was my apprentice. I was her mentor in the mysteries of the new found faith. She had her own battles on the way. I had mine. We were just meant to prove that true friendship can exist. She was aware of this truth. She didn't ask me for anything except that I help her get closer to God and to her destiny, but at the same time and with an undeniable enthusiasm, she was ready to risk everything she had to help me fulfill my own destiny. For this very reason, I dare to write about her. And I know her so well that I allow myself to share all about her in pride.

Brida was not just one of my disciples; she was the presence we all need in times of trouble. She carried a joyful, healing force, not in physical terms, but beyond what I was able to understand. She was always positive, a convincing positive force, but not like those who try to sound positive by quoting famous people's sayings. I can't put who she was into words! She also was able to see beyond things. That's something poets are very good at, especially Haiku writers. She didn't even need to look at me to find out if I had a bad day, and she could even feel it when we were miles apart.

One day I was badly sick with a terrible flu. Pouyan was on a trip to his parents' place in their town, and I was alone at home. I was so sick that I couldn't even crawl on the floor to get something to eat, and there she showed up at my door with a homemade warm soup and flu medicines. She told me she was at home reading her Bible, and then all of a sudden she felt a pain in her stomach. Then something or someone told her I was sick. So she got up, made some soup, and bought some cold medicine on the way to my place. There were many other examples of how strangely we were connected, just like what happened the first day I called her.

Somehow we turned into each other's conscience. She even introduced me to her family, but just as a friend and her teacher, to assure them she was not crazy about all she was sharing with them. She did the same with Pouyan. As a result, her sister, Tata, began to show up at church.

To me, she was a helper and comforter from outer space. There was no misunderstanding between us, no lies, no hidings, no excuses, and no judgment. She always had time for me and my naggings, and she laughed while I was complaining. That part was my favorite part! She was a joy. She kept reminding me about how proud she was to know me as her mentor, about my music, my books, and about all the years I had been serving God, no matter what I was going through. She was ridiculously supportive! She read all of my books and attended all of my concerts later on. Words are truly inadequate to picture who she was, not just for me, but for everyone else around her. That's what Pouyan believed about her, too.

She was more Christ-like than any other Christians I'd ever seen since those days with those young missionaries in Japan. From time to time, she felt she needed to remind me that no matter how I felt about myself, God loved me and He was there for me. In one sentence, she was a God-send to prove to me that He had not forgotten me. Through Brida God reminded me of what He was doing for other rejected souls in the whole world. Sometimes healing of a soul comes through another soul, and this is the work of God.

The painful thing was that we both knew we would have to say goodbye to each other sooner or later, but we both had decided not to talk about it. We didn't want to spoil the friendship by thinking and talking about what was going to happen.

I knew that eventually Kathy would learn about her, and as I had predicted, she reported the news to Pastor Vartan and told him I was cheating on her (while I was convinced later that she was seeing her ex). So Vartan felt that he needed to see Brida and spend some time with her to see if Kathy was right. Plus, it was customary for pastors to meet with new believers and check on their progress.

They met. After an hour, he was convinced in spirit that there was nothing immoral between me and her. He liked Brida so much that he asked her to start serving at church by writing dramas and plays for Christmas and Easter. As I learned later, he called Kathy and told her what he thought and that she was wrong about her.

Paulo

It was in those days of rejection, frustration, disappointment, and loneliness that I had the honor of knowing a man whose life experience and the consequences of those experiences brought me a great amount of discernment, understanding, and hope. His approach to life and his reaction to situations in life, along with his naked sincerity and honesty, drew my whole attention to his works and character; Paulo Coelho. God was preparing me for the next step in my life.

When I came to know him, not many people knew much about this Brazilian author. The first book I read from him was *Maktub,* as far as I remember. For me, he was a reminder of the years I had lived (figuratively) with Carlos Castaneda. But Paulo had a hopeful and bright approach to mysticism. And since he was not an atheist, but a Catholic, I was more interested in him. There was something in his writings that spoke right into my heart, especially after reading his testimony of how a bible saved him from a black hole he was drowning in one day during the period he was in sorcery and Satanism (see the book of *Valkyries*).

The experiences he had gone through were very familiar to mine, and in some cases, they were exactly the same. I remembered how identical were our experiences of being drawn to that black hole where we both felt death at the back of our necks.

Since I loved literature, I had already begun to write down some of the conclusions I had reached about life issues. Every time after I'd read one of his books, or during the reading, I would go to my notes and surprisingly find that I had reached the same conclusion on the same subject, sometimes using the exact sentences and words he had used. Brida, Pouyan, and I used to sit down together and talked about the same experiences Paulo had gone through in life and the similarities with what we had experienced in a different situation, like living in Iran.

A couple years after I discovered Paulo as an inspiring writer, other translators began to notice him and started to translate his works. When Arash Hejazi (Paulo's exclusive translator and publisher in Iran) began to directly and closely work with him, Paulo was almost very well known among the Iranian young generation. In fact I began to look for other books by Paulo in English to translate when I noticed that Kathy had filed a divorce. I wasn't surprised because I knew she would do that sooner or later. I didn't have much time, and leaving seemed to be the only option; I had no time for another translation job.

Kathy informed me, through one of our mutual friends, that she needed a letter from the church expressing that there was no other way for us except the divorce. She didn't want to ask Bishop Edward personally for the letter. She asked me to do that and I didn't care if she came up with her famous saying that I was the one who wanted the divorce. So I went to Bishop Edward and told him about the letter. He was reluctant to issue such a letter for an Islamic court because it could have been an indication that the Assemblies of God had been giving Christian marriage certificates to Muslims converted to Christianity. Until then, there was no official paper that could show this was a presumably illegal act. Issuing such a letter could be dangerous both for the church and for us.

Bishop Edward was not the same with me anymore. I guess what Kathy had told me, had come true. Yet he finally agreed to issue the letter. A week later, he asked me to go to the church to get the letter. It was the first time, after a year and half that I was allowed in the building. It was filled with memories, mostly good and unforgettable. I went down the stairs where he was holding a class. During the break, as I approached him with a smile, he grabbed the letter and handed it over to me without even looking at me or returning my hello. That was the last time I saw him in Iran. I left the church with another sad memory.

Kathy told me (through a friend) that she needed the letter and $2000 to pay the judge (under-the-table money) to issue the divorce papers. Two thousand dollars was a lot of money considering the terrible economy of Iran. That was all the cash I had at the time. I had invested all my money in publishing my books. Thousands of copies of my last three books were still in our storage waiting to be released. Years later after we were officially divorced and I had already left Iran, a friend of mine told me that Kathy gave all my books away. (It was a polite way of saying they were all thrown out.)

Meanwhile, I did some research on the legal (and illegal) ways of leaving Iran. For Iranians, getting a visa for any country in Europe or North America was tougher than winning a lottery; we were counted as terrorists in almost every country! I decided to write to some Christian organizations and explain my situation. Some of them sent me some applications to join them for missions, but the fees were so high that I wasn't able to afford them. Others were churches with not much authority to get a missionary visa for me, even for a short period of time. Some other organizations promised me to do everything in their power as soon as I got out of Iran; but how was I to do that? No country was willing to issue any kind of visa for Iranians. In those days, many who wanted to escape Iran claimed to be a minority under persecution; therefore, governments faced the problem of discerning the false cases from the true ones. Some of these people had paid lots of money to get fake documents. Others preferred to take their own way through the mountains to other neighboring countries. Those who were richer could easily buy fake IDs or travel documents. But those who didn't have enough money had only two or three options. One was Pakistan; the other one was Turkey, or if you were on the black list of the Government, the only option was to take the risk of crossing the borders through the mountains.

My parents were in Canada, but they were under my sister's sponsorship, and therefore, were not able to help. Since she had already sponsored my parents she couldn't do it again for me at the time. She had her own problems, like most of us. Plus, in those days, going through the immigration process could take two to three years, even if you met the required scores.

I kept corresponding with Christian organizations, but so far was having no success with any of them. As I mentioned before, many were asking for thousands of dollars for missions. The last money I had was what I gave Kathy to bribe the judge (I've done things I'm not really proud of).

Sometimes spiritual and mental pain is far worse than physical torture. I guess that's why, in all dictatorship governments, they start with the mental torturing first when they want to force you to cooperate with them.

It is very challenging to remain faithful to an unseen God and defend His cause in such situations like mine when you feel you are all alone, like

Elijah in the Old Testament after he ran away from Jezebel (see 1 King 20). I thought, *Well, Jesus was 100 percent God, and 100 percent human; it was easy for Him to remain faithful to God, especially considering the fact that He knew everything from the beginning.* I was just trying to make the situation more understandable for myself by thinking, *I'm only a man; it isn't easy.* I guess having these kinds of thoughts is normal when you're at such a dead end. The only way to sustain your mental health is to hold on to the goodness of God as a loving father.

Paulo Coelho, who is occasionally mentioned by some Christians as a bad influence (even recently by the Iranian regime, who accused him of practicing sorcery) happened to be my *another helper* after Brida. In the previous three years of challenges that I had in my marriage, in the church, and with the government, in all those dark and lonely days, only my Bible and his books motivated me and pushed me toward accomplishing my dreams. My name, Bijan, also means warrior, (some dictionaries have mentioned *warrior of light* too) and what Paulo revived in me was the idea of wrestling with life as a warrior and keeping my dreams alive, no matter what others or even I felt about myself.

Of course, that's what Jesus wants for all of us, too (fulfilling our destiny by embracing the fullness of life in Him), but as humans, when we are desperate, we need to see a miracle, whether in tangible form (like Brida) or in unseen form (like Paulo and his works). Jesus is able to be both for us—a close friend and a coach. But in my case, for some reason, He decided to use Brida and Paulo instead.

Anyway, as an early fan of Paulo Coelho, beginning in 1997, I began to make him known to as many of my friends as I could. I even talked about him in my concerts in between the songs. It was in the year 2000 that Mr. Arash Hejazi, by inviting him to Iran, got the chance to become Paulo's exclusive publisher in Iran. Even though as a translator I wasn't pleased with the Arash translation style or vocabulary I was somehow happy because some of the translations of Paulo's works that were already published by others were really lame translations. So when I heard that Arash had organized a visit for Paulo, I was so happy that, along with Pouyan and Brida, we began to spread the news everywhere, especially in my concerts. I felt so close to Paulo that I decided to write him a letter and explain my situation to him. The rest of the story you know from Chapter 1 in this book. I went to the Airport. I met Paulo. I gave him the letter.

While Brida, Pouyan, and I were waiting to see if Paulo would write back to me during his stay in Iran, we went to His lecture in Talar Vahdat

(Hall of Solidarity) in Tehran. Pouyan decided to leave because of the huge crowd; he thought we could never get in. Brida and I stayed and, through her charm, we found a corner in the balcony. The building was packed with young people. I guess there were at least 3,000 people there (just an estimation), and at least a thousand were left behind the doors. It was the first time that the Islamic regime had issued permission to a foreign author with such popularity to speak in such a huge place. That day, for the first time, after two decades of Islamists' rule over Iran, I noticed the thirst that our young generation had in spiritual matters, and I was proud of them. I thought, *One day God will help me share His love and greatness with this passionate generation. They don't know who He really is. All they know about Him is what they heard of Allah from an Islamic point of view.* And I said to Him, "You are the only one who can fill their vacuum and satisfy their thirst. And You will make it happen." I knew He would, one day.

After Paulo shared with us about the rich Iranian culture and how he was inspired by Iranian ancient poetry and literature and how he was impressed by that young crowd, he said that he wished he could truly show his gratitude toward such an awesome audience, but no words were able to express his feelings. Right in that moment, I turned to Brida and whispered to her ear, "Hey, listen, I bet he will do one of these two things, I just have a feeling!"

"What two things?" she asked me, laughing.

"Seriously," I replied, "Believe me, he will either dance like a Native South American Indian sorcerer (I didn't even know what kind of dance it could be!), or he will cry and weep like a baby!"

"Oh yeah, you're right! Imagine Paulo Coelho in the Islamic Republic of Iran dancing on a stage!" she laughed again.

"Then he will weep!" I said.

After thirty seconds of silence, Paulo began to cry! He was really weeping. The whole audience was in total silence as long as he wept. And he wept for a long time.

I turned to Brida and said, "Didn't I tell you, didn't I tell you?!"

She looked at me with unbelief in her eyes and whispered, "Yes, you told me, my mentor!"

Then the whole crowd stood up and began to clap for him, for a long time.

He was busy for the next few days with the meetings and probably some trips that his Iranian publisher had already arranged for him, but I didn't care to follow up, for it wasn't him who I wanted to follow, but the legacy he was trying to share; following our dreams.

Long after that night, I received a fax from him which read:

Dear Bijan

I only read your letter in Brazil—today. But I hope that in my next visit to Iran, we can meet and discuss your letter.
May God help you.

Paulo Coelho

I've kept a copy of the fax with me ever since.

The Last Temptation

I WAS HAPPY THAT, DESPITE all of the talking behind my back at the church, those whom I had trained had kept the torch of faith flaming. Brida, Pouyan, and many of the other new friends I'd made were all happy with their new faith. Some of them began to write plays for the church events. Some got involved in music, and others were active in evangelizing to their friends and relatives. What else did I need to be happy again?

My last concert, which was in early November 2000, went very well. Thousands of people were talking about our band. It was at Shafagh Cultural Centre in Tehran. We didn't have enough seats for all who had heard about us and had come to hear our music. It was the last night of our three-night performance, three nights in a row. At the end of the concert, while the band was performing the last piece, the manager of the Centre called me to the back stage and asked me if we agreed to go for another round. He told me that there were more than a thousand standing outside the Centre demanding another performance. I was surprised, and to be honest with you, very proud.

I told him that the permission by the Ministry of Culture and Guidance was only for three nights and that we were not allowed to go for another round. He reminded me that the permission was for three nights, but what he wanted was another performance on the same night. He was right. There was nothing against that. So when I got back on the stage, right before saying goodbye to the crowd, I asked the band members if they agreed to another performance right after that one. I told them there were a thousand new fans standing outside waiting for another performance. They agreed.

Among the new crowd, there were a few representatives from recording companies. They were sent there to invite me to have a meeting with the owners. From among them, I picked one recording company, which was the most renowned one: Tannin Records. After the concert, I made the arrangement with the representative to meet with Mr. Abtahi, the owner of the Tannin Records.

Abtahi was a young, ambitious man who had come back to Iran a couple years after the Islamic regime was established. He had left the United States to start a business in Iran. His representative told me that her boss was very excited about our genre and style. We made the arrangement for the next morning. He was waiting for me in his office. I was surprised by what I saw! He was wearing black leather pants and a black leather jacket. I saw a black motorbike helmet on his desk, which indicated that he was riding a nice motorbike to his work place, probably black. Considering Iran and its Islamic culture, I thought he had probably lost his mind to dress like that. After the normal greetings and formal introductions he began the talk.

"Bijan, I heard your songs two nights ago, and I should say I'm very impressed! I wanted to see you as soon as possible and tell you what I feel about your work in person. You guys are very talented!"

"Thank you, Mr. Abtahi. And I should say that I'm impressed, too, by you and your appearance!" I said that with a smile.

"I know it may seem too much for here, but I'm not afraid of being who I am," he replied. "Of course, I still have challenges for dressing like this, but it's getting normal for the official authorities to see me this way. But let's talk about your songs."

"Sure, I guess that's the reason why I'm here. But first I'd like to hear your opinion on my songs," I wanted to see what elements exactly attracted him.

"Well, I should mention that I'm a musician and an enthusiastic music listener. And as someone who's been living in the States for quite a long time, I have a good taste in music. But to be honest with you, I haven't been hearing any good music suiting to my taste here in Iran since I got back from the States. Most young musicians here are trying to copy the great bands of the 70s and 80s, but in their best, they're just copying the original and repeat the same tunes and melodies from, let's say, Pink Floyd, Deep Purple, Led Zeppelin, Dire Straits, and Metallica. Even those who play Iranian Pop music are, in fact, copying the same old Iranian songs of 30 years ago. They don't create a new genre or anything new at all. Honestly, what they do is not what I'm looking for as a music producer."

"Then what are you looking for?" I asked.

"I've been looking for people like you, people with a different voice," he continued, "not necessarily a Mark Knofler, Roger Waters, or Steven Taylor or even Ebi and Darioush, for that matter." (Those last two are the most popular Iranian pop singers, both before and after the Revolution in Iran, who live in the States now.)

"I'm a fan of 70s music too, but I never considered myself a good singer. I'm just trying to do new things," I said, "Did you hear about last night?"

"Yeah, and I'm not surprised. Two shows in a row, one after the other! It proved me right." He smiled.

"Well, I believe that we have many good musicians and songwriters," I said, "but not everybody has the chance to shine, I mean here in Iran."

"You are right, especially in other cities and small towns. That's why I thought I needed to help you," He said.

"Help me? What do you mean?" I asked.

"Well, I thought if I help you accomplish your dream, we can prepare the way for others who write different songs or play different kinds of music to be encouraged and step out to try their chance. I also like the fact that you write spiritual/inspirational songs that speak to the new generation.

"Yes, I agree with you, but what about the Ministry of Guidance? In the end, they are the ones who should issue the permissions for concerts or even an album," I said.

He smiled and confidently said, "Don't worry about that part; we will get the permission. We have our connections!"

"Wow! If you say so, then let's get to the business!" I teased him.

"Sure. But before that, would you please tell me what inspires you to write these songs?" He seemed curious.

Despite the fact that it was the first time I had met this guy, I trusted him, and briefly told him my story. He listened and nodded a few times. When I finished my story, he said, "Well ,as someone who's lived in the States, I'm familiar with the situation, and I'm glad you chose music to communicate your beliefs instead of going door-to-door forcing people to believe what you believe," he laughed aloud. I laughed too, for I knew he was talking about Jehovah's Witnesses! I was familiar with their method from my days in Japan.

He paged his secretary and asked her to bring us some coffee.

Then he asked me to join him by the window. The whole city was there in the view, Tehran—with its foggy poisonous sky and all those flat houses and out-of-order high towers. While we were drinking our coffee, he began to share about what he wanted to offer me, if I agreed to join his fulltime staff and write only one song in a week. I asked him if he was offering me a fulltime job at Tannin.

He said, "Yes."

His offer sounded a little bit weird to me. I thought he wanted to invest in us for an album! I told him I had already made up my mind to leave Iran and pursue my dreams in Canada or the States.

When he heard that, he again showed me the whole city from his big window. He said "Bijan, I like you and your character. Why do you want to go through many troubles to fulfill your dreams in the West? Things are different there. You have no idea how difficult it is to get into the system there in the States or even in Canada. I have the power to give you all you could imagine right here in your own city. Believe me when I say I have the power to make it happen! I can make all these young people worship you like an idol! Stay and work with us."

I was shock by his words; they were very familiar. In that moment, the only thing that came to my mind was the scene in which Jesus was being tempted by the devil in the desert. He was offered the whole world if He would just agree to be in Satan's service. He could have had all He wanted at the price of abandoning His mission. I already knew my destiny was not to stay in Iran anymore. But his offer was a tempting one. My whole existence was telling me to leave while, my heart was telling me to stay and work with the Tannin Records.

I was so excited, not because of the offer, but because of being considered so important that something or someone wanted to stop me from fulfilling my destiny (just like that old man's offer in Tokyo). The bigger God's plan is for you, the stronger the temptations become to distract you from that plan. If you think you have a great destiny to fulfill, and there's something or someone trying to stop you, that will be a sign to assure you that you are on the right path. Sometimes even the biggest money offered to you is not comparable to the joy of fulfilling your own dreams. But that's why most people in the world are not happy; they take the offer in exchange for their dreams, the dreams God had for them in the first place when He decided to create them before the world was founded.

To assure me that his offer was true, He said, "I buy your songs, the music, and the lyrics. I can write a check for you now. I will also give you a room here in the company, your personal office equipped with the most recent musical technology, if you just accept my offer. Just think about it. I'm not asking you much. And I'm willing to offer you a good deal. And he told me the amount he wanted to pay me as a salary. It was five times bigger than what I was expecting to hear!

"What do you say?" he asked.

The number was very tempting. I was pretty sure none of the other musicians I knew were regularly making that much money on a monthly basis. I asked him to give me some time to think about it. I knew I wasn't going to accept it, but it was wise not to give him a "no" right away. I was willing to sell some of my works because I needed that money to leave Iran.

We met again a couple days later, and I told him I was ready to sell some of the songs to his company. He agreed, and in a minute, he wrote me a fat check. I cashed it the same day. It was more than enough for the plans I had. I had already made up my mind to go to Turkey and find a third country to immigrate to; the money was enough to keep me going for a year.

The next time I went to his office was to say goodbye and thank him for his generous offer. I told him the truth about my decision. He seemed upset and admitted he was not very happy with my decision. His enthusiasm was a little suspicious to me. Why should someone like him offer me such an unusual job proposal with such a huge salary? I guess I'll never know.

"There was another young man. I wanted him to stay and work with me," he said, "but he, just like you, told me that he had to leave Iran. He was very talented. His name was Gilbert Hovsepian."

I was so surprised to hear Gilbert's name. He was a close friend of mine. In fact, we had made some good music together, and he had helped me with few arrangements. We used to play together at the Assemblies. He was the middle son of Rev. Haik Hovsepian, who was murdered by the Islamic regime. I told Abtahi that he was a close friend of mine. Abtahi was surprised, too, and said, "He was a genius. Believe me, you guys could capture the whole city if you wanted. Where is he now, by the way; do you know?" he asked.

"He's probably in the States, maybe in California, but I'm not sure," I replied. I wasn't really sure.

"Well, Bijan, my offer still stands, and if you, under any circumstances, changed your mind, you know where to find me." He sounded very kind and caring. I thought, *I wish I'd met him under different circumstances.*

We shook hands and said goodbye. I never saw him again. He was a cool guy.

The difficult part of the process was to say goodbye to Brida! We both knew this would happen sooner or later, but we had never openly talked about it. Kathy had already finished the procedures with the divorce and was waiting for me to sign the papers to make it official. One morning, I called her at her office and told her I was ready to sign the papers. We made the arrangements for the day after.

We met at an Islamic Marriage and Divorce Office, and we both signed the papers. It was a cold but sunny winter day in late December 2000.

The lawyer said, "I wonder why a beautiful couple like you, so sweet, and so good looking are getting a divorce?"

Kathy replied with a sentence that baffled me again, "It's going to be alright; he will come back!" and they both laughed. I was confused, but preferred to ignore what she had said.

When I was signing the last paper, I noticed that the divorce request was in my name! We had already signed a mutual agreement that said the divorce was a mutual decision we made together. When I saw that the paper was in my name, as the one who had requested and applied for the divorce, I was shocked and asked Kathy about the other paper we had signed.

"I have no idea; this is what they gave me. My dad was the one who made all the arrangements; otherwise they wouldn't issue the official papers, just because you, mister, are a Christian!"

I stood there speechless. I was so mad at her and at her dad that I just wanted to get the signed papers and get out of there. So I just signed the last one, grabbed the papers, said goodbye to them, and walked out.

Maybe it made no difference who had requested the divorce. But the thing is that, in Iran, if everybody thinks that you, as a man, have divorced your wife, they will curse you for destroying a young girl's life. They never forget what you did, and they hate you and blame everything on you forever. What mentality was behind what Kathy and her dad had done? I didn't have time to think about what people might think of me—a monster, a cruel man, or a cheater, perhaps. I didn't care.

I never gave in to the thought that she might have been cheating on me, and I still, to this date, fight that thought, for I don't want to believe that. Although I have forgiven her completely, I will always remember her as the one who left me. Forgiving doesn't mean that you have to go back and live with the same person who caused you so much pain; it rather means letting go and moving on, sending your best prayers and thoughts to them forever. And that's what I did, of course later on.

I went to a big store and bought two big suitcases. The time had not yet come for me to leave, but buying the luggage was actually a reminder that I was leaving soon, and the thought gave me peace.

The same day, I called my parents in Canada and told them it was over, officially over. Then it was my younger sister's turn. I called her too and told her what happened. She invited me over to their place. I accepted.

When I got there, she hugged me and cried in my arms and said she was sorry for what happened between Kathy and me. We sat down and drank a glass of wine, and then she told me that they were, in fact, invited to a small party, and she asked me to go with them and have some fun. Since I knew the person who was throwing the party very well, I accepted.

The person whose place they were invited to was a French Journalist who had married my brother-in-law's sister in France. We knew each other very well. He liked my story, my conversion story. He was a Catholic believer and had been very interested in having an interview with me for a long time, but because of his reputation as a Journalist in Iran and because of my safety, we never did the interview.

That night, he provided me with all kinds of information about his friends all over the world in case I needed any help. He also blessed me with few hundred dollars as a gift from a brother to a brother. He asked me to be in touch with him in future, and before we left, he prayed for me.

That night, the whole night, I was thinking about Brida. She was on a vacation to northern Iran. She called me the next day at my sister's place and told me she had a weird feeling the night before; she wanted to make sure I was alright. I laughed and said, "Come on! Again? How do you feel these things?" Then I asked her about when she was coming back.

She said, "Tomorrow night." I assured her there was no reason to worry and that we would talk sometime after she had a rest. She agreed.

The reason she felt that way was not just because Kathy and I were now officially divorced, but because I was not doing well. After signing the divorce papers, something dark took over me; all of a sudden, everything seemed so meaningless to me. Did I do wrong to let Kathy go? Maybe I wasn't sacrificing enough. I was supposed to save my marriage and fight for it. Maybe I didn't do my best! I thought I was the worse person in the whole world. I knew I didn't want all this to happen. The negative force, the dark side, the enemy, the devil was trying to nail me down again.

Suddenly the unbearable fear of an unknown future became so real to me. Plus, I didn't want to say goodbye to Brida. How was I supposed to tell her I was leaving? That was the toughest part. I didn't know how to tell her that I had already made up my mind. Only two or three people knew about my decision, and Brida was not among them. I really didn't know how to bring up the subject, even though we both knew it was going to happen.

All the past insults, disgrace, rejections, accusations, mental breakdowns, and sleeping pills had wearied my body and soul. I was broken and worn out inside. I had given myself away to God so that He could use me in the forms and frames He wanted. And I was happy about that. I always thanked Him for even the worse things that happened to me. We should not just be thankful for what we have, but we should also be grateful for what we don't have. I always knew all things were working for my good, even if that good seemed so bad to me at the moment or even for years! I really preferred to be up there with Him, in His warm and assuring arms, but deep inside, I knew my job wasn't done yet, and this very reality made everything harder for me to bear. This heavy feeling came upon me after I signed the divorce papers, and I knew the heavy shadow of being a divorced person would follow me everywhere I'd go, especially among Iranian Christians, who generally think anyone who is divorced has actually committed adultery. It was like I had nothing left to live for anymore. Even fulfilling my dreams didn't sound so great to me at the time. I felt as empty as a void, as a vacuum, but I knew it was just a temporary feeling.

In fact, not knowing what was waiting for me in Turkey after leaving Iran and the fear of unknown along with mental and physical pains and shame had kind of crippled me. I had to trust God and remind myself again that He was able to fulfill what He had started in me.

That night at my sister's place, I wrestled with God for hours. And as we know, no one can overpower God. I finally gave up fighting and decided to do whatever it cost to become who I was created to be. I had to show Him I wasn't a noisy cymbal. I needed to prove it to myself, too, that I was a man of my word and a man of my dream, both for the glory of God and for the sake of people who were destined to be touched by me, just like other men of faith who had touched my life.

I now believe that touching people's souls and lives is the highest purpose of God in letting us live on the earth. This is the destiny of humankind. Some believe in this and live their lives to the fullest to bring the good out of people around them, and some get it completely wrong and live in a way that they abuse and misuse others for their own selfish desires. For some people, everything orbits and circles around them so that they can live happily. But I'd rather be abused instead of abusing others. I'd rather be belittled in order to lift up others, even if I have to sacrifice my own rights.

You may think of it as a sickness, but that's what Jesus did. He let them insult Him. He let Himself go through suffering in order to show humankind how worthy they are. Each and every one of us has the chance to carry a little of God inside. We can accept this and live accordingly, by trusting God to fulfill His marvelous plan through us, or we can deny this fact and live our own lives as we desire, making stairs out of people on our way up. I decided not to be sorry or feel pity for myself anymore. I said to myself, *Enough of that already! If that's my destiny, I'll live it without regrets.*

Before I talked to Brida, I needed to see Kathy and tell her that I had forgiven her, whether she believed she was innocent or otherwise. I needed to do that to free myself from the prison she had put me in. She knew very well how sensitive I was to my faith, and she wanted to break me to the point that I finally admitted all she had accused me of was right, just because of one verse in the Bible that says husbands should love their wives like Christ loved the church and gave Himself away for her. That was the only verse she kept quoting. Since she had started to present our case to the church in that way, three more young married girls had begun to take complaints to the leaders of the church regarding their husbands. And all three husbands were good friends of mine, but now didn't even want to see me. The subject of divorce, all of a sudden, had become an option for others who had small problems.

Many years later, I met with those three guys again, outside of Iran. Two were living in a hell (according to them), and one was divorced, blaming Kathy for brainwashing his ex-wife. In the eyes of the leaders of the church, I had sowed a bad seed among our young couples, and all I went through was a payback by God. That was one of the reasons why they excluded me from the church even long before the divorce took place. Perhaps they were right in doing this; maybe they wanted to help Kathy, maybe I *was* a bad example. Only God knows.

Of course I won't do the justice if I don't express my appreciation to the Assemblies of God in Iran and the great leaders I worked with, leaders who were ready to give their lives for Christ and His bride. Some of them are still among my heroes. And let's not forget that in a country like Iran, it's not an easy job for pastors and church leaders to run a church, a church with 70% Muslim born Christians. So I won't take hard on them, for I was one of them.

Talking to Kathy and telling her that I had forgiven her was what I had to do before moving forward.

I called her and told her I needed to see her. She accepted. She was still living in our old apartment. I guess she was a little afraid when I asked to see her, for when I got there, I noticed that one of her friends was there. I didn't care, because she was there almost every weekend, since we moved in to that apartment. Maybe it was better to have a witness. The only problem was that I never trusted that girl. There was something suspicious about her; she kept telling me that Kathy was not the right person for me, and I needed a girl who was sensitive to my interests in music and art! I never told Kathy that she had these conversations with me. She was one of her close friends, and I was worried about their friendship. Maybe I was wrong. Maybe it was one of Kathy's calculated plans to test me. But it didn't matter anymore. I hadn't done anything wrong; I ignored her presence there.

We sat down. Her friend also came and sat down with us! I opened up first, "Kathy, I know this has been a difficult journey for us. We both might have done and said things that we shouldn't have or things that we regretted later. You may think you lost many things, but if you try to be honest and think back, you would also admit that I've lost many things, too. Neither of us won anything; we both lost."

She said, "I didn't lose anything; I won!," then they both laughed.

"So you admit I lost many things, right?" I asked her.

"You started it. You first mentioned about divorce. We all know that," she replied.

"Not again. Don't start over. You don't need to pretend anymore. I'm not going to let you start this game all over again and put the blame on me. You know it's over now. And I'm not giving in to any argument anymore. I'm just here to tell you that I have forgiven you from the bottom of my heart, even though I still don't understand why you put us both through all this—to prove what? I just want to tell you I have nothing against you in my heart. I'm leaving Iran soon. I got my ticket reservation. I'm moving on!"

All of a sudden, her friend stood up and began to yell at me like crazy, "You forgive her? You are here to say 'I forgive you'? Do you know what have you done to this girl? Do you have any clue what she's gone through? You messed up her life. You stole her youth days and left her in this jungle, and now you tell her you have forgiven her? You're out of your mind. If it was up to me, I would have never let you in today. She's a fool still talking to you!"

Kathy jumped in and told her to keep calm. Then she asked her to leave us and go to the guest room so that we could talk.

My lower jaw was on the floor, like Jim Carry in *Mask!* I couldn't believe what I had just heard. This girl was crazy! How dare she talk to me like that? She had told me many times that she knew Kathy was aggressive and in many cases wrong, but she never dared to tell her that to her face!

After she left the living room, Kathy moved closer to me and took my arm and put it around her shoulder. She then put her head on my shoulder and began to cry gently. I was confused again. Was she playing another game? Looking back over all the schemes I had seen from her, I wasn't able to discern when she was her real self!

All I did was hold her in my arms, letting her cry for about a minute in total silence. I closed my eyes to all I had gone through and tried to be supportive. I didn't want to think about who I thought she was. I only wanted to be a shoulder for her tears. I didn't pity her; I felt empathy for her. Even if she felt it for a moment, that was enough for me.

I was right. It was only for a moment. I kissed her forehead, held her face with my both hands, looking eye-to-eye, and told her, "I wish you the best. I have to go now."

"Are you really leaving?" She sounded unbelievably mad and surprised! "Why, why are you doing this to me?!" she asked me, shivering.

I couldn't understand what she was talking about. "What do you mean by that? I'm not doing anything to you. This is what you have done to both of us; there's no turning back now. You knew this when you started it, but it's over now," I said.

"Don't you love me anymore? Don't you know what I will go through as a divorced woman in this society? I thought I was doing the right thing to win you back, because I love you!" she said.

I didn't want to listen to her. I thought about what she had told the lawyer when we signed the divorce papers, "He'll be back." I felt I was talking louder, "What kind of love is this? You are not serious! I can't go through this anymore. For God's sake, don't do that again to me," I said.

"I still love you! Can't you see? I did all this to prove to you that, at the end, no one stands by us except us. You were getting away from me by church and your stupid ministry," she replied.

"Kathy, I don't understand what you are talking about! I don't understand it, and I never did back then," I said. "I've never let my church activities come between us. Don't you ever say that. It was not about the church because you even asked me to find a second job while you knew it would put more distance between us. So it never was about the church. I was always there for you. Where have you been all those lonely nights when I cooked for us, waiting for you to come back home until midnight? Tell me, where have you been all those nights? Having fun with your friends? Who left me and disappeared three times each for at least a week? Me or you? Who locked the door of our bedroom on me? Who kicked me out of bed? Who destroyed my reputation? So please stop pretending and be yourself for once in your lifetime." I was almost yelling. I had lost my energy.

"Can't you see that all I did was to help you see the reality of life? You can't, we can't, just live by faith." She seemed serious. She continued, "We needed more; we needed a better car, a better house, a better job, a better life! You were walking in a wrong direction. That's what all my relatives and friends agreed on. I just wanted you, us, to be a happy and successful couple and to have everything we deserved. Don't you see how successful other people are? They have everything."

"What? Your relatives and friends?" I shouted, "You mean all these years you've been trying to teach me a lesson, a lesson your relatives taught you? You destroyed our lives because of what they believed to be the right thing? No, no, no, I can't believe that. I can't believe you lied to me, lied to my church, my family, and friends about me just because your relatives told you that you could change and correct me? This is ridiculous. This is not love. This is evil. We had more than enough, even more than many couples we knew. You're still not telling me the truth. I refuse to believe this nonsense! It cannot be the reason. This is unbelievable. This is the most stupid thing I ever heard."

"Bijan, please listen. I thought that if you would lose your trust in everybody and especially the church people, you would come back to me.

I thought you would learn that faith, religion, and those kinds of nonsense cannot put food on the table. I did that for us, for our future." She kept repeating the same thing.

I said, "Now I really think you are out of your mind. You have a psychological problem, you and your family, except your mom. She is the most reasonable person I've ever seen among your family members and relatives. Except her, all of you are fake, pretentious, and selfish." I was shaking.

I continued, "I don't want this love of yours. I don't need that kind of love! A love that destroys is no love at all!"

Suddenly I remembered why I was there—to tell her I had already forgiven her! I had not! Forgiveness is not conditional. Forgiveness flows out of a true godly love, and it's unconditional.

I cried gently. I couldn't look at her. I didn't want to again go through all she had made me go through in the last three and half years. The damage was beyond repair. But it didn't matter anymore. I had to forgive her once and for all, no matter what she did or why she did them.

She was waiting for me to say something she wanted to hear, something like, "Oh, Kathy, thank you so much for doing what you did to me. Now I know I was wrong, walking in a wrong direction. I appreciate you for putting me through all this misery so that I would understand I was wrong and how dearly you loved me. Thank you for your amazing love!"

I was staring at some non-existing spot beyond space and time. I felt I was lost again. My brain was not able to analyze all that had happened. How could she start such a dangerous game, ignoring what might happen at the end?

My heart was telling me to stay with her for a little while more. I still loved her, not as a spouse, but with a godly love that cared about her future. After all, I had listened to my heart four years before regarding her, and I had ended up where I was. Not everything our hearts tell us is right. I had to move on. Contrary to what we usually consider a right thing regarding listening to our hearts, I decided to leave that place immediately. The heart is a deceitful thing, for it always wants, longs, desires, and never thinks.

Maybe you are thinking I should have stayed with her, but I knew I shouldn't. I was filled with sadness. It was the same feeling I felt when she told me she would kill herself if she'd go back to live with her parents in Gorgan a year before our marriage. I wouldn't fall for that again. If I had stayed there and thought more about the possibilities, I would have gone crazy. I was in my thoughts when she spoke again, "Yes, I guess you better go, before I change your mind." she smiled. I said, "You are right." Then I kissed her forehead and left. That was the last time I saw her. To this day I haven't understood why she did what she did. It's still a dilemma to me.

What happened that day didn't stop me from asking everybody I knew about her in the next eleven years up until today. Even though she didn't want me to know where she was living or what she was doing, still, somehow, I felt responsible. I kept getting news about her through our mutual friends for years until I eventually lost contact with all of the people we both used to know. The last person I knew who she was still in touch with won a green card lottery in 2009 and moved to California. No more news about her since then.

The Ring

I KNEW BRIDA WOULD TAKE it easy on me. She was my real other half, I would say, if I believed in that kind of stuff! I called her, and we met in a coffee shop. She asked how things went between Kathy and me. I told her it was over and preferred not to talk about it. She accepted. I asked her to tell me about the trip. She told me a little bit. Then there was a long silence.

"I'll leave for Turkey in few weeks," I said.

"Good! I'm glad you are moving on." she said. "Now you can follow your dreams. There are many good things out there that will never happen without you. Now I wish I could be with you on your journey, but I know you need to face it alone!"

Knowing she was right, I said, "You will have your own adventures. You too need to fulfill your destiny."

She smiled, and drank a little bit of her iced caramel mocha.

To change the atmosphere I said, "We still have a few weeks ahead to challenge life and enjoy defeating it," I laughed.

"And we will always win," she replied.

"And we will always win," I repeated.

I thought, *She has no idea what she did and who she was for me. She was the manifestation of Jesus' love. She was ready to give everything she had to protect me. In her dream, she never said a word when I showed her the way in that dark cave; she just ran toward the light, no looking back. But in reality she stayed by my side to the last moment and sacrificed many things to help me be back on my feet again. She risked her reputation and tolerated all my selfish complaints. She was a hero to me.*

We left the coffee shop and went for a walk. The weather was cold, but it was pleasant. The only thing that was hurting me was the fact that

I knew she was sad. But I had to fulfill my destiny, and to do that, I had to depart. In fact, by doing that, I knew I would also prepare the way for her to move on and fulfill her own destiny, too. Deep in my heart, I knew it was the only right thing to do.

I had to leave Iran. I was a danger to everyone around me. I never told anyone that I knew I was watched. I knew I was followed day and night. Sometimes it was a trail motorbike, and sometimes it was a certain dark blue Hyundai with the same guys sitting in it. Once, the same bike passed me by in a dark ally, and its rider hit me from behind. It was dark, but I could see him staring at me, sitting on his roaring bike from a distance. I couldn't see his face. But the way he hit me was more like a warning. Nothing serious happened to me, just few scratches.

On another occasion, I was attending a funeral ceremony of a relative when a bunch of young, tall, well dressed and muscular guys came to me and asked how I was doing! I didn't know them, but they knew my name. One of them said, "You may not know us, but we are familiar with you, Mr. Bijan!"

I was about to ask them how they knew me when my cousin came to us and said, "Hey Bijan, these are my new friends. They work in the Ministry of Information. It's so cool to have some people in such high class places." He seemed very excited and proud of being friends with them. Then he said, "I see you guys have already made friends!" Then he introduced them to me by name. I knew what was going on, but my pitiful cousin had no idea they were using him. After a short formal talk, I asked them to excuse me because I had to go home. My cousin left us for a minute to give his condolences to the diseased family.

One of them turned to me and said, "How about we give you a ride?" I thanked him and declined, but they insisted. I told them that I lived far from there, but the same guy said, "Mr. Bijan! We know where you live, and it's not far from here." After taking a deep breath, I said, "Alright guys, we all know what's going on here. I don't need your ride. I don't know why you are using my cousin, but you need to know I'm not doing anything anymore!"

"We know." he said, "Don't worry, we like you, and we hope we can work together."

"I'm not going to work with anyone anymore. So if you excuse me, I need to go now," I said.

They offered me a hand shake and a smile, one-by-one. There were five of them. When I left the funeral, I just walked in the streets aimlessly for about three hours before I went home. I didn't want my cousin to get in trouble because of me.

So I knew I had to leave Iran as soon as I could, but so far, I had no news from any church or organization outside of Iran being able to help me. I asked the Assemblies to at least give me a letter of membership (not even a service record), but I received this answer, "A disgraced divorced man asks for a letter of membership? And the letter is not going to be issued, for he is not a member of this church anymore!" Can you believe that? When I finally went to Turkey I went through many unexplainable, horrible hardships and a membership letter could have definitely saved years of my life. I'll tell more later.

For the next few weeks, Brida and I met regularly. She was a great encourager. I guess it was her gift. All we talked about was our dreams. Mine was to freely make music, write a book about my life, and then continue the legacy with whatever God had in store for me, whatever I could share with others that would make life easier for them. I also had the dream of having my own TV Talk Show. God was able to accomplish all those dreams (which later on I understood them as God-given visions; my destiny). Hers was to publish her poems, write short novels, edit literature, travel around the world to mystic places, sharing Jesus, and have an adventurous life.

Once she asked, "Are you going to mention me in your book?" then she playfully smiled and winked at me.

I gave in to her game by saying, "No. Why should I?" I laughed.

"Why? Because without me your story is incomplete!" Now it was her turn to laugh.

"Yes. You are right. In fact, life is incomplete without you, without Brida!" I paused and looked deep in her big playful eyes.

"Yeah, yeah, yeah! The world is not complete without me, you should say," she said, "Nothing is complete without a Brida!" she said.

I replied, "Life is bigger than the world. World will end someday, life won't," I said.

"You have no idea," she added, "but God has a Brida and a Bijan for everyone who needs one. They are everywhere. He puts one on the path of every seeker. Believe me." She spoke like she knew a secret. Then she asked, "Do you think we'll see each other again?" She asked the question with the voice of a little five-year-old girl.

I replied with a voice of a wise old man, "Definitely child, we will, trust your mentor!" We both laughed.

"I'm sure we will see each other again when you are rich and famous." she said. "You will fulfill your dreams and then sit back and enjoy the outcome."

"Don't be silly. As long as life's going on, we need to live our dreams. Every day is pregnant with new dreams and visions. There's always something to do." I said.

After a short silence I asked, "You know what? You may laugh, but sometimes I ask myself what or who I have been for you! Have I been the same for you as you've been for me? Did I do anything that brought more value to your life? You never told me what you think of me."

She looked at me with eyes half closed, scanning my face. I immediately read her mind. She was saying, "What a silly question! You already know who you are for me!"

Then she said, "OK, you want to know who you are for me? You are Jeje (she liked to call me that!). My Mentor! The one who showed me the way. The one who brought me Jesus. The one who gifted me a friendship that is bigger than life. You are my teacher and my best friend. You showed me something that no one was ever able to. You brought me hope. You motivated me. You made me write again. You made me feel again. You gave me back my wings again. You opened my eyes to a new world, where love is not just going through pain, but it inspires you to soar like an eagle and fly higher than any limit anyone has set for you...And now you are leaving! I know you must go. I knew you would go. I knew it from the beginning, from my dream. You knew it, too. And now I need to learn to fly alone, by myself. It's alright, I get it. But if I tell you that right in this moment I'm not sad, I would be lying. I am. And the only thing that can take away this sadness is to make sure you will follow your dreams, at any cost. That's all I ask of you. I don't ask you to remember me or call me or write to me or anything else, even though I will kill you if you won't," she laughed and pointed her index finger at me. Then she continued, "I just want you to follow your dreams, and know that I'm there for you. Wherever you are, whatever you do, I'm there with you. Just keep the fire burning. I will pray for you as long as I live. You are the most important thing that has ever happened to me so far. This is who you are for me. Do you want me to say more?" She was smiling, but I could see the tears in her honest, childish eyes like the waves of an ocean.

I was speechless. I wanted to cry like a baby and laugh like a clown at the same time. I asked God in my heart, "What have I done, Lord, to deserve her friendship?"

And I heard a gentle voice saying, "If you are all that to her, just imagine how precious you are to Me!"

I took a deep breath and said to her, "Thank you! That's all I can say. Now let's go out for a walk in the snow. Shall we?" Then I added, "By the way, remind me later about a surprise; I got you something!" Her eyes shone like a little girl when you tell her you got her a new beautiful pink bike!

"No way! I want to know what it is right now! Come on, Bijan; tell me what you got me!" She kept asking.

With a voice of an old man again, I said, "Sorry, little girl! It will only happen in the latter days." like I was talking about the end times.

"You are mean!" she said with a smile.

———

I bought a train ticket to Istanbul, Turkey—the first passenger train to Istanbul from Tehran. It was supposed to be a three-day long trip. But it sounded good to me because I would have enough time to ready myself for the future challenges. It was foolish to think everything was going to be alright. Every state of life has its own challenges. But I never thought some of them could be worse than what I had already been through!

During the rest of my time before I left, I had nothing else to do except try to make some connections with those I knew outside of Iran and spend time with Pouyan and Brida. I was training them by transferring to them all I had learned and all I had to offer. They were spiritually growing fast because they were humble enough to let God work in them through His word.

None of the people I knew in Japan were living at their old addresses anymore. Even the Harvest Church had changed its location and probably changed its name, too. Even the missionaries I used to know had changed their addresses. I had hundreds of contacts from the States, Canada, England, Nigeria, France, Germany, South America, Australia, and New Zealand. (A good friend of mine from the time I was in Tokyo was from Christchurch, the city with that horrible earthquake in February 2011. I still don't know how she's doing, and I hope she will let me know of her safety, hopefully after she will read this book. Her name is Lisa.)

I needed to continue my search, for if I wasn't able to find someone to help me, I would have to apply for asylum to UNHCR within ten days of my arrival in Istanbul. So I was doing my best to find someone to help me. Brida had bought me a fax machine so I could get faster responses.

Pouyan was also talking to his friends and relatives to see if they were able to help.

I was still being watched by the same bike rider and the same people in that Hyundai. I'm not sure what they were doing when I was at home, but whenever I was out, there they were. It was so annoying because I wasn't even able to pick my nose (just joking). I'm not sure if you can understand how it felt to be watched day and night by those who are not hesitant to harm you for no reason, if they want. It was like an everyday walk on the green mile! But as long as I had my God, my guitar, Brida, and friends like Pouyan, there was no reason not to be happy! Yes, my guitar was also a good friend of mine. I wrote many songs during all those challenging days. They were the same songs I sold to Tannin Records. They carried a message of love, hope, encouragement, and forgiveness. It was on one of those days that I wrote a song for Brida. That was my surprise gift for her. I knew she would love it. I still believe it is one of my best songs in terms of lyrics.

On one of those last days before I left, I finally played and sang it for her. She cried as she listened to the song. She hugged me and told me that it was the best gift she had ever received in her life. Since that day, she called it "my song," and that's what it is, Brida's Song. She was an angel to me. And I hope, one day, you will be touched by one like her on your own path, when you are so close to giving up; then you will know what I'm talking about.

Finally, the last day arrived. She came to my place to help me pack. All I wanted to pack was my books, the ones I had translated and published. I had already given away all I had to those in need in the streets. I used to walk in the streets to find homeless people. I liked sitting beside them and talking with them. Some of them had great insights to share. I joyfully shared my cloths and money with them; that was all I could do for them after I prayed with them. I remember once my friend and I talked to a young homeless man on a street in our neighborhood and encouraged him to renew his mind and start a new life. He was so desperate and hopeless that, while we were talking to him, he began to cry. He agreed to cooperate. We took him to a public bath and then gave him some new clothing to wear. He looked completely different, like a totally new person. He was a very handsome young man in his mid-twenties. We were blessed to be able to help him with enough money for his travel expenses to his hometown, to his parent. He was ashamed of who he had turned into and could not face his parents who, despite their poor life condition, had supported him to come to Tehran to find a better future. We bought him a ticket and accompanied him to the bus terminal. He pulled me into his arms and cried a river. He said that no one had ever been so kind to him in his whole life. He then got on the bus and waved at us until the bus was out of sight. A few days later, when I was downtown to buy a music gadget, I saw him sitting on another street in some dirty, worn-out clothes. He hid his face under a dirty blanket as soon as he saw me. I decided not to embarrass him. That day I learned a truth; we are not a victim of our circumstances; who we become in life is a choice we make for ourselves!

My train was scheduled to depart at 3 p.m. Since it was the first train to Turkey, I was pretty sure no one would be able to trace me unless they had followed me to the train station! I thought, *Well, it is much better for them to let me leave the country than to have me stay and continue to poison the young generation,* which is how they referred to what I was doing.

After Brida helped me packed, I sat on the couch and played some tunes with my guitar. She asked me to sing "Her Song" again. She came and sat by my side. She closed her eyes and listened to the words. She gently cried. I stopped singing. We held hands in total silence. We had no words to exchange. In fact, we didn't need any words at all. I held her in my arms for a while, but to avoid any temptation at the last moment, I kissed her forehead and told her that everything was going to be fine. I needed to be strong; that's what she wanted me to be. I called a cab.

When we were getting in the cab, I saw that dark blue Hyundai again. Maybe they knew all about my plans, and they were probably happy I was leaving. I never told Brida about them; I didn't want to worry her. For some reason, they were taking it easy on me, and I think there were only two reasons for that: 1) the Khatami administration was against any violence, and 2) God's favor was upon me.

We arrived at the Train Station thirty minutes before the departure. I had my Bibles and many Christian books and CDs in my bags. Brida created a diversion so that I could pass them through the inspection point. She was smart. What she did was spontaneous and clever. She just distracted the old man by talking to him with the same baby voice she used to talk to me, telling him I was her brother and that she needed to pass through the checking point to be with me until the last moment. She sounded very cute when she was doing a baby voice. I remembered the story of Abraham and Sarah. Meanwhile, I pushed my bags to the other side; there was no electronic spot check.

The whistle sounded. She looked nervous and a little bit shaky. I knew she had been keeping things inside for a long time. All of a sudden, she burst into a heavy cry while resting her head on my chest. She couldn't help it. I felt she was fighting with something. I knew what it was. She was fighting with her desire to tell me not to leave. I admired her strength. I held her in my arms until the train's whistle sounded for the second time.

I took her tiny beautiful face in my hands and told her, "We'll be in touch. I promise we'll meet again. Keep praying for me; I need your prayers. I'll do the same for you." She just nodded and tried to smile while tears were rolling down on her face.

She said, "Wait, I need to give you this," then she gave me a letter and asked me to read it only after the train left the station. For the first time in our friendship, I was frightened.

She asked me again, "Please promise me, only read it when the train has left, OK?" I assured her.

For the last time, I put my arms around her shoulders and kissed her forehead and said, "We'll meet again, don't forget that." I moved toward the passport check booth. The man in the booth looked at my passport and checked it with the black list he had on his computer. I took a deep breath and asked God to intervene. It only took about thirty seconds. He stamped my passport and let me go. When I turned around to wave at her; there was no sign of her. She was gone. I thought she had run outside in order to not see me getting on the train. When I turned around to walk toward the platform, there she was standing right in front of me! I don't know how she had done it, but she had tricked the security again and passed to the other side!

We both laughed. She accompanied me to my wagon and watched me getting on. She waved at me from outside. She was the only civilian on the platform.

She told me not to forget to write her long letters every day, with all the details. She knew I loved writing.

"Yes Madam," I said, while saluting her with my right hand like a soldier. She laughed. I said, "Here you are; it's better now. You're much prettier when you smile!"

The train embarked slowly, and she began to walk with it until it sped up. We kept waving until I saw her no more.

I greeted the two young men in our compartment and then sat down, took the letter out of my pocket, and opened it. Then something came to my mind, and I decided to put it back in the envelope until the train was far enough; after it had passed the border.

I thought about the old man in Tokyo who told me I would have two decades that would divide my life into two completely different eras. It had been exactly ten full years since I had given my heart to Christ. I didn't care about what he had said. All I cared about was the fact that God was in control of my life, not a ghost or a spirit or the devil or even myself. The thought gave me a peace beyond understanding.

I was so exhausted that I just wanted to rest for a few hours without thinking about anything, absolutely nothing at all. So I decided to go to the washroom before I took a long nap. While I was washing my hands, my silver ring with the golden carved cross slipped out of my finger and dropped in the sink. My reflex was very slow, and I couldn't catch it; it was gone.

Standing there looking at the hole in the sink, I thought, *Alright God, an era is over now. That was a sign. I agree. But I need a little rest before we go through the next round together. Please don't take it hard on me. I need some time to rest. Thank you!* And I winked at my reflection in the mirror.

God is serious about His business. No time to rest. Healing was on the way, but only within the process and form of another life-changing challenge. To God, even resting time could be another form of stretching our capacity.

I did read Brida's letter after the train passed the border. I'm not going to disclose the content of the letter. It was very emotional and personal. Three years after I left Iran, while I was still in Turkey, she married a filmmaker, a tall, handsome fellow, a Christian. I was the first to know about the good news! The first thing she shared with him was the magical story of our friendship, and I believe that story drew them closer to each other. To be honest with you, I even knew they would eventually marry long before they became close friends! In 2011 they finally left Iran and now they live in some part of Europe. She is the best thing that ever happened to me so far, and she will remain the same until the end. We are still in touch. She feels responsible to check on me regarding my dreams.

I needed to take a nap, but before I did, I decided to pray for Kathy. I asked God to protect her, to reveal more of His love to her, to keep her safe, to bless her, to give her joy, and to lead her steps. At the end, I asked Him to forgive me again for any shortcoming from my side on her behalf, even the ones I wasn't aware of.

I heard the train whistle. We were getting close to a tunnel. The sleep rubbed me away.

My lovely parents on their wedding day - 1960

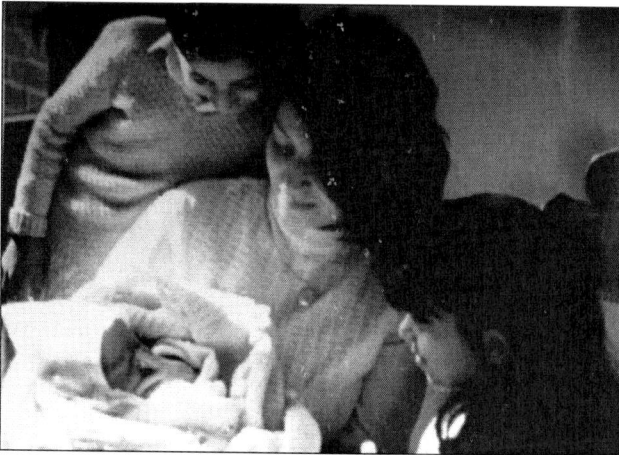

Birth of my youngest sister - 1969

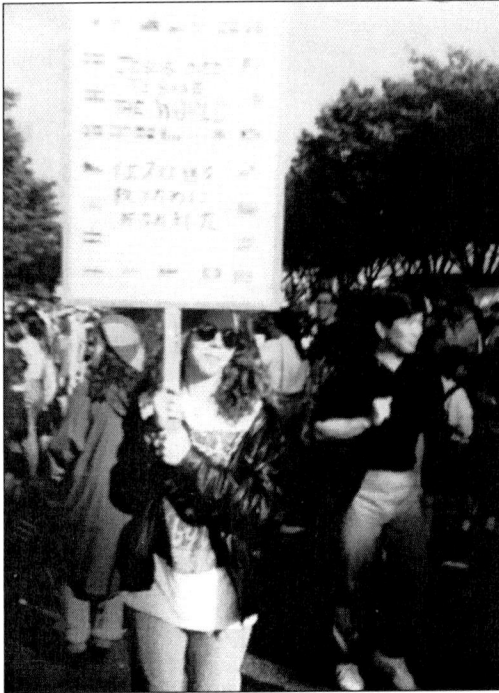

Bonnie in Tokyo – 1991

Playing gigs at a coffee shop in Tokyo called White
Spot - a few weeks after my new life began

My last day in Tokyo at Shibuya Harvest - 1992

My first public Concert in Iran – 1996

Guest speaker in a popular Iranian TV show,
Pezhvak, Los Angeles, CA - 2009

Right before recording a TV program with
Voice of Freedom, Dallas, TX - 2010

My concert in Vancouver - 2010

Cover of my first English album "Unconditional" - 2012

Last words

I ENTERED TURKEY ON MARCH 11 of the year 2001. After going through lots of hardships for three years, I finally found my way to Canada on March 11 of the year 2004 and became a Canadian citizen on the same day in 2008. Today, again, is March 11, but the year is 2011, while I'm writing these concluding lines. Yes, I did plan the book to end on this day, the beginning of a new era in my life.

Before God opened the sea (figuratively) for me to come to Canada, horrible things happened to me during my three-year stay in Turkey. I was beaten and robbed many times by gangs and mobs. I had to live with gay and lesbian prostitutes for a period of time. I suffered hunger for months. I got a terrible stomach disease that stayed with me for years. And even Iranian Churches in Istanbul were reluctant to be in touch with me. I was still a leper to them! For two consecutive years I received letters of deportation back to Iran from the Turkish authorities—all because my church refused to issue me a simple letter of membership. United Nation High Commissioner for Refugees (UNHCR) closed my file as a false one within three months of my arrival, and as a result, I was forced to remain in Turkey three years regardless of all my attempts to prove the truthfulness of my claims, and every year God intervened miraculously to keep me in Turkey for the plans He had for me.

During my stay in Istanbul, I became the worship leader of the River in Istanbul Church, which now is broadcasting TV programs all over Turkey, thanks to Erman Family. Later I was also blessed with the privilege of founding and shepherding a Farsi-speaking Church for Iranian refugees in a town called Kastamonu in the north of Turkey. I served them as their pastor for two years. They all are another unforgettable part of my life.

274

Right now, many of them are active in humanitarian activities in their capacity around the world, and some serve as pastors or worship leaders in Europe and North America. Some of them were arrested by the Turkish authorities and were deported back to Iran, where they planted house churches and for that very reason were arrested but thank God they were released later.

After three years, and after receiving three letters of deportation, when another circle of life passed, my file was miraculously opened by UNHCR. Up to this date, I have no idea what made them open my file again, neither did those who interviewed me know how my file appeared on their desks. After a short interview I was accepted and was sent to the Canadian Embassy in Ankara for another interview; the result is me in Canada writing this book!

I started a new life in Canada while still some hard-headed Christian leaders in Iran think I'm a junkie sleeping in the streets of Tehran. Let them live in their selfish bubbles. Since then, I have travelled to the U.S., England, the Netherlands, Belgium, Armenia, and many other cities and towns throughout Canada for conferences and concerts. I have worked with Iranian and non-Iranian charities or Christian organizations around the world, such as 222 Ministries International, Global Exploit Ministries, and Intercede International, just to name a few. And I have appeared on CBN Mohabat Channel, CTS Canada, Sama TV, and Nedaye Azadi on TBN Nejat as a guest speaker.

I also had the wonderful chance of recording my first studio album in Canada with Jam Music Productions, which also was released on March 11 2009. I achieved many other goals, which would not even be possible to imagine if I was still in Iran. The freedom in Canada and Canadian hospitality helped me break my hardened shell of solitude and enabled me to overcome my boundaries, giving me the chance to experience life in its fullness once again.

I'm not very much changed, but I grew to learn so much more about God's grace and love, about life, and about people in general. Life is not about being changed; it's about growing in grace and doing your part in integrity, which is to become a hope-giver and a lift for others. That's what I learned, thanks to every single soul I came in contact with on my adventurous journey.

I should mention that years later, after Canada became my second home, God allowed me to meet with my lovely pastor—Edward, who I invited to Toronto for a conference for Iranians. We had so many things to share. He was changed. We reconciled. Two years after I left he also had to leave Iran because of a challenge with the leadership regarding his re-marriage after his wife went to the Lord. Life has a sarcastic sense of humor. He was not God, and there was no way for him or Vartan to be 100 percent sure which one of us, Kathy or I, was the true victim. Or maybe we both were. My past was another gigantic mountain I had to move, and by meeting them again and clearing the past misunderstanding, I was finally free to move on. But to be honest with you my divorce story is still affecting my life and ministry whenever and wherever I try to work with Iranian churches. It is sad to meet with ministers who don't even know you but have already judged you.

I still need to continue this journey and do what I'm here on earth to do. Thank God for putting so many wonderful people on my path exactly when I needed to be touched by their spirits, as I have probably touched their lives, too.

My life's philosophy has not changed. I believe in Christ as my Savior and my Lord with all my heart, all my soul, and all my strength. My greatest desire is to make Him known to everyone I meet on my journey, but I do not think in a box anymore, just like He never did. You may be able to put beliefs in a box, but you can't put faith in there because faith gives you the ability to fly beyond all your earthly limitations. Any kind of faith presented in a form of law and regulations is nothing but mere belief, and beliefs have no power to change you or set you free. That's what the Master Mind behind all challenges of life wants for us—to know the ultimate truth. Only the truth can set us free, and faith is the only way to activate the truth to act on our behalf. Let the truth of faith in Christ set you free. Give Him a chance to speak to your soul. Let Him speak life into your dead circumstances. God says that He will turn our mourning into joy and will comfort us, and make us rejoice rather than sorrow (Jeremiah 31:13). Beliefs cannot lift a finger for you and me when we need a miracle. Faith (and not a belief system) is able to show you the extraordinary side of life, where everything can turn into a miracle.

I strongly believe that faith, even in its smallest form, is able to move mountains. But in moving mountains, it's not the uprooting that matters; it is where you put them down that has value.

These days are very difficult, but important days for my country, Iran. I pray for the lost souls to finally find their way back to what they have lost—a loving relationship with the Creator. And I pray that God would heal the wounds of the broken hearted and take away the hatred they feel against the Islamic regime in order to enable them to embrace the true freedom, not just in its political form, but in every area of their lives. And I pray for peace in Iran and for all Iranians around the world, a peace beyond understanding. I also pray that God may have mercy on the leaders of Iran, because they do not know what they are doing. May God be with all who love freedom and fight for it, not by guns but by sacrificing their own freedom as our young men and women are fighting for their simple right to have a voice, not just for themselves, but also for the generations to come. May thousands of memoirs and true stories find the chance to be heard and published—stories of a brave and tolerant nation called Persia.

All the divine forces of creation, along with the people who helped me in my battles under the leadership of the Master of the universe, taught me how to move my mountains using my faith (your past can be your greatest and heaviest mountain). And now, by putting these mountains into words in this memoir and in my songs, I hope I'm encouraging others in their battles according to their purpose in life, no matter where they are born or live. And I am so happy that I still have other mountains ahead to move. Maybe my story doesn't sound so remarkable in comparison to those of many others who have gone through tougher challenges in life, but if I have learned one thing and only one thing from this journey, it is the reality that none of us can fulfill our destiny by ourselves alone; we need each other. Some people believe that we must put aside our differences and get along with each other but I believe that we need to embrace our differences as privileges and celebrate them while looking for common grounds so that we can join our earthly abilities with our heavenly gifts in order to touch one person's life at a time. And if we have a chance to touch more lives, let's do that too—whether through music, literature, film, a picture, or whatever else we are capable of offering the world at the moment. This gives me the motive to move forward.

In last few years I've been helping many refugees in Turkey to find their ways to a third country where they can live in freedom of speech, life style, and peace of mind. I helped others who were financially in trouble by raising awareness about their situation through speaking in churches and charity organizations, appearing on TV shows and reporting to news agencies I've been in touch with. We helped release of a number of Christian and political prisoners back in Iran; the battle still goes on. And life goes on too like a never-ending challenge, and we all are warriors. Our swords should not remain unused, but they should not be pulled out without a cause, either. Our reward is not what we gain, for what we gain will only turn into a victory when we share it with others. So here is my question for you, "Where are you going to put your next mountain down; in a book, in a song, in a painting, in a helping hand, or in a voice against hunger and poverty? Or perhaps all of the above. That's the only thing that matters—sharing our common experiences by whatever we can in order to be able to look at the world from a new angle and with a new perspective, to value life as we are called to unfold its mystery together.

Bijan Ilyaie
March 11th 2011

Acknowledgment

As you read the book you understand that I have valued everyone who came across my path and taught me something about life, even those who hurt me and brought so much pain to my life.

But since this section is consecrated to those who had believed in me and in my dreams, I would rather express my deep appreciation to those who had a role in bringing those dreams to reality.

I would like to thank Angie, who revived the passion in me to write this account when she heard a short version of the story over a cup of coffee four years ago back in Toronto. Thanks for rekindling the flame.

To Hengameh who, within a short period of time, not only became a good friend of mine but also the most passionate fan and sponsor of my vision to share my story with the whole world.

To the Mohajers; Taghi, Zahra, Ebrahim, Esther, Michael, and Elisabeth, for believing in me and supporting me. You all did so much more than I expected, even beyond your limitations. I'm thankful for your friendship.

To Sherrie A., who provided me with a quiet place to concentrate and write the book. I will never forget your kindness and generosity.

To my Pastors Giulio and Lina Gabeli who unconditionally loved me and encouraged me not to give up on my visions whether it was my music project, concerts, or the book. I'm so thankful for your friendship and I'm privileged to be part of the Westwood Community Church's mission. Giulio, Lina and all of you Wetswooders, your love and support have always given me another reason to rejoice every day since the day I knew you.

To Pastor Steven who brought a word from God and that word helped me make my final decision to write this book and record my first English album. By the way, I love jamming with you!

To my parents and sisters whose arms were always open to me not only in the times of success but also in my failures and falls no matter how desperate I was. Your happiness is my greatest prayer as long as I live on this earth.

To Marina Nemat for being a mentor and a friend. Your book *Prisoner of Tehran* gave me the boldness to finally start writing my own memoir. Thanks for all your advices and suggestions.

And before I give all the glory to the only true, living God, my best wishes go to the first person who believed in me whole-heartedly in the first place and became a precious vessel in God's hands to heal my broken heart. To the one who never judged me, never condemned me, never lied to me and never blamed me, but remained a true friend when everyone else had left me stranded and alone; to the one who truly valued my dreams as her own, and became a living part of them all; to the person who sacrificed many things to see me fulfill my own dreams even at the cost of losing hers; to Brida.

But none of these was even possible if the lover of my soul, Jesus Christ, had not found me, washed me, cleansed me and given me a new destiny; a destiny He had already designed and planned for me, and for you, before the creation of the universe, a plan of hope and success; a greater destiny, when we embrace His unconditional love. Jesus, You are the greatest gift to all humanity. Thank You for what You have done in me and for what You have done through me. And thank You for all the marvellous things that You are willing to do in everyone's life if they just receive your love. I will always love you.